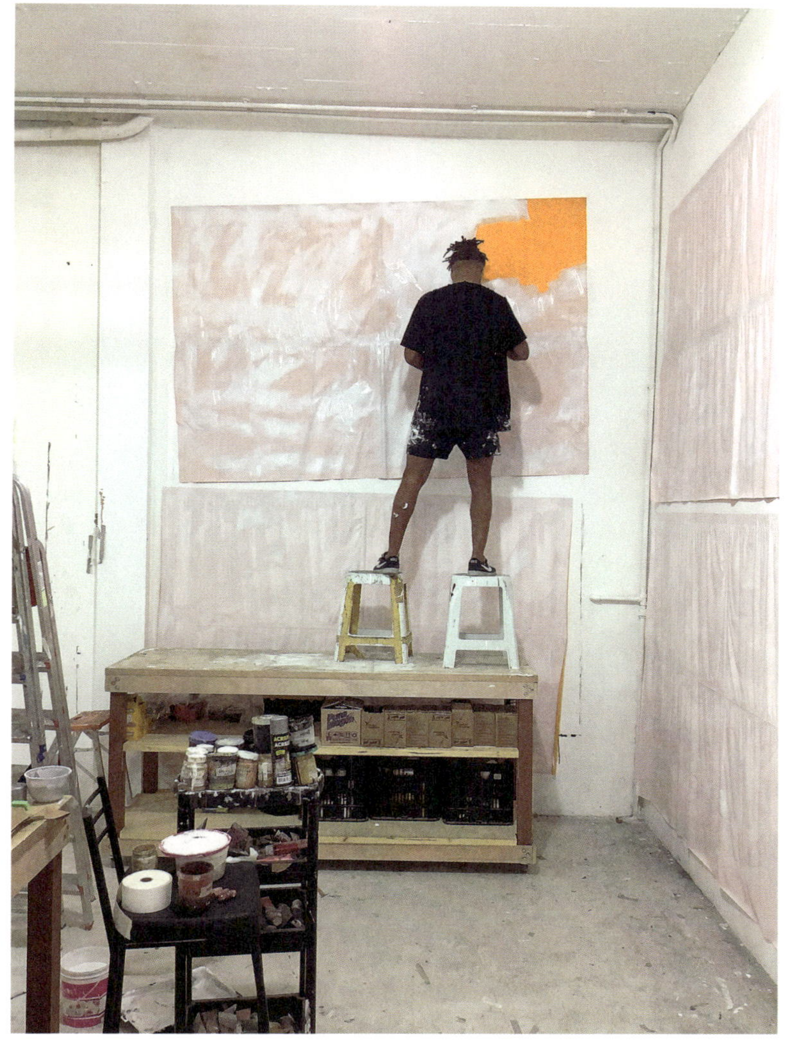

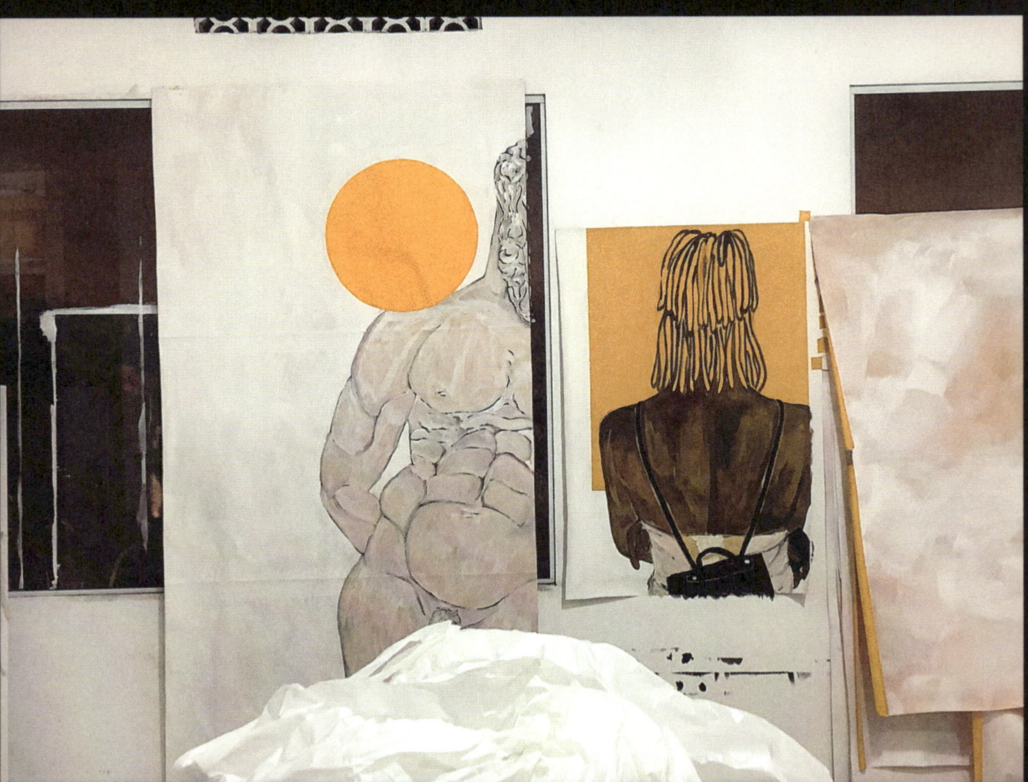

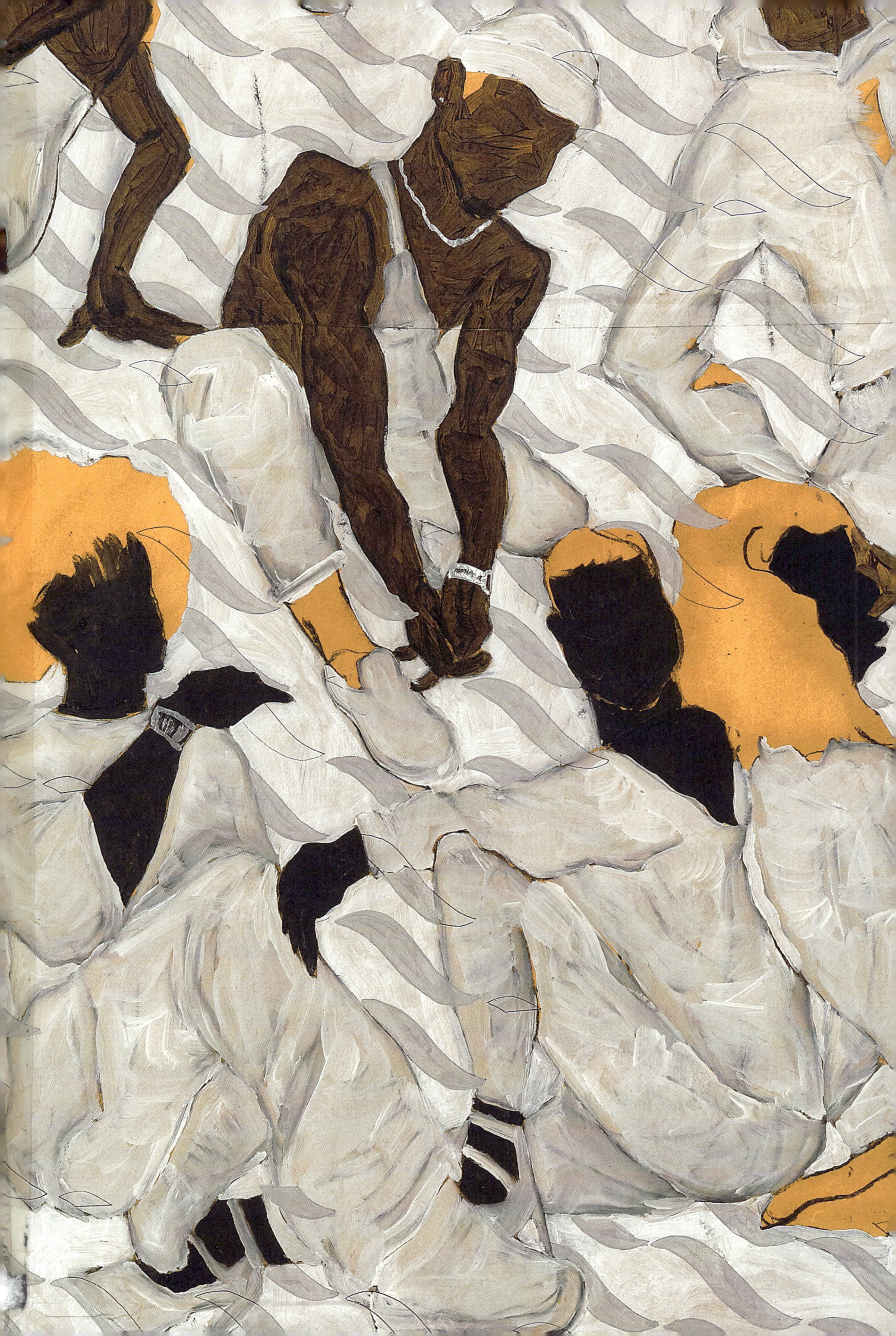

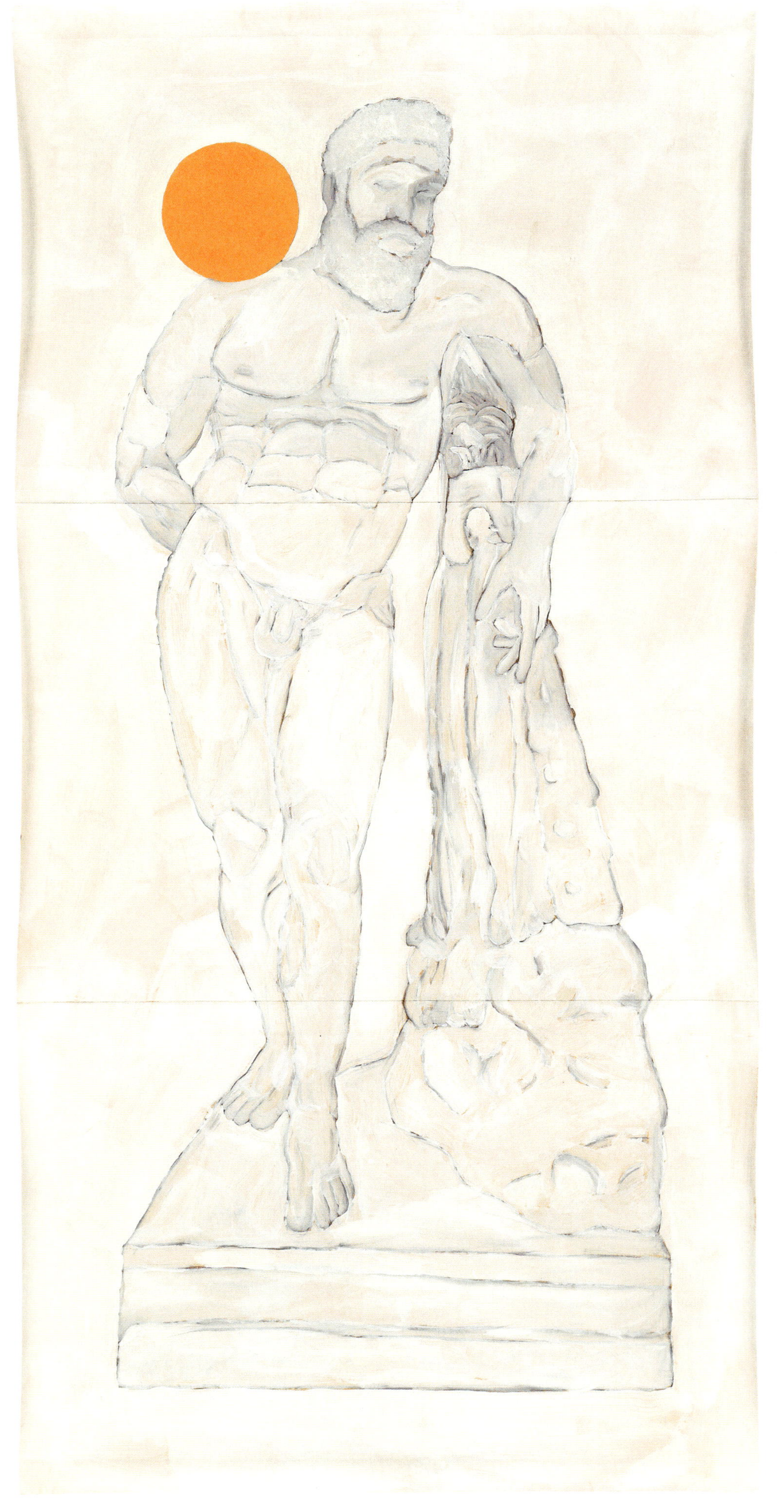

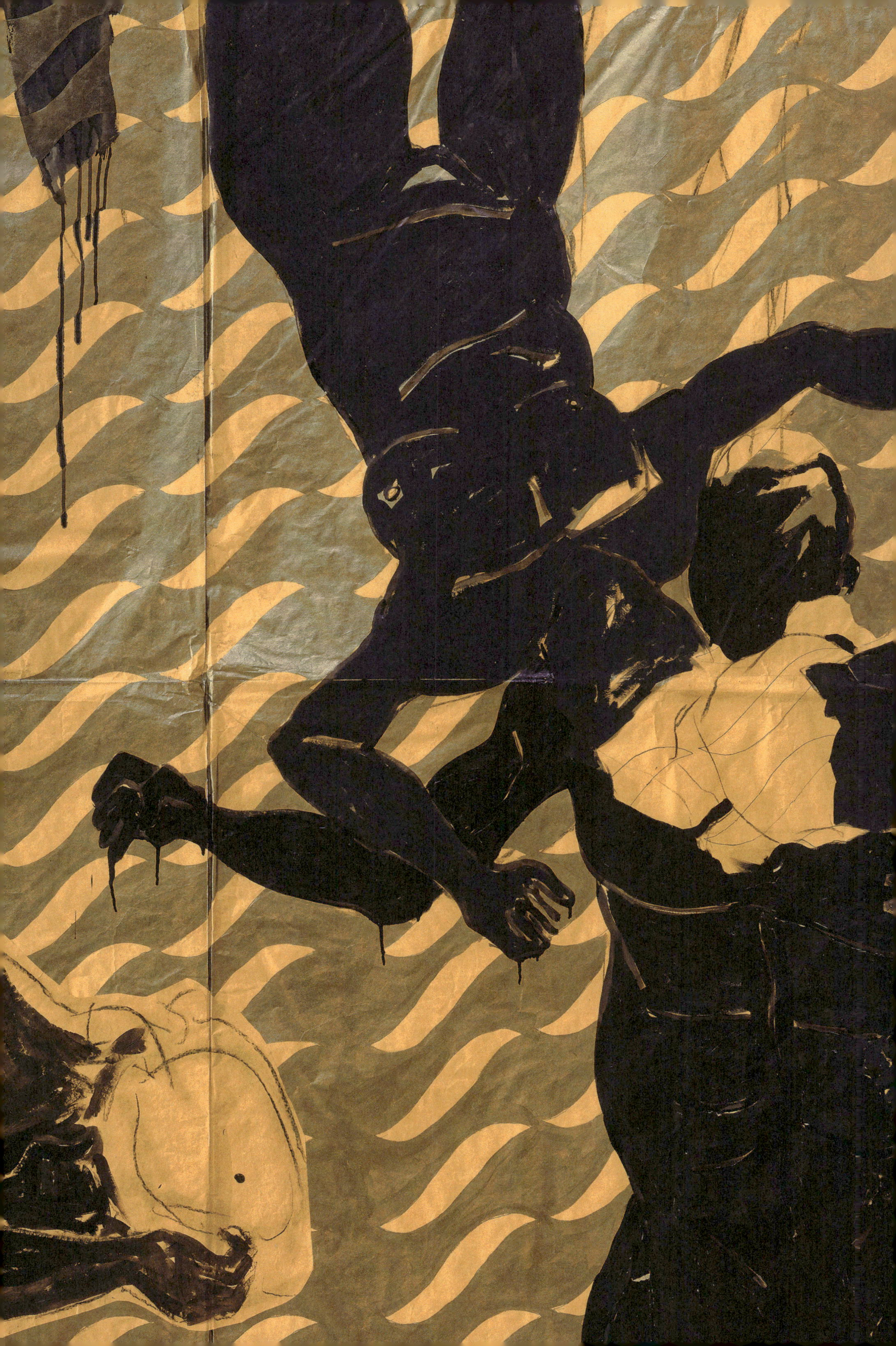

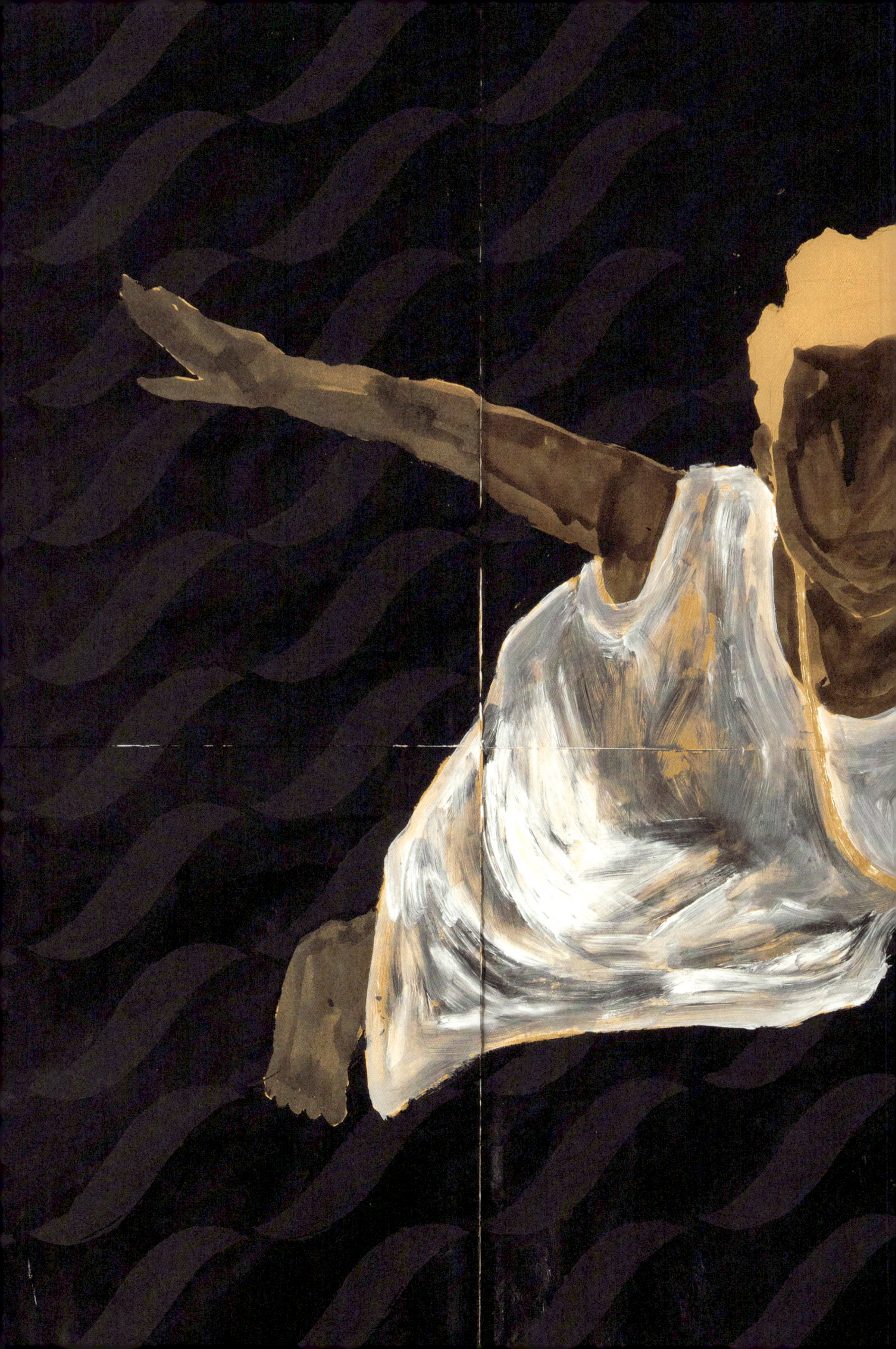

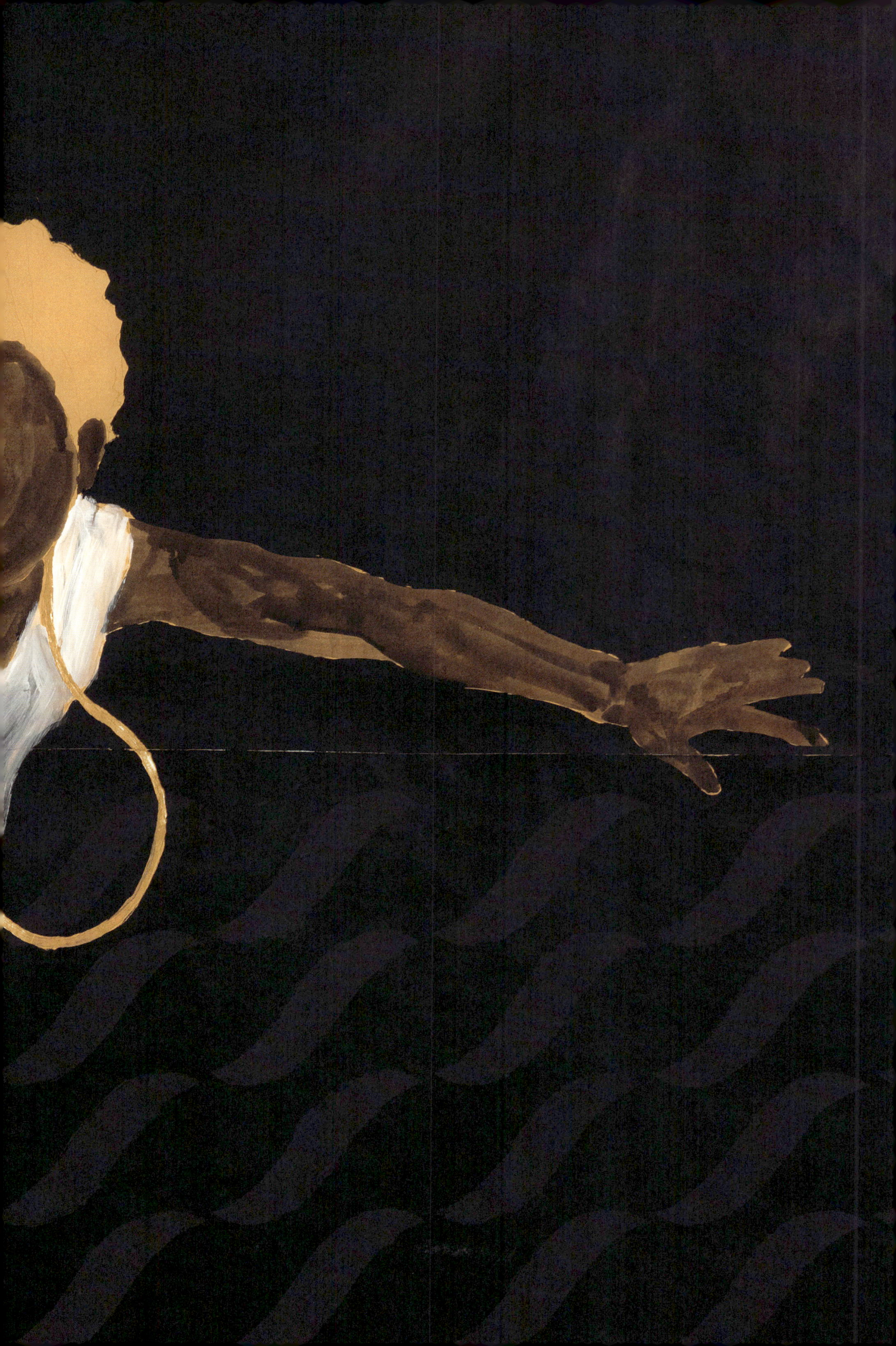

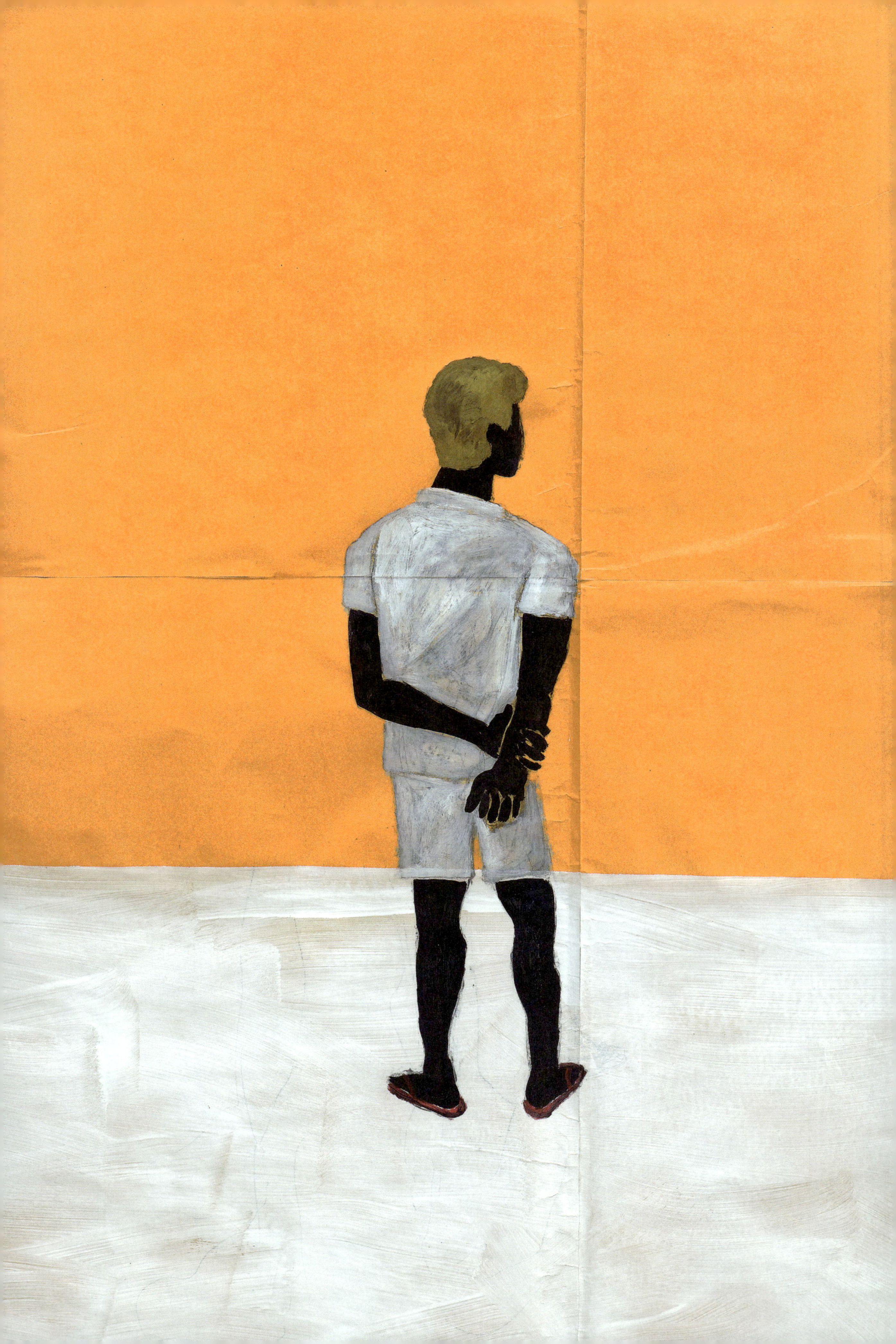

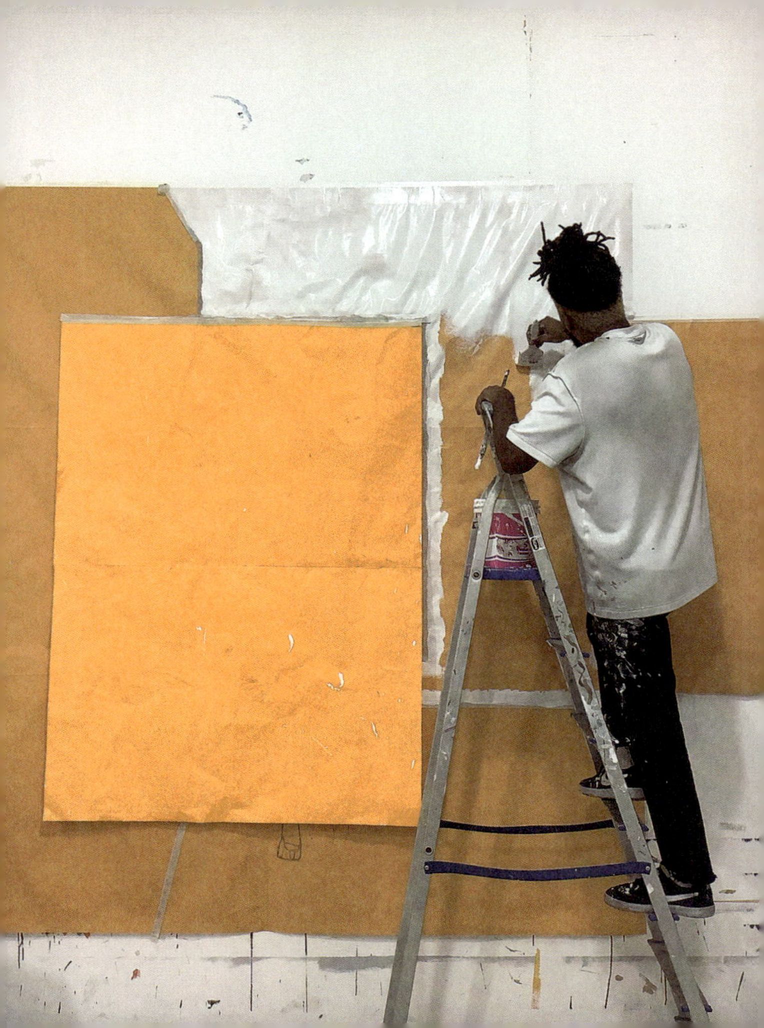

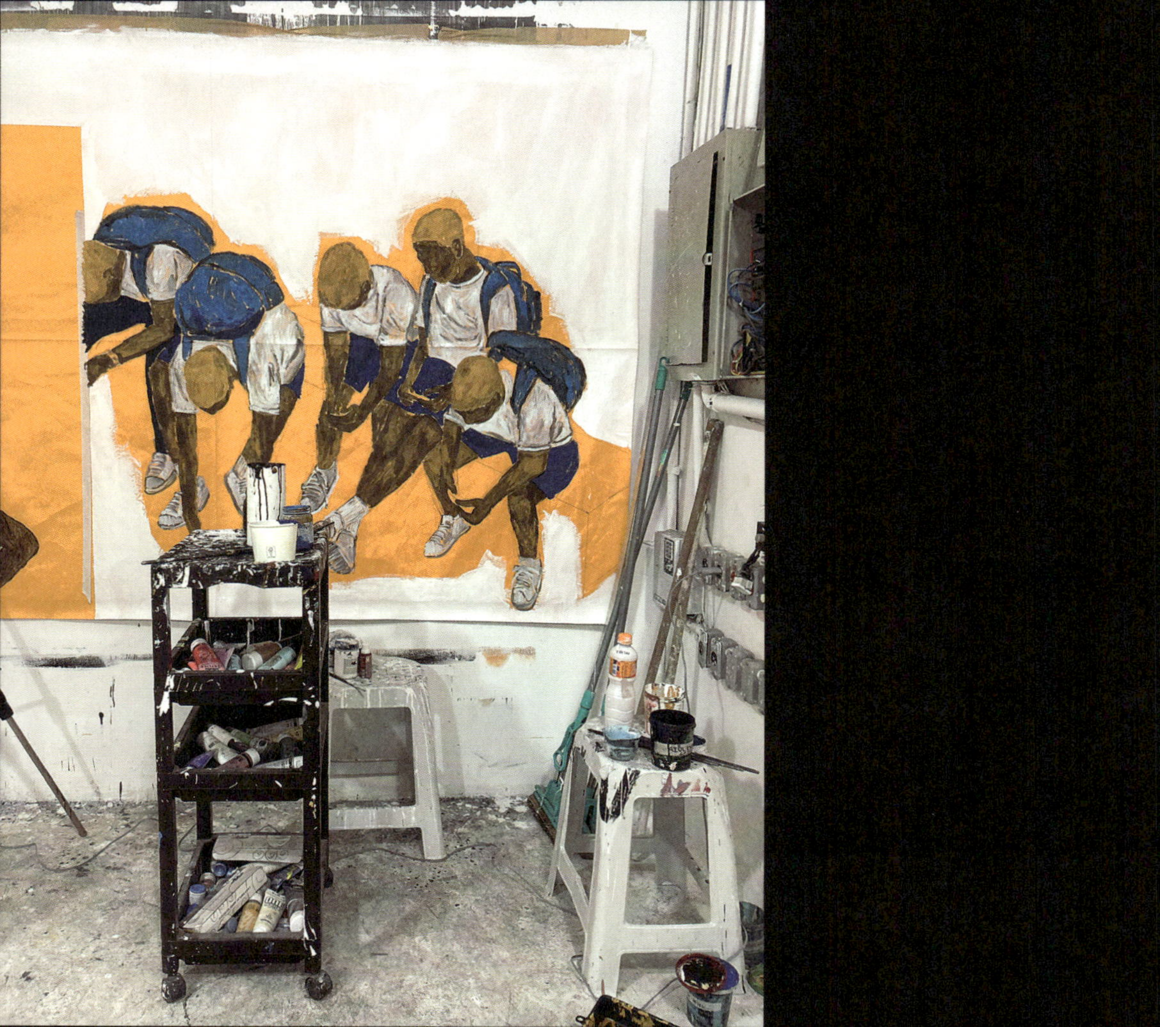

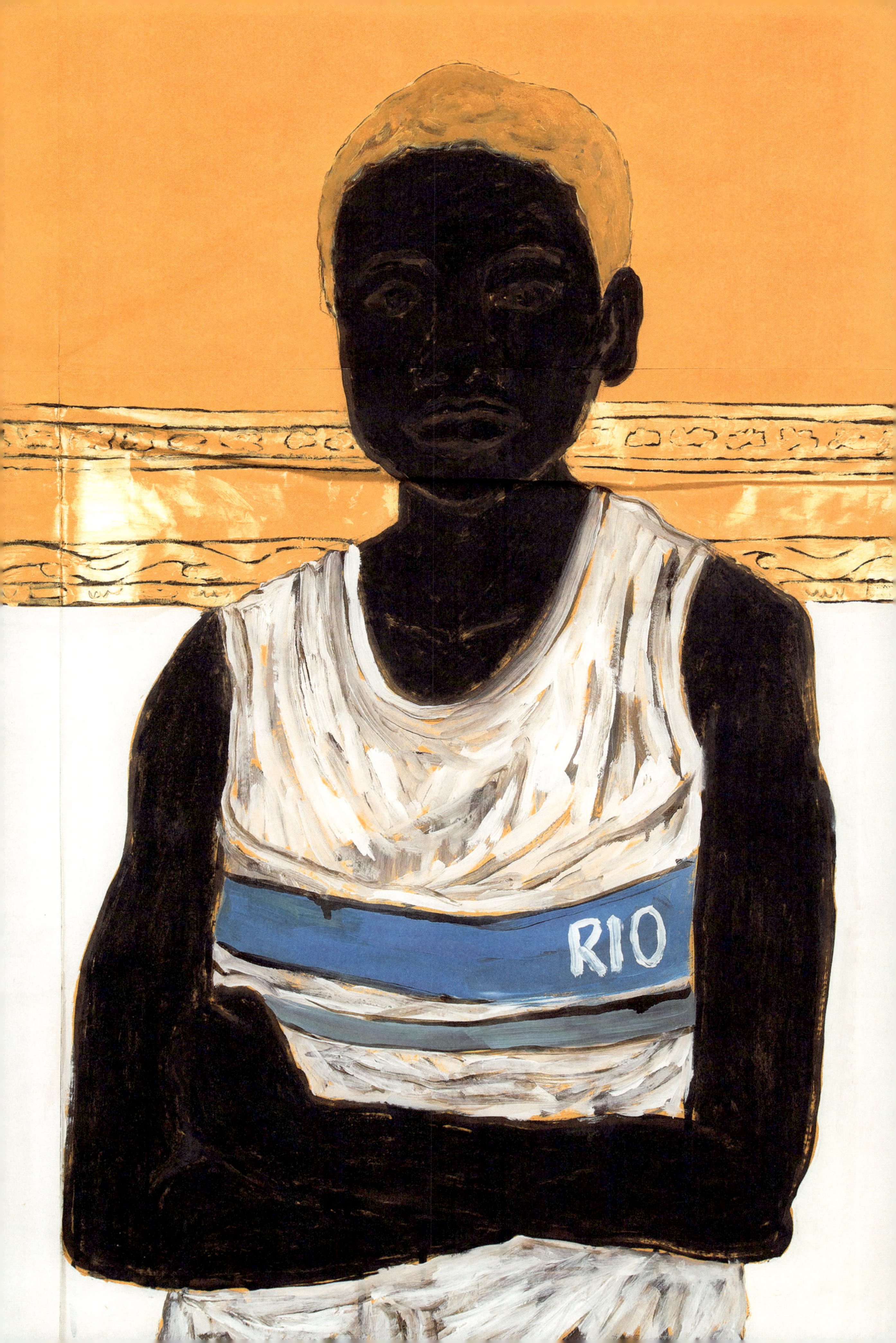
RIO

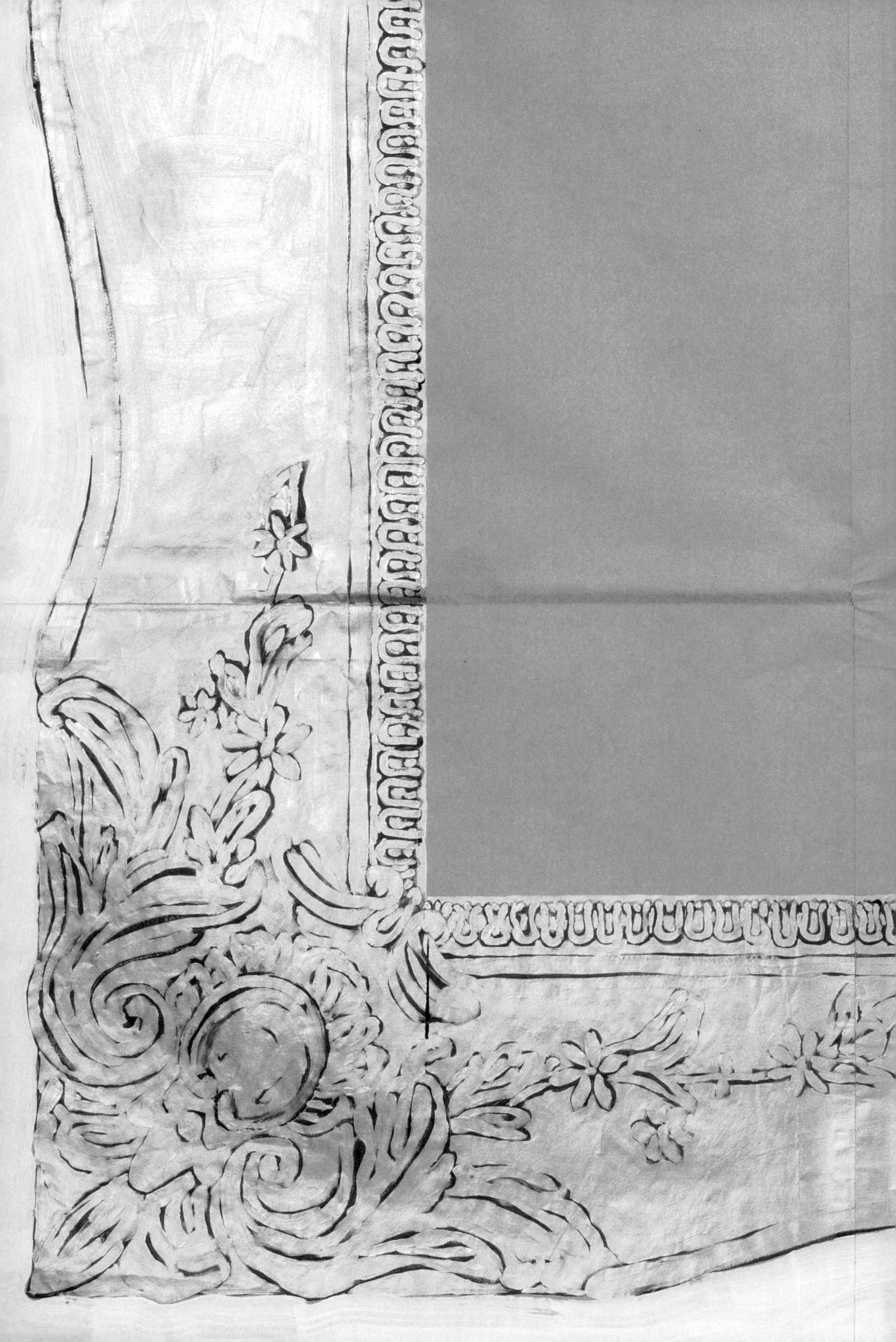

MAXWELL
ALEXANDRE

PARDO É PAPEL

The Glorious Victory and New Power

Edited by
Alessandra Gómez

Verlag der Buchhandlung
Walther und Franz König

With *Pardo é Papel: The Glorious Victory and New Power*, we are proud to present the first North American solo exhibition of work by an extraordinary emerging artist, Maxwell Alexandre. At The Shed, we're committed to nurturing rising talent, supporting innovative artistic practice, and broadening global art historical narratives: these are a few of the many reasons why we've invited Alexandre to share new and existing work from two strands of his series "Pardo é Papel," called "New Power" and "The Glorious Victory."

Born in Rio de Janeiro, Alexandre uses art, rap music, and hip hop culture as powerful tools to connect with his community. Inspired by his expansive vision of how these cultural forms intertwine, Alexandre set off on his journey as an artist in 2017, when he began painting Black subjects on *papel pardo*, a popular and distinct type of yellow-brown Brazilian kraft paper. In Brazilian Portuguese, *pardo* is also a complex term that refers to the skin tones between black and white, and for years it was also an official government category used by the Brazilian Institute of Geography and Statistics to hide Black identity on birth certificates, résumés, and ID cards. Alexandre shares that pardo has colonial connotations, ultimately making it difficult to translate into English. As he shares in the "Testimony" included in this book, he soon realized his choice to paint Black subjects on papel pardo was a political gesture.

Alexandre celebrates Black identity through his own expressions of empowerment—found in pop culture, music, and contemporary art, as well as within Brazil. His paintings are impactful not only because of their scale but also because of the statements Alexandre makes about the importance of Black identity, representation, and his community. He's dreamed of touring this incredibly impactful series around the world beyond Brazil to connect with international audiences who share experiences like his own, and The Shed is honored to be a part of this vision. He is a remarkably gifted artist who has a distinct ability to connect with other disciplines. We are thrilled to be able to share this body of work with our audiences.

I'd like to extend my deep thanks to Maxwell and his studio, to his gallery A Gentil Carioca, and to Frances Reynolds from Instituto Inclusartiz, all of whom have been enthusiastic partners in helping us realize this exhibition. I'd also like to express my gratitude to my talented colleagues at The Shed across all departments, in particular to our chief curator, Andria Hickey, as well as our senior program advisor, Hans Ulrich Obrist, and our former chief curator, Emma Enderby, for their roles in introducing Alexandre and his work to The Shed. Above all, I'm grateful to this exhibition's very talented curator Alessandra Gómez for her commitment and thoughtfulness in bringing this important work to new audiences at The Shed and providing scholarship on Alexandre's practice in this publication. I thank Tina M. Campt for her illuminating essay in this catalogue, along with Alessandra, Maxwell, and Hans Ulrich, who have each contributed incisive texts to this publication, which has been beautifully designed by Normal studio. This catalogue will undoubtedly serve future generations as Maxwell continues on his artistic trajectory and expands his oeuvre.

The work we present at The Shed would not be possible without our wonderful Board chair, Jonathan M. Tisch, who this year has boldly taken over from our founding chair, Daniel L. Doctoroff. I'd also like to thank the entire Board, listed in the acknowledgments, for their continued and thoughtful support. The creation of new work at The Shed has been generously supported by the Lizzie and Jonathan Tisch Commissioning Fund, together with our visionary group of Shed Commissioners, whose names can be found at the back of this book.

Alex Poots
Artistic Director and CEO, The Shed

Alessandra Gómez

Variations of New Power

Monumental paintings float just above the gallery floor, delicately suspended by thin wire and binder clips, disrupting conventions of displaying paintings on walls to create intricate pathways and intimate enclosures in the gallery. These vibrant, large-scale works from the Brazilian artist Maxwell Alexandre's series "Pardo é Papel" (2017–) depict collective portraits on brown kraft paper, or *papel pardo*, and celebrate the empowerment, self-esteem, and prosperity of Black people. Drawn from his own memories of living in one of the largest Brazilian favelas, Rocinha, these paintings present striking figurative scenes of communal leisure interspersed with recurring religious, art historical, and pop culture symbols of capitalist excess, status, and desire. These are depicted alongside Black cultural icons, including Beyoncé, Nina Simone, and Elza Soares, and commercial products from his childhood, such as the popular plastic blue Capri pools, Danone yogurt, and the chocolate drink Toddynho. Moving through these scenographic paper passageways as if traversing a cityscape, each visitor confronts the paintings' commanding physicality as they pull one closer to examine details or push one farther away to take in their expansive compositions (fig. 1). Alexandre implicates visitors' bodies in the experience of viewing these monumental images, which oftentimes hang parallel to one another on multiple spatial planes (fig. 2).

These works, included in *Pardo é Papel: The Glorious Victory and New Power* at The Shed, offer a sweeping introduction to the artist's oeuvre. Alexandre conceives various bodies of artwork within the "Pardo é Papel" series and describes some as albums, making connections to his rap music influences. For his first North American solo exhibition, Alexandre debuts new and existing artwork from the album "A Vitória Gloriosa," or "The Glorious Victory" (2017–), alongside the self-referential subseries "Novo Poder," or "New Power" (2019–), which centers Black spectators enjoying and contemplating artwork in galleries and museums to draw attention to these spaces and their inherent power in legitimizing art historical narratives. These spaces are often exclusionary and inaccessible to communities of color as a result of inequitable practices and the white Western value systems that uphold them.

Though both "The Glorious Victory" and "New Power" are interrelated through Alexandre's explorations of race, Black empowerment, and pride, "The Glorious Victory" primarily centers the prosperity of Black communities through sonic, visual, and linguistic references to hip hop culture and rap music. In contrast, "New Power" focuses on the physical occupation—and disruption—of power dynamics in dominantly white contemporary art spaces. Together, these series capture the architectural density and rhythms of life in Brazil not only from the artist's memories but also from speculative contexts and reimagined representations of power.

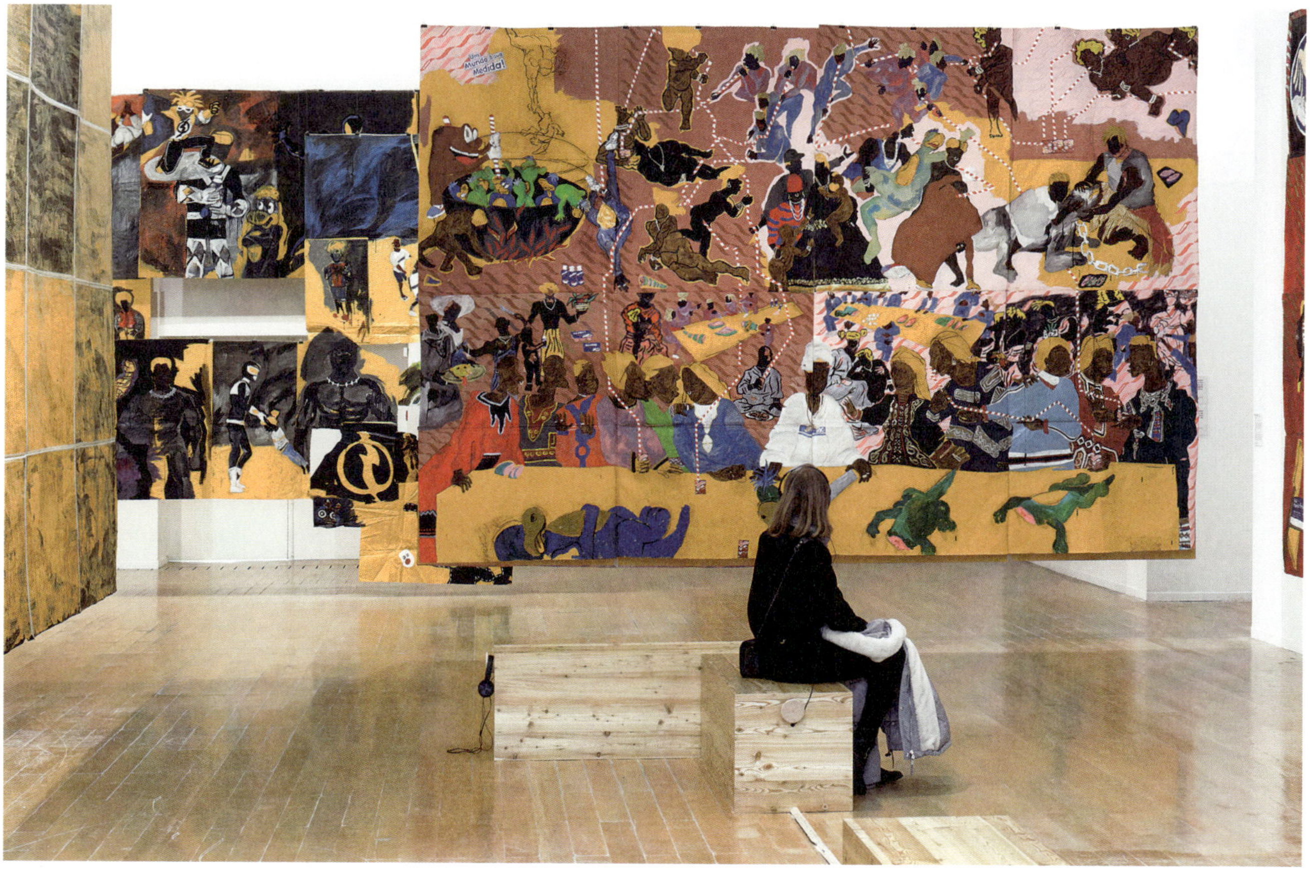

Fig. 1: Installation view: *Não foi pedindo licença que chegamos até aqui* [We didn't get here by apologizing], 2018, from "Pardo é Papel: The Glorious Victory," 2017–. Pardo é Papel, MAC Lyon, March 8–July 7, 2019.

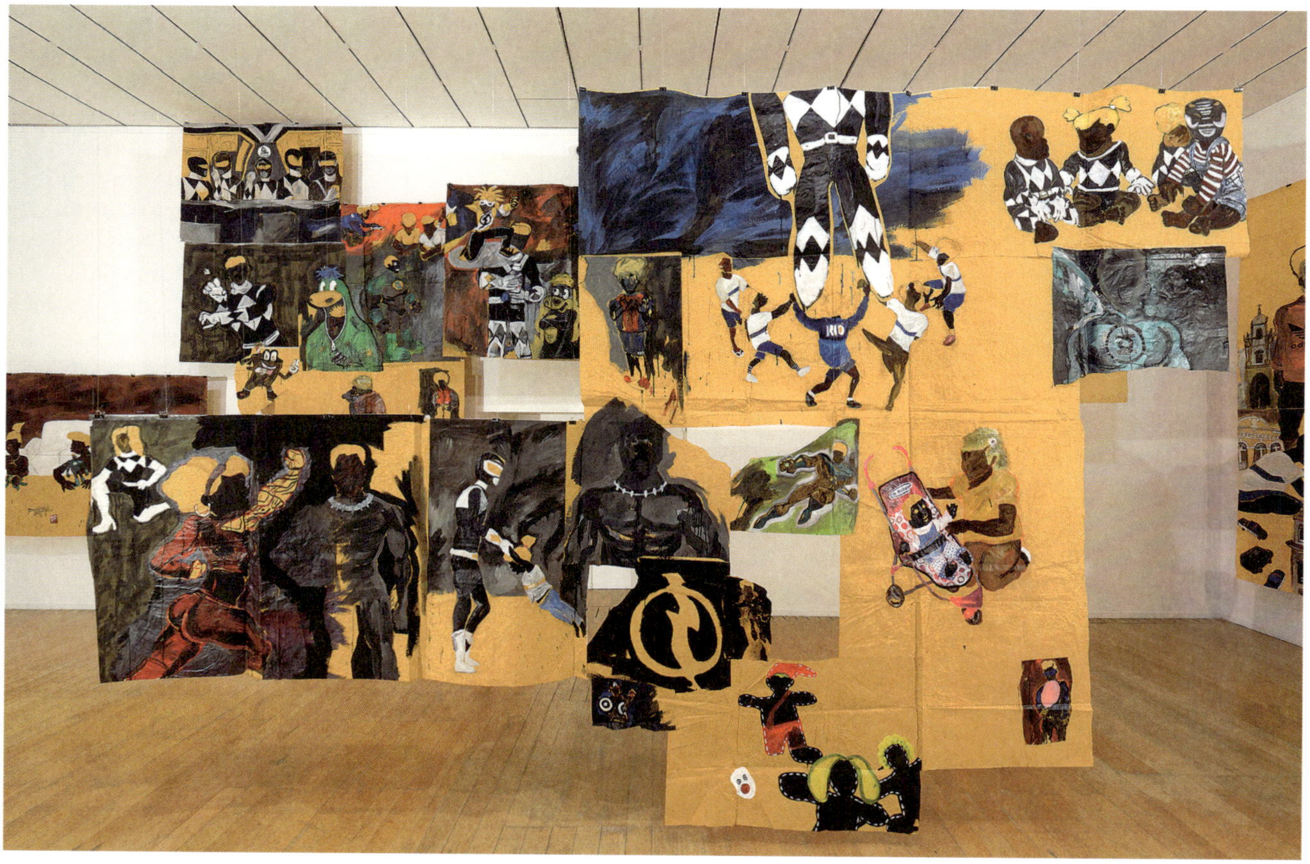

Fig. 2: *Megazord só de Power Ranger Preto* [Megazord only with Black Power Rangers], 2018, from "Pardo é Papel: The Glorious Victory," 2017–. Pardo é Papel, MAC Lyon, March 8–July 7, 2019.

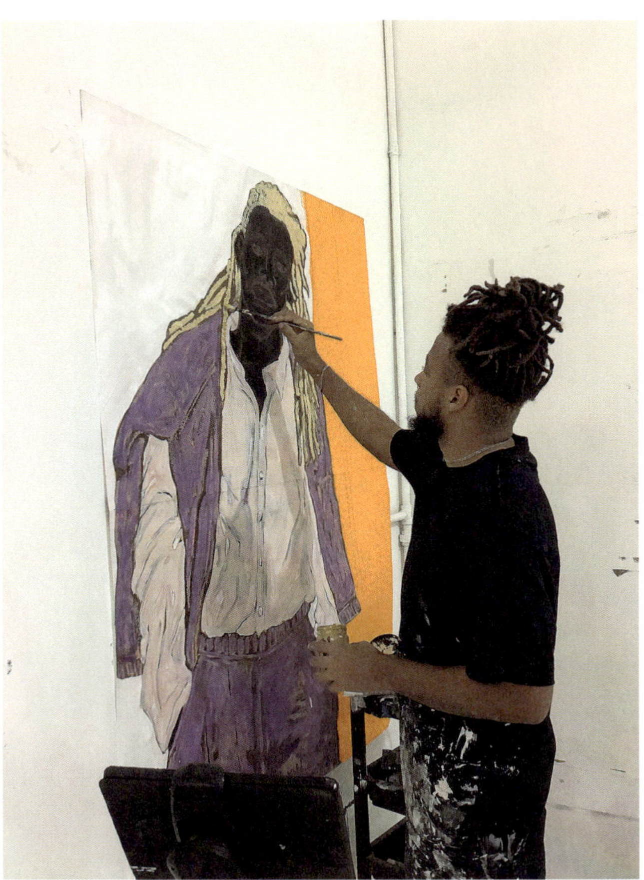

Fig. 3: Maxwell Alexandre in his studio in Gávea, Rio de Janeiro, 2021.

Born in 1990 in Rio de Janeiro, Alexandre served a mandatory term in the army and pursued a career as a professional in-line skater for nearly 12 years before developing an artistic practice. In 2017, after graduating from Pontifical Catholic University of Rio de Janeiro the previous year with a degree in design, Alexandre began painting Black subjects on leftover kraft paper (fig. 3). His work often incorporates graphite, acrylic paint, and unconventional liquids including bitumen, a dense, durable infrastructural mixture used for roofing and roads, and everyday cosmetic products such as brown liquid shoe polish and henê hair relaxer. At first, these unconventional painting materials were chosen for their accessibility to the artist, acrylic and oil paints being too expensive an investment at the time. After completing many portraits on kraft paper with them, Alexandre soon came to realize the paper's own conceptual and material significance. This type of yellow-brown kraft paper is commonly referred to in his native Portuguese as *pardo*, a word that also transmits racial and colonial connotations. Alexandre describes pardo as an ambiguous racial category used to whiten and trivialize Black identity in Brazil; in this category, one is considered "less Black, yet not white."[1] Unlike in the United States, Brazil avoided segregationist laws during the 19th century and, instead, promoted eugenicist principles to whiten populations under the guise of racial tolerance. The term pardo is a product of this fraught history. "Pardo é papel," a phrase popularized by Black activists in Brazil, roughly translates in English to "brown is paper" or "brown is a type of paper." However, this English translation fails to capture its origins in those racist 19th-century ideologies.

In Brazil, racial categories refer mostly to one's skin color, regardless of history and ancestry.[2] Because of this, Brazil's census conflates racial identities with skin tones, ultimately resulting in "ambiguous categories that allow people to move in and out of them."[3] Developed by the Brazilian Institute of Geography and Statistics as part of the 1950 census, the term pardo is tied to the history of Brazil's racist ideology of miscegenation, an anti-Black process advocating for the eugenic engineering of lighter-skinned populations across generations, actively promoted by the Brazilian nation-state. Many activists involved with Brazil's Black Movement argue that the term pardo was implemented to hide the ancestry of Afro-Brazilians, obscure Black identity, and distort true demographic depictions of Brazil. Anthropologist João Pacheco de Oliveira describes the term as "[having] no other function than to serve as an instrument of the discourse of miscegenation and to gather numerical evidence that reinforces the ideological assumptions regarding the tendency toward the progressive 'whitening' of the Brazilian population."[4] Alexandre shares

1 Maxwell Alexandre and Judith Benhanmou-Huet, "Maxwell Alexandre, Palais de Tokyo, November 2021." YouTube, December 2, 2021. Video, 9:55. https://www.youtube.com/watch?v=oLmXg74vscc.

2 Edward Telles and Tianna Paschel, "Who Is Black, White, or Mixed Race? How Skin Color, Status, and Nation Shape Racial Classification in Latin America," *American Journal of Sociology* 120, no. 3 (2014): 869. https://doi.org/10.1086/679252.

3 Karla Mendes, "'I Am Indigenous, Not Pardo': Push for Self-Declaration in Brazil's Census." Pulitzer Center, July 6, 2021. https://pulitzercenter.org/stories/i-am-indigenous-not-pardo-push-self-declaration-brazils-census.

4 Ibid.

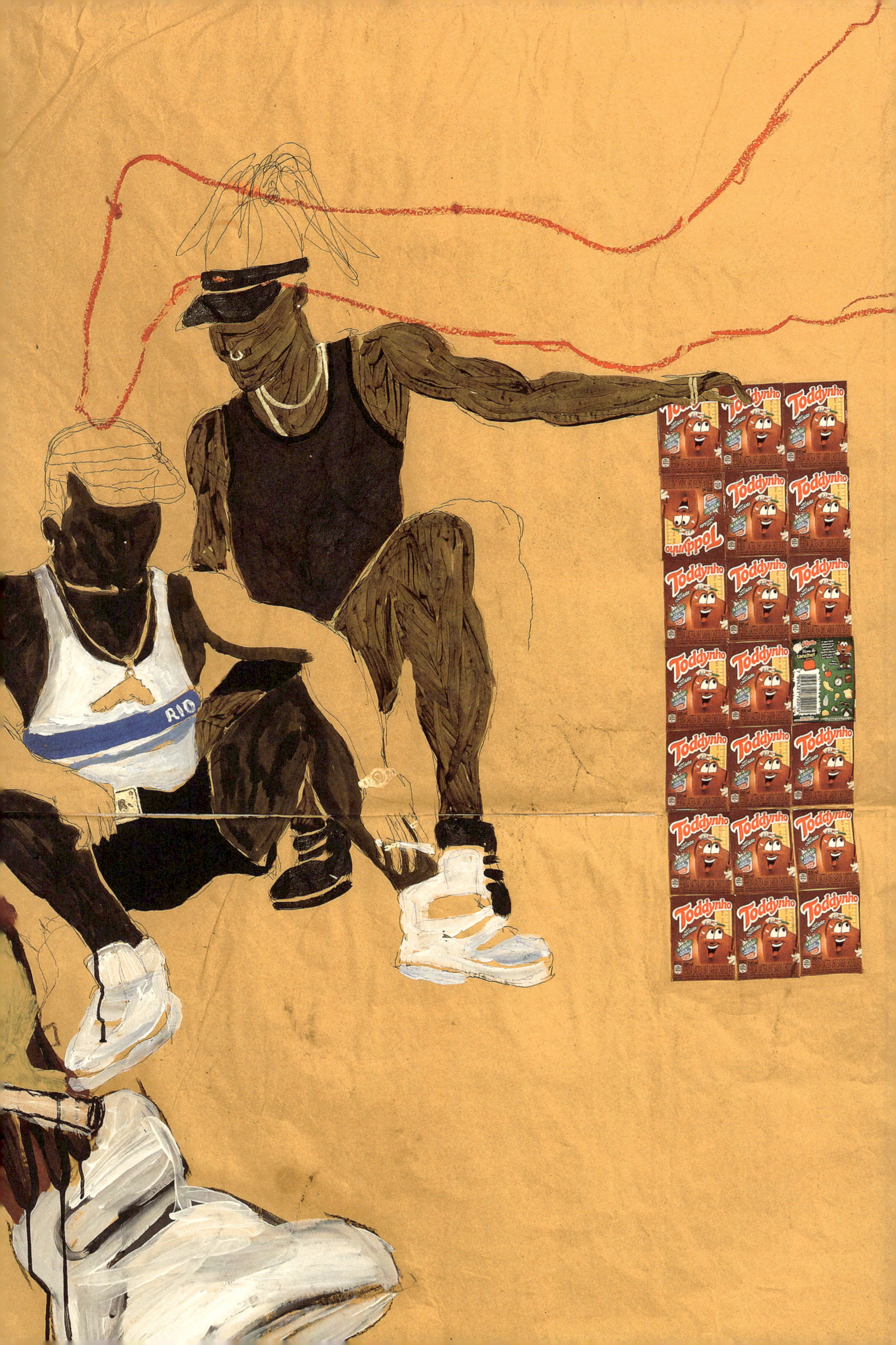
RIO
Toddynho

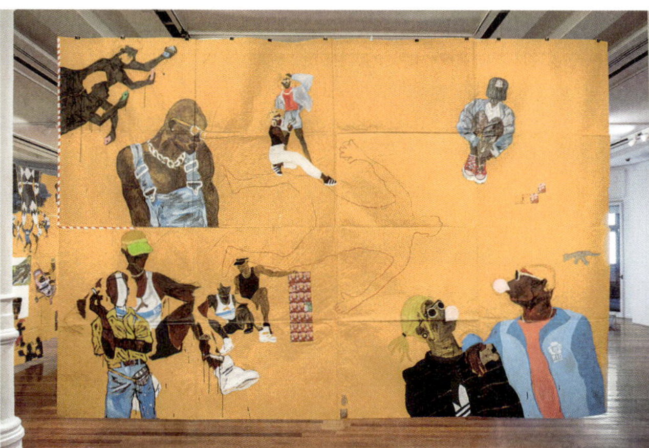

Fig. 5: Installation view: *Bilionário escuro* [Dark Billionaire], 2018, from "Pardo é Papel: The Glorious Victory," 2017–. Pardo é Papel, Museu de Arte do Rio, November 2019–May 2020.

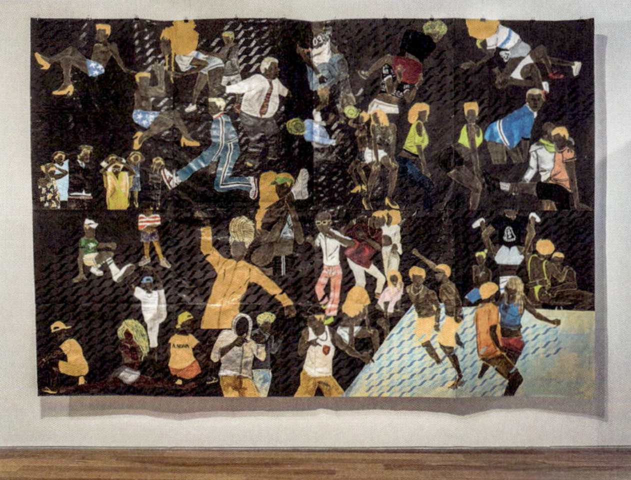

Fig. 6: Installation view: *A lua quer ser preta, se pinta no eclipse (diss)* [The moon wants to be black, it paints itself in the eclipse (diss)], 2019, from "Pardo é Papel: The Glorious Victory," 2017–. Pardo é Papel, Museu de Arte do Rio, November 2019–May 2020.

Fig. 4 (opposite page): *Bilionário escuro* [Dark Billionaire] (detail), 2018, from "Pardo é Papel: The Glorious Victory," 2017–. Latex, grease, henna, bitumen, dye, acrylic, vinyl, graphite, ballpoint pen, charcoal, oil stick, and powdered chocolate wrapping paper on brown kraft paper.

Pacheco de Oliveira's belief; as the artist explains of his intentions behind "Pardo é Papel," "I created this series to talk about self-esteem and Black pride [because] the term pardo has been used for whitening."[5] Grappling with the historical weaponization of this term specifically against Black people, Alexandre deliberately paints Black subjects on pardo paper as an empowering political and conceptual statement, one that requires viewers to look well beyond the formal qualities of his work in order to contend with these painful legacies that continue to affect how Black identity is stratified in Brazil.

Throughout "Pardo é Papel," Alexandre leaves sections of the kraft paper unpainted to highlight its own color as well as its conceptual significance, exposing all of its wrinkles, creases, softer textural qualities, and even tears (figs. 4, 5). By taping together paper rectangles to create larger surfaces without hiding edges, he allows his artworks to retain a quilted, grid-like quality. And unlike the resilience of traditional canvas, suspended kraft paper is a delicate, precarious material that sways in response to any nearby movement. Reflecting on the importance of an artwork's materiality, contemporary artist Kerry James Marshall observes, "[Images] may have the capacity to transport, but the thingness of the thing, the materiality of the painting, has a profound impact on the way you relate to the object," which is why the history of pardo, not just the captivating scenes within his artwork, is crucial to this interpretation.[6] By adapting kraft paper as the conceptual and material foundation of his paintings, Alexandre insists on the term pardo as a descriptor of paper rather than a masking of Black identity to make Brazilian society seem whiter, or less Black.

Unlike one of his earliest painting series, "Reprovados" (2017), which portrays scenes of racial oppression and injustice toward Black communities, "The Glorious Victory" focuses on their prosperity and empowerment through sonic, linguistic, and visual references to international and local rap music alongside cultural references to Rocinha. Often set against a backdrop of shimmering gold or patterned monochromatic blue waves, famous Black political and religious leaders, activists, students, musicians, and other community members occupy all corners of Alexandre's towering paper paintings (fig. 6). All the figures share the same dyed-blonde hairstyle as their creator, hinting that they are extensions of the artist himself. The recurring symbols that Alexandre incorporates to honor his community with broader artistic representation (the wave patterning derived from Capri pools, the brands Toddynho and Danone) may be recognizable luxuries to communities from Rocinha who are represented in the artwork itself, or to those with connections to Brazilian culture. For instance, Alexandre derives

5
Hans Ulrich Obrist, "Maxwell Alexandre," in *Hans Ulrich Obrist–Entrevistas brasileiras*, vol. 1, ed. Hans Ulrich Obrist (Rio de Janeiro: Cobogó, 2020), 403. (Unpublished translation by Matthew Rinaldi.)

6
Luc Tuymans and Kerry James Marshall, "Luc Tuymans and Kerry James Marshall in Conversation," *BOMB* no. 92 (2005): 54. http://www.jstor.org/stable/40427228.

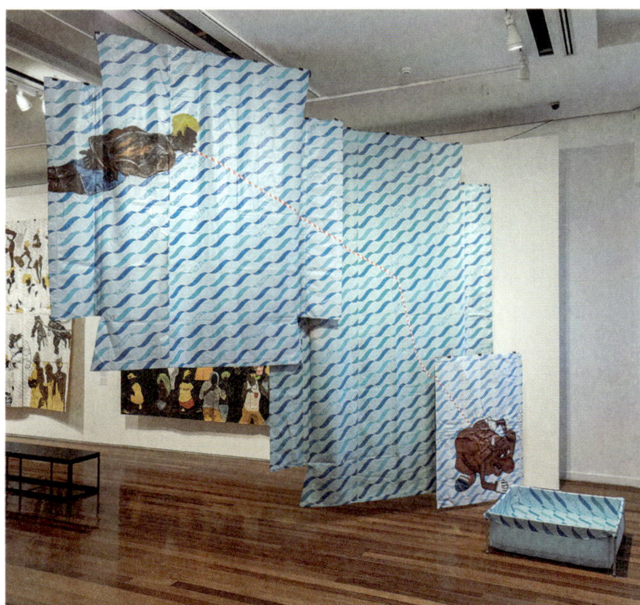

Fig. 7: Installation view: *Até Deus inveja o homem preto* [Even God envies the Black man], 2018, from "Pardo é Papel: The Glorious Victory," 2017–, Pardo é Papel, Museu de Arte do Rio, November 2019–May 2020.

Fig. 8 (opposite page): *Close a door to open a window* (detail), 2020, from "Pardo é Papel: Close a door to open a window," 2020–. Latex, shoe polish, hair relaxer, bitumen, graphite, acrylic, pigment, charcoal, and oil stick on brown kraft paper.

the wave patterning in the background of his paintings from the aforementioned inflatable Capri pools commonly found atop favela rooftops, legible as a status symbol only to those living in Rocinha (fig. 7). Outside of Rocinha, Capri pools are not considered luxurious, but by incorporating the patterning throughout his work, Alexandre asserts their value, giving them equal standing alongside the more universally recognizable luxuries, such as iPhones, private aircraft, and sleek convertible cars (fig. 8).

In addition to the status symbols that Alexandre elevates from the Rocinha community, he draws on musical influences. Alexandre incorporates lyrics by local Brazilian rappers Baco Exu do Blues, BK', and Djonga into his titles as a way to meaningfully connect with his community in "The Glorious Victory" and a subsequent album, "Close a door to open a window," which borrows its title from a song by US rapper Tyler, the Creator. Alexandre observes that contemporary art is not necessarily valued in conversations he has with his Rocinha community, whereas rap music makes up a more intrinsic part of the culture (figs. 9, 10).[7] According to linguist, scholar, and anthropologist Jennifer Roth-Gordon, "[Brazilian] rappers and their fans' understanding of race and racial inequality is heavily influenced by the US civil rights movement," given their shared experiences of racism, police brutality, and social inequity in both countries.[8] To bridge these experiences across two artistic disciplines, Alexandre translates rap lyrics, sometimes abstractly, sometimes figuratively, constructing an entire visual universe around one phrase.

One of Alexandre's most prominent portraits and an inspiration for the larger subseries, "New Power" (2019–), depicts a scene from rapper Jay-Z and singer-songwriter Beyoncé's *Apeshit* music video, from their collaborative album as The Carters, *Everything Is Love* (2018) (fig. 11). In the video, wearing sharply tailored green-and-purple pastel suits, lavish diamonds, and gold jewelry, their hands clasped tightly together, chins slightly raised, and looking down upon us, The Carters pose in front of Leonardo da Vinci's *Mona Lisa* (1503). Art historian and performance scholar Alexandra Thomas discusses this music video as "an embodied intervention of Western art," further explaining that white people attend museums to "romanticize empire, to think about genealogies of white male artists."[9] Directly referencing this scene in his painting *Novo Poder* (2019), Alexandre includes an ornate gold frame surrounding raw pardo paper in a nod to his own artistic oeuvre (in the same position that the *Mona Lisa* was situated in Jay-Z and Beyoncé's music video). By replacing the famous Renaissance painting with pardo paper, Alexandre inserts his own artwork, community, and locality into

7
Obrist, "Maxwell Alexandre," 406.

8
Jennifer Roth-Gordon, *Race and the Brazilian Body: Blackness, Whiteness, and Everyday Language in Rio De Janeiro* (Oakland: University of California Press, 2017), 166.

9
Thomas, quoted in Cady Lang, "Art History Experts Explain the Meaning of the Art in Beyoncé and Jay Z's 'Apesh-t' Video." *Time*, June 19, 2018. https://time.com/5315275/art-references-meaning-beyonce-jay-z-apeshit-louvre-music-video/.

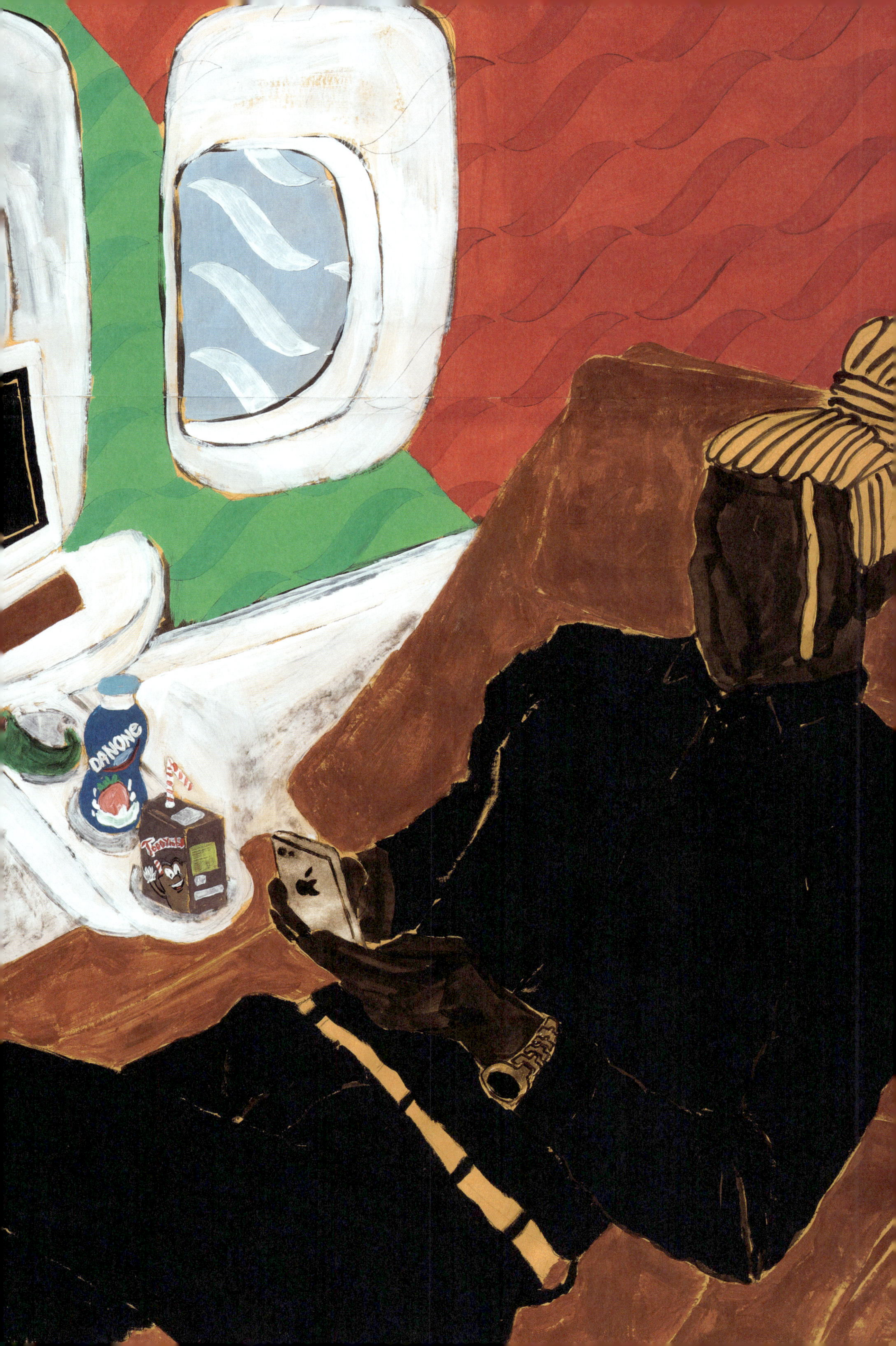
DANONE

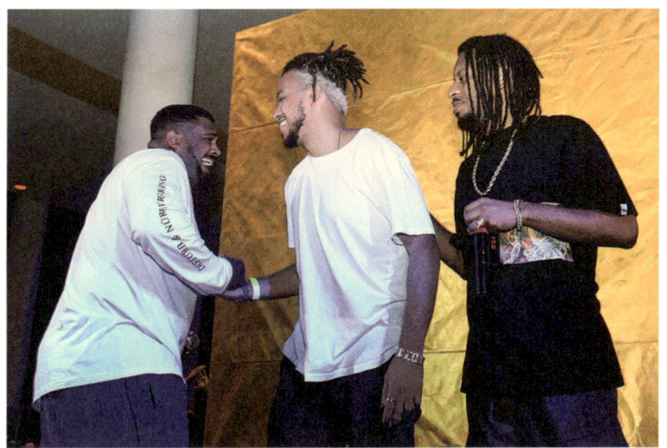

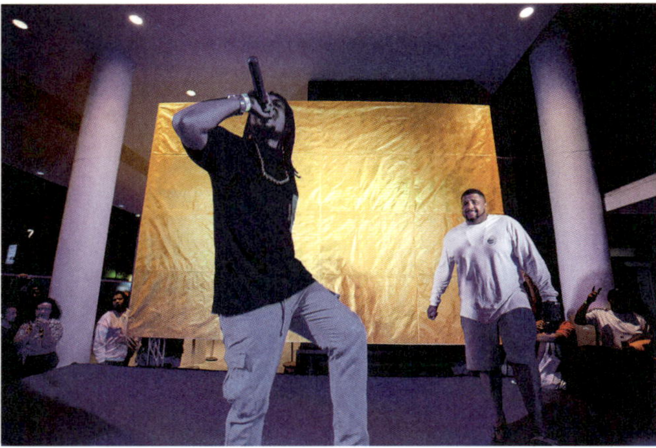

Figs. 9, 10: Scenes from a "Pardo é Papel" performance with BK' and Baco Exu do Blues, Museu de Arte do Rio, 2019. Top image, left to right: Baco Exu do Blues, Maxwell Alexandre, BK'.

white contemporary art spaces that exclude Black artistic representation and subjects. Surrounding the iconic duo are attentive visitors observing multiple versions of Alexandre's bare pardo paper artworks, scenes that serve as a subtext to the exhibition itself (fig. 12).

In contrast to his figurative works throughout "Pardo é Papel," and serving as another precedent to "New Power," Alexandre's only abstract piece, *O mundo é nosso* (2018), whose title translates to "The world is ours," shares its name with a Brazilian rap song by Djonga featuring BK'. In this monochrome, consisting of four sheets of kraft paper, each rectangular surface of the painting is consumed by a black substance (figs. 13, 14). Rather than using paint, Alexandre returns to the liquid polish he used for his daily shoe maintenance while serving in the army from 2009 to 2010. Although the work is monochromatic, the semitransparent nature of the shoe polish on the paper, along with the visible texture from the paintbrush hairs, dried drips, and paper creases, animates its surface. Because of the inspiration Alexandre finds in music, *O mundo é nosso* could be interpreted as a visual translation of Djonga's poetic chorus:

> Como se fosse a noite, cê vê tudo preto
> Como fosse um blackout, cê vê tudo preto
> São meus manos, minhas minas
> Meus irmãos, minhas irmãs, yeah
> O mundo é nosso, hã
>
> Like the night, everything is black
> Like a blackout, everything is black
> My bros, my sistas
> My brothers, my sisters, yeah
> The world is ours

Against the soundscape of Djonga's captivating lyrics, Alexandre explores the symbolic possibilities of an abstract black monochrome, shifting away from figurative subjects (i.e., my brothers, my sisters) yet still referencing them.

With the absence of a Black figure in this artwork, the connection between Djonga's lyrics and Alexandre's abstraction is what scholar and curator Adrienne Edwards deems "an attempt to understand how artists negotiate and exhaust the paradigm of Black representation in visual art."[10] The artist's own words affirm Edwards's observation that "[i]f you're Black, from the favela, and you're an artist, [there is this assumption that] your art has to be political. [. . .] The Black artist has less room to talk about sublime subject matter, about the spirit."[11] Acknowledging that his artwork occupies a political context through his use of pardo paper, Alexandre mentions that there isn't necessarily a separation between abstraction and figuration in his artwork.[12] In another, earlier series, "Afirmações de Terreno" (2015),

10 Adrienne Edwards, *Blackness in Abstraction* (New York: Pace Gallery, 2016), 68.

11 Alexandre, quoted in Obrist, "Maxwell Alexandre," 405.

12 Tash Nikol, "The Divine Comedy of Maxwell Alexandre's Brown Paper Universe." *Highsnobiety*, December 2, 2020. https://www.highsnobiety.com/p/maxwell-alexandre-interview/.

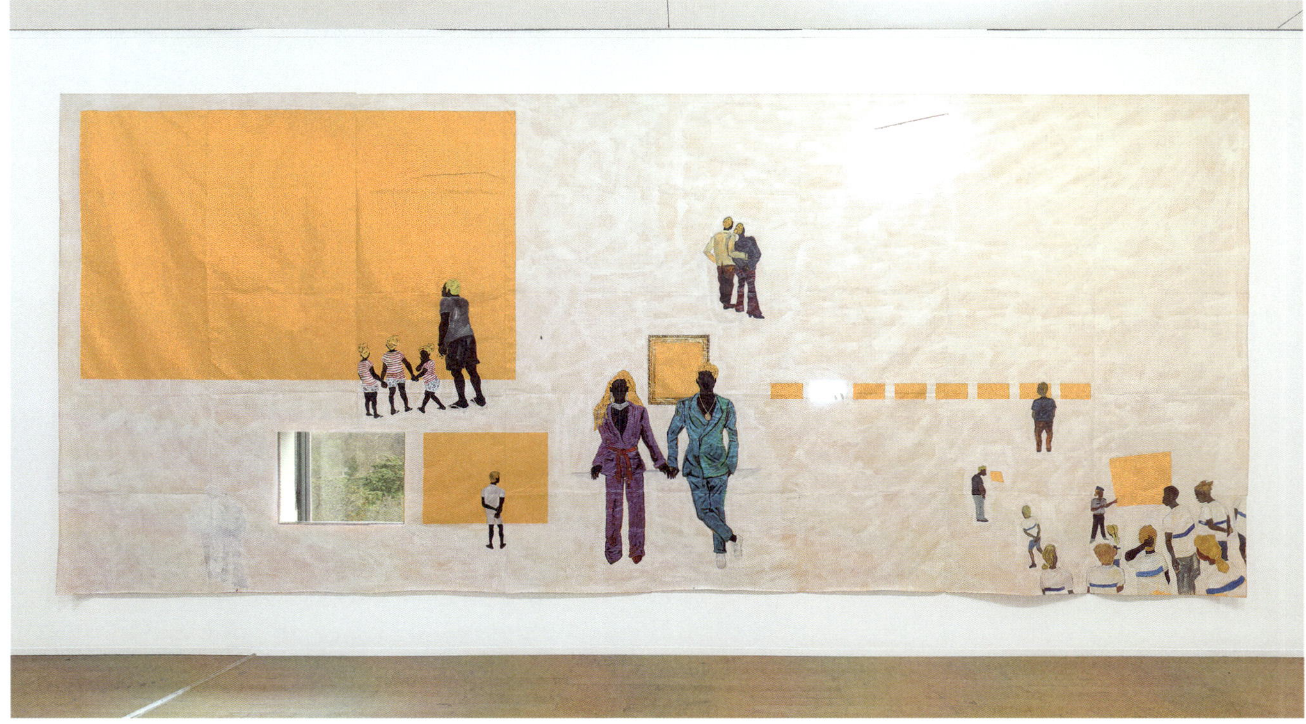

Fig. 11: Installation view: *Novo Poder* [New Power], 2019, from "Pardo é Papel: New Power," 2019–. Pardo é Papel, MAC Lyon, March 8–July 7, 2019.

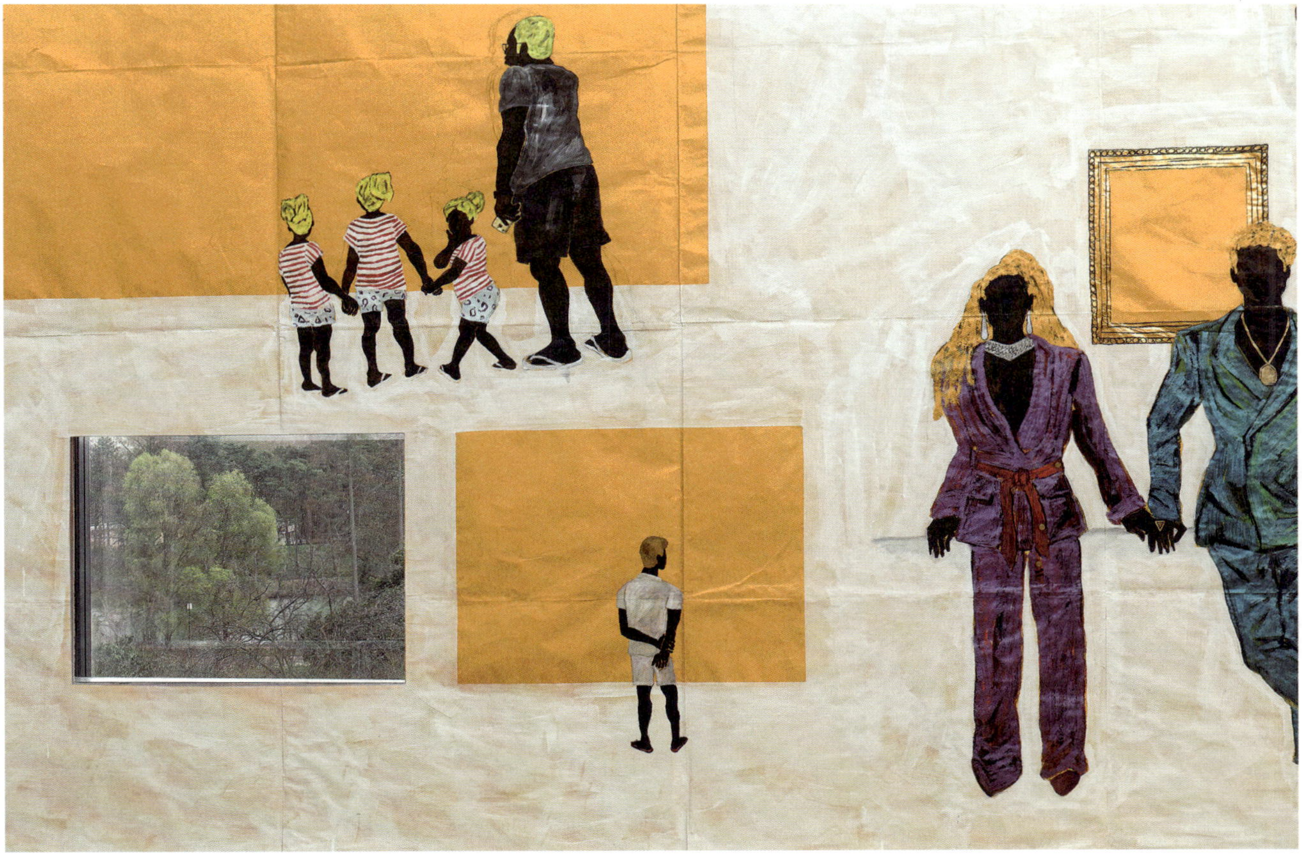

Fig. 12: *Novo Poder* [New Power] (detail), 2019, from "Pardo é Papel: New Power," 2019–. Latex, shoe polish. Bitumen, dye, graphite, charcoal, acrylic, and oil stick on brown kraft paper.

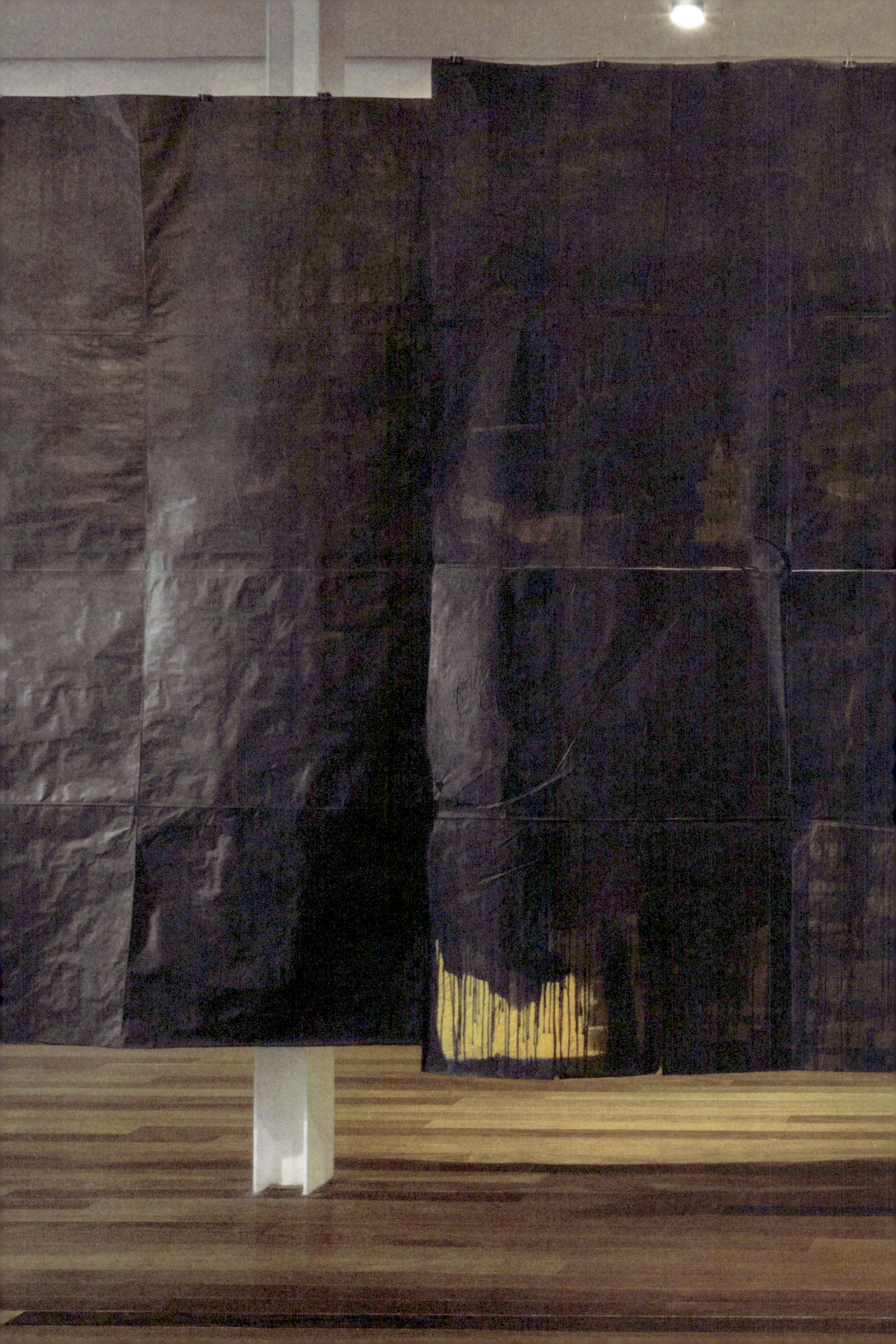

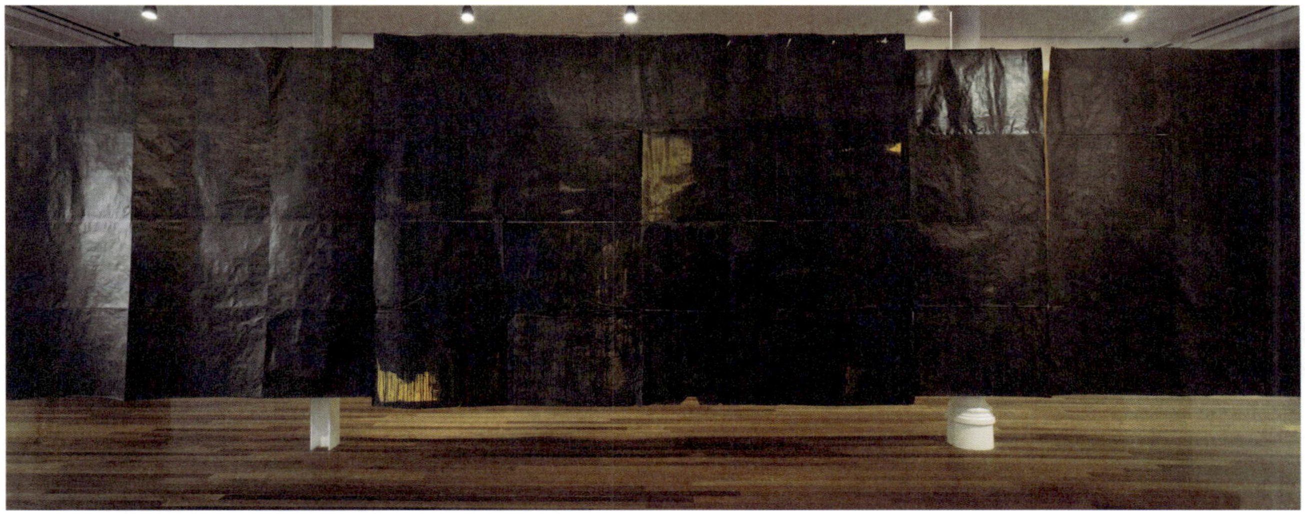

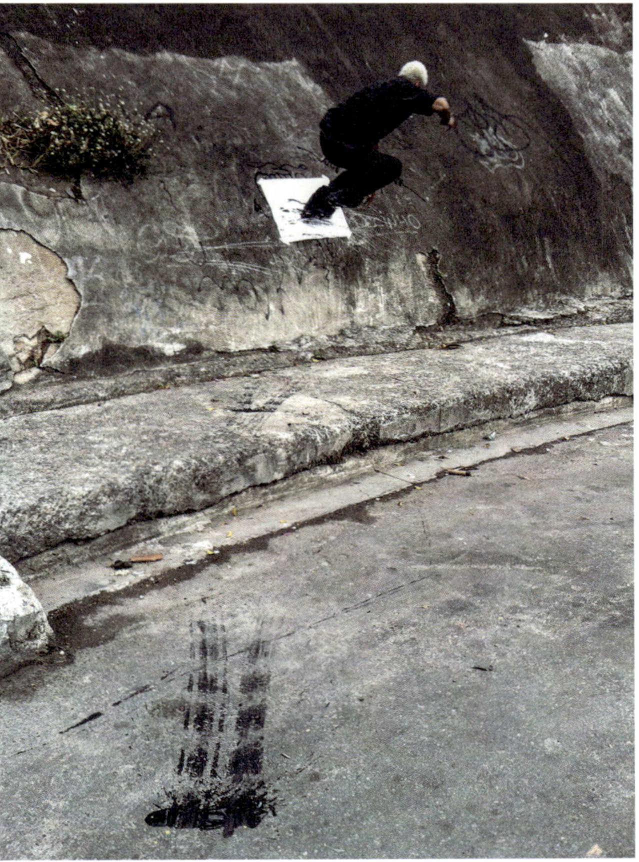

Fig. 15: Alexandre creating *Afirmações de terreno* [Terrain statements], 2016.

Fig. 14: Installation view: *O mundo é nosso* [The world is ours], 2018, from "Pardo é Papel: The Glorious Victory," 2017–. Pardo é Papel, Museu de Arte do Rio, November 2019–May 2020.

Alexandre created paintings by placing large canvases on the floor or on walls throughout the city, then coating the wheels of his skates in paint and rolling across the canvases to document his movements, resulting in abstract linear compositions (fig. 15). Although the composition is formally abstract, the works still contain corporeal references as they document the artist's exhaustive physical movements across the surface. As in this series and *O mundo é nosso*, these abstract sensibilities reappear in subtle yet compelling ways in later works, including his most recent subseries, "New Power."

In the "New Power" subseries exhibited at The Shed, which Alexandre has expanded with new work since its debut at the Palais de Tokyo (November 26, 2021–March 13, 2022), white monochromatic paintings on pardo paper organize the space, replacing freestanding exhibition walls and extending the gallery architecture (fig. 16). Alexandre depicts Black audiences observing and enjoying art in museums and galleries and considers contemporary art or intellectual capital as a form of new power. In these moments of the visitor's self-conscious spectatorship alongside Alexandre's subjects, he creates a mise-en-abîme, or formal technique that reproduces a copy within a copy. In this case, it's a gallery within a gallery, a painting within a painting, an audience aware of another audience, surveilled by human museum guards and illustrated museum guards, each watching over their respective audiences sitting, posing, photographing, and contemplating art. Most of Alexandre's figures in these paintings turn inward, with the occasional exception of a watchful guard observing the materiality of pardo artworks, just as a visitor does (fig. 17). In viewing these artworks, visitors and painted figures share space as a collective audience (fig. 18).

Fig. 13 (opposite page): Installation view: *O mundo é nosso* [The world is ours] (detail), 2018, from "Pardo é Papel: The Glorious Victory," 2017–. Pardo é Papel, Museu de Arte do Rio, November 2019–May 2020.

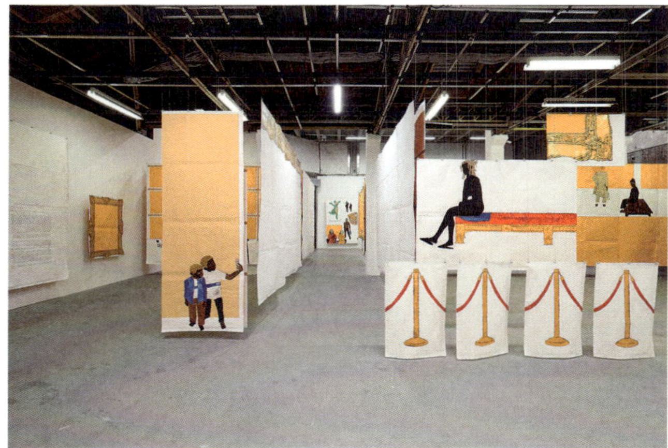

Fig. 16: Installation view: *New Power*, Palais de Tokyo, Paris, November 26, 2021–March 13, 2022.

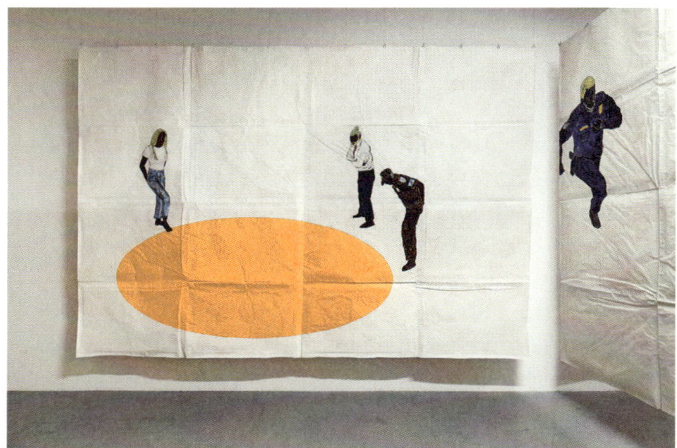

Fig. 17: Installation view: *Descent into limbo*, 2021, from "Pardo é Papel: New Power," 2019–. New Power, Palais de Tokyo, Paris, November 26, 2021–March 13, 2022.

Despite the similarities between pictorial representation and the physical gallery space and surroundings in which the audience resides, Alexandre destabilizes the symmetry of the mise-en-abîme. Like Jay-Z and Beyoncé's assertion of Black representation at the Louvre in *Apeshit*, Alexandre describes how his paintings demonstrate a reality not always reflected inside of predominantly white institutional art spaces: "[A]s a Black artist, I was concerned about having an exhibition where the audience is white and Black people only occupy service-oriented roles," such as that of a museum guard who cares for the artwork.[13] The presence of white audiences ruptures Alexandre's intended desire for the mise-en-abîme, to have Black audiences that are both physically present in the gallery and reflected in his work. This rupture serves as a critical reflection back onto white spaces of the art world, where the inclusion of Black artists does not necessarily equal substantive representation when the same inclusion is not also extended to audiences, board members, and arts workers through equitable practices. Alexandre prompts visitors to bring a level of self-awareness to art institutions by observing who inhabits them, who is represented in them, and who holds the power within their organizational structures.

Inclusive of paintings commissioned specifically for this exhibition at The Shed, this expansive new era of Alexandre's "Pardo é Papel" series presents a powerful expression of Brazilian Black identity. Through these captivating bodies of work that transition from Rio de Janeiro's dense landscape to the interiority of white-cube art spaces, Alexandre issues a vigorous response to the call put out by Carioca rapper BK', whose celebratory chorus declares, "Nós somo' o novo poder."[14] For Alexandre and the Rocinha community and the musicians who inspire his artistic practice, this declaration will continue into the future as an enduring, uninterrupted vision of this mode of existence. Otherwise, as BK' asks in his song, "Se tu não avança, tu vai ser o quê?"[15]

13 Alexandre, quoted in Obrist, "Maxwell Alexandre," 409.

14 We are the new power.

15 If you don't move forward, what will you be?

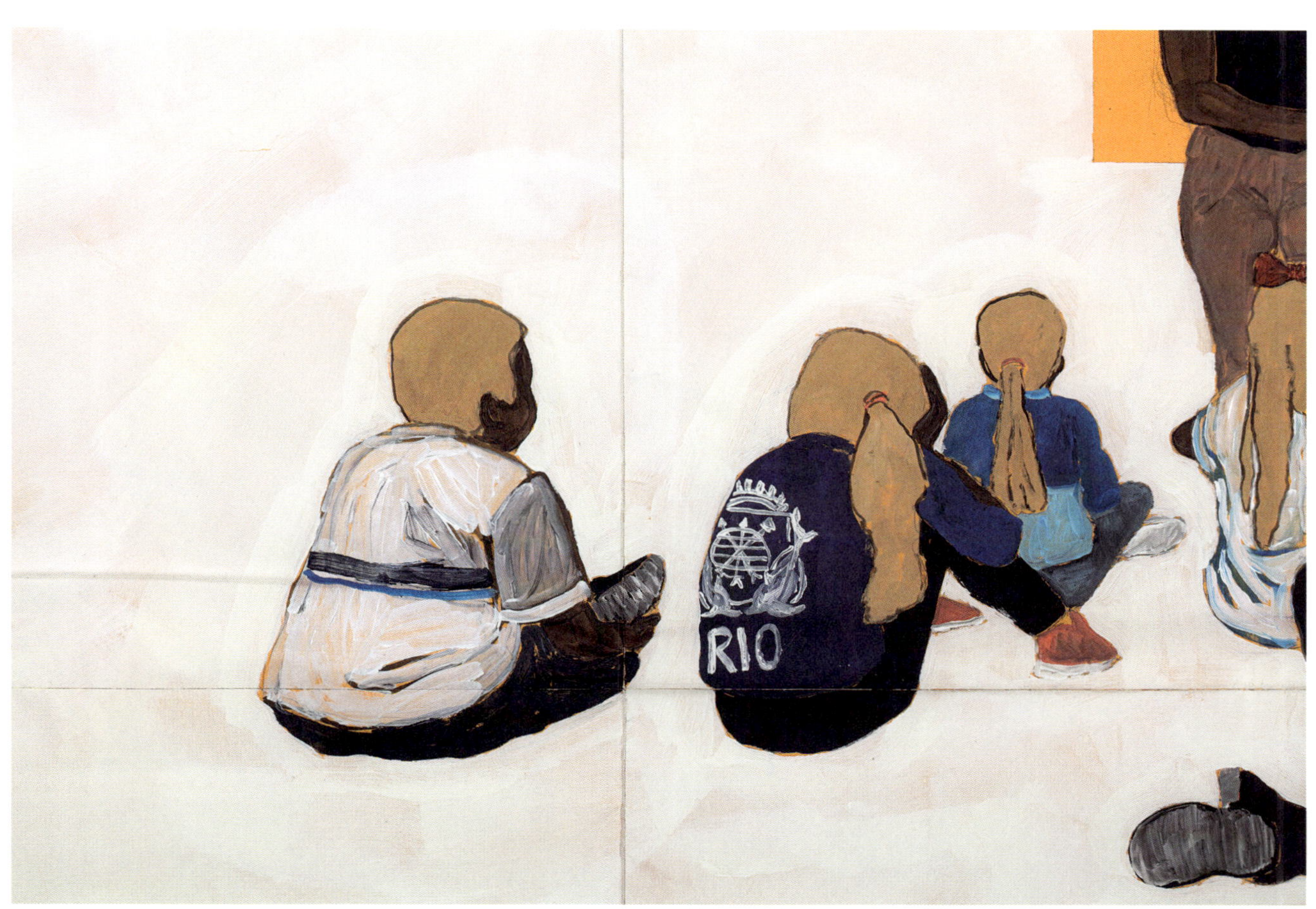

Fig. 18: *sem titulo* [untitled] (detail), 2021 from "Pardo é Papel: New Power," 2019–. Shoe polish, bitumen, charcoal, graphite, latex, and acrylic on brown kraft paper.

sem título [untitled] (detail), 2021.

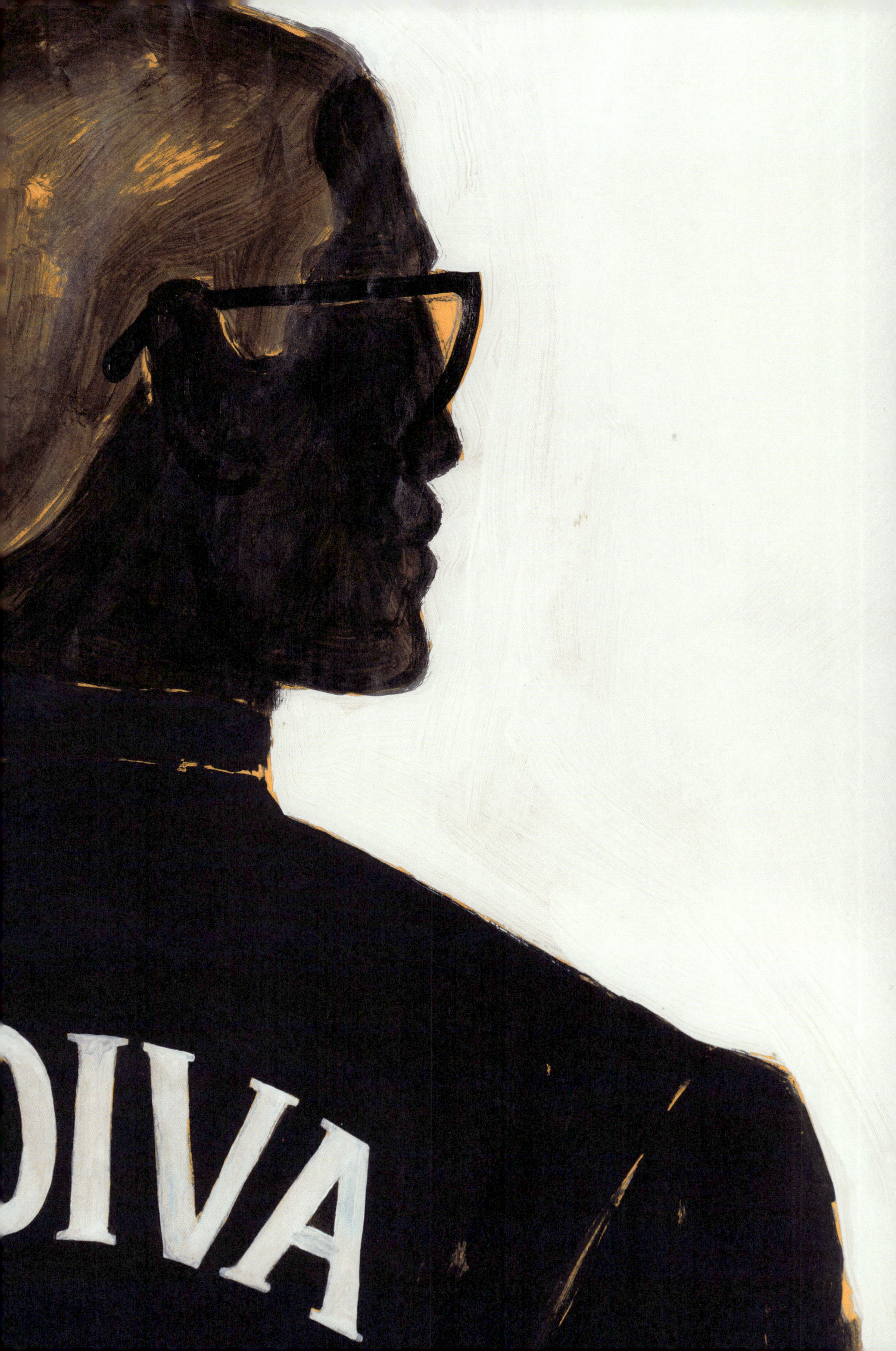
DIVA

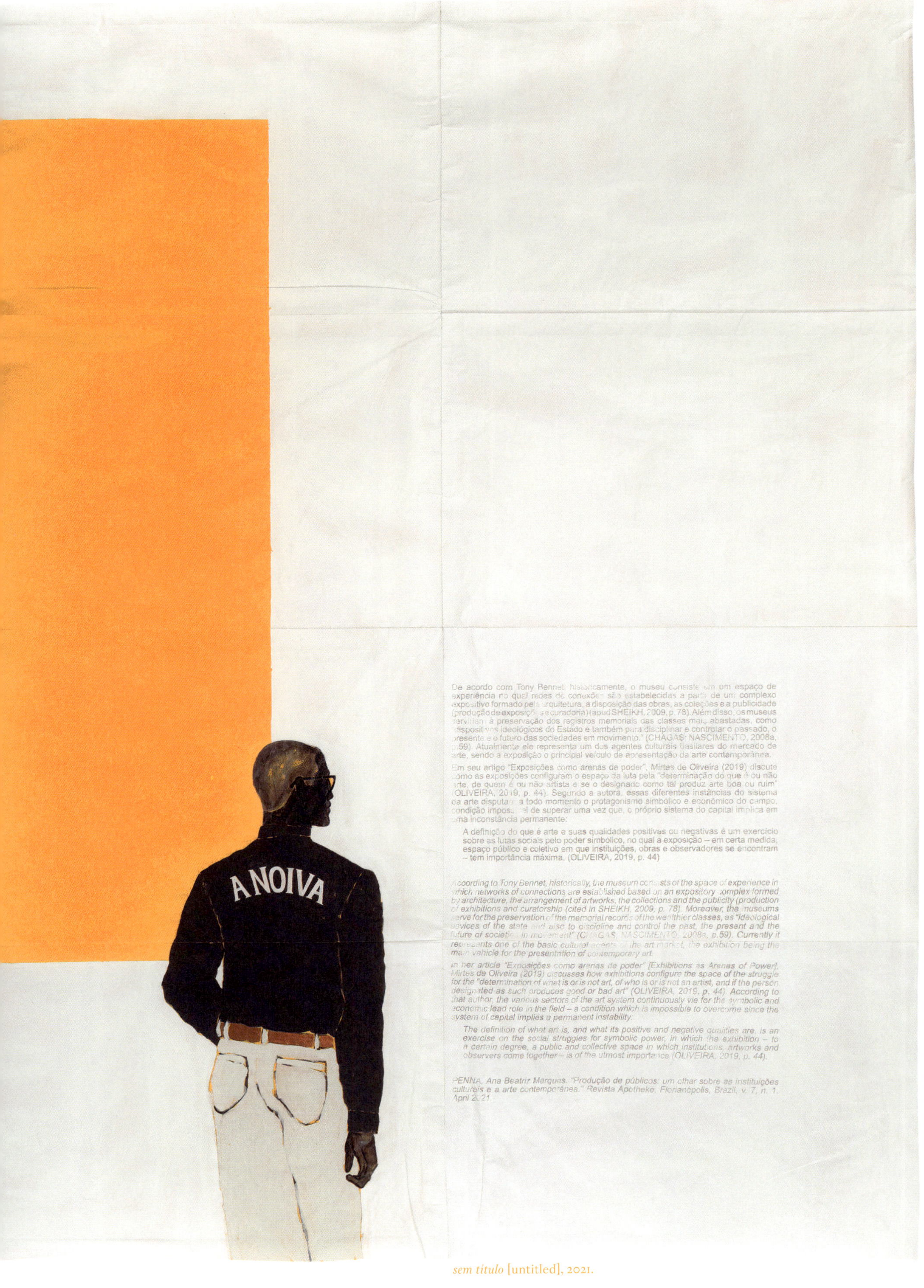

sem título [untitled], 2021.

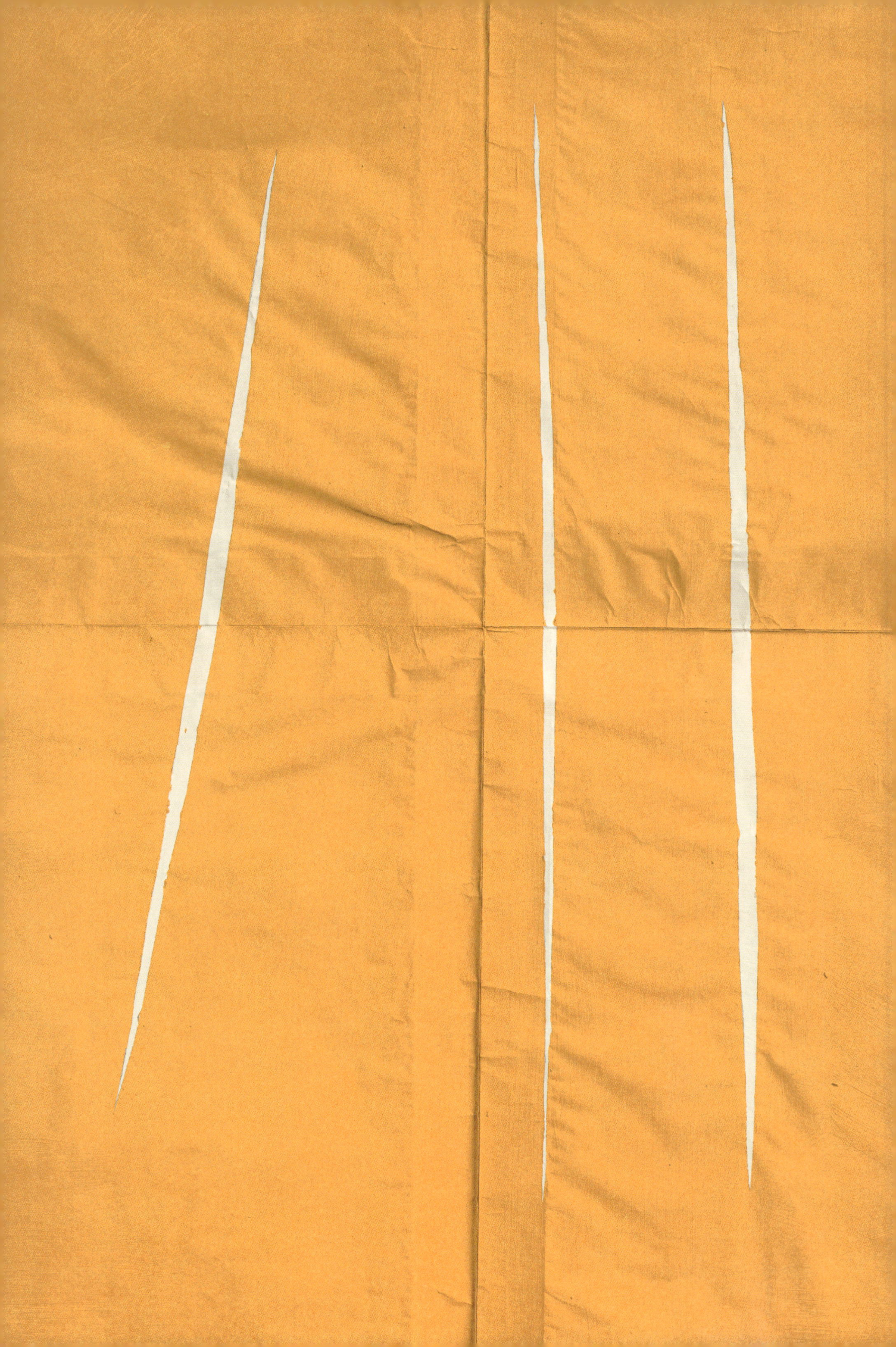

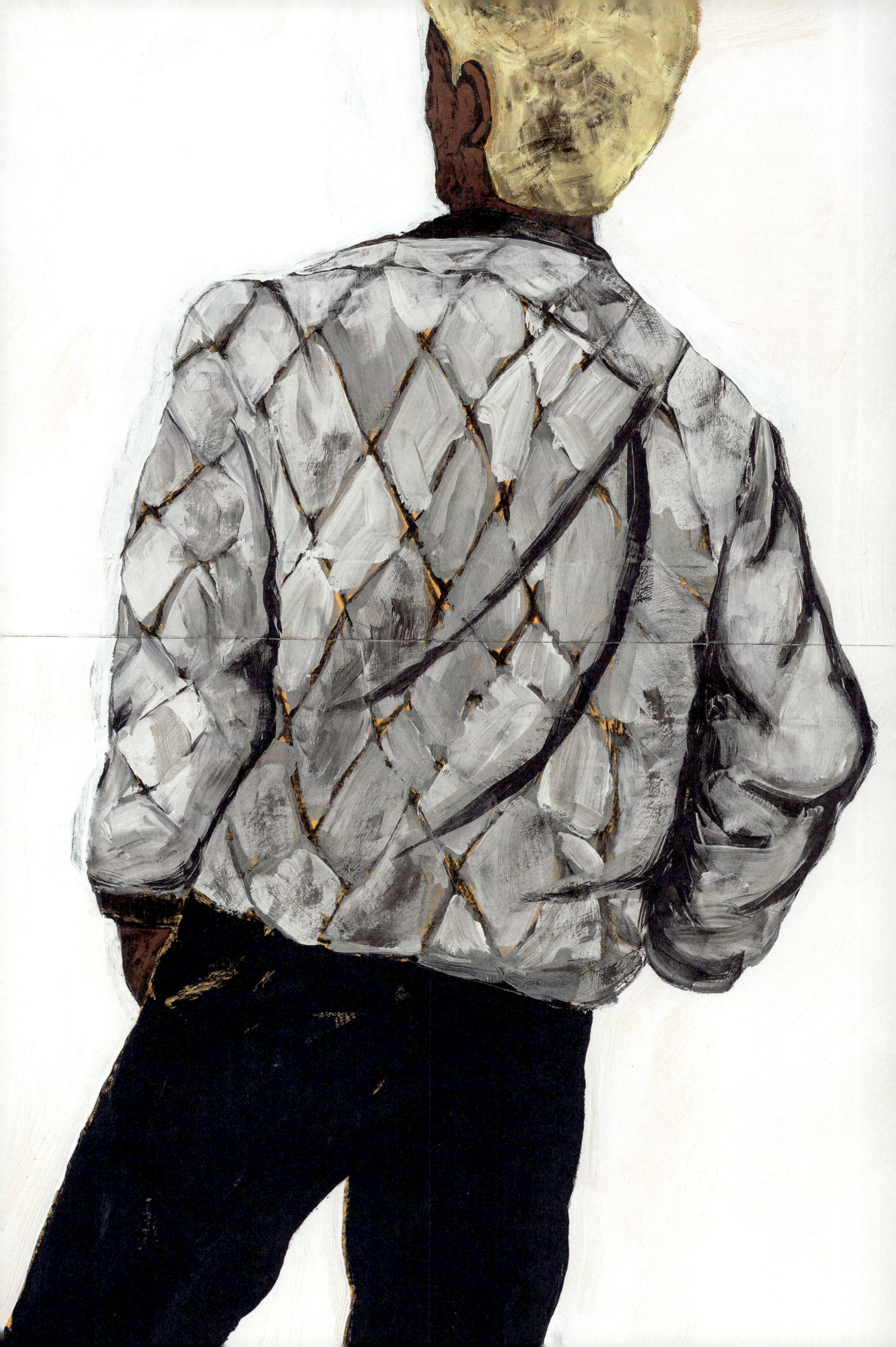

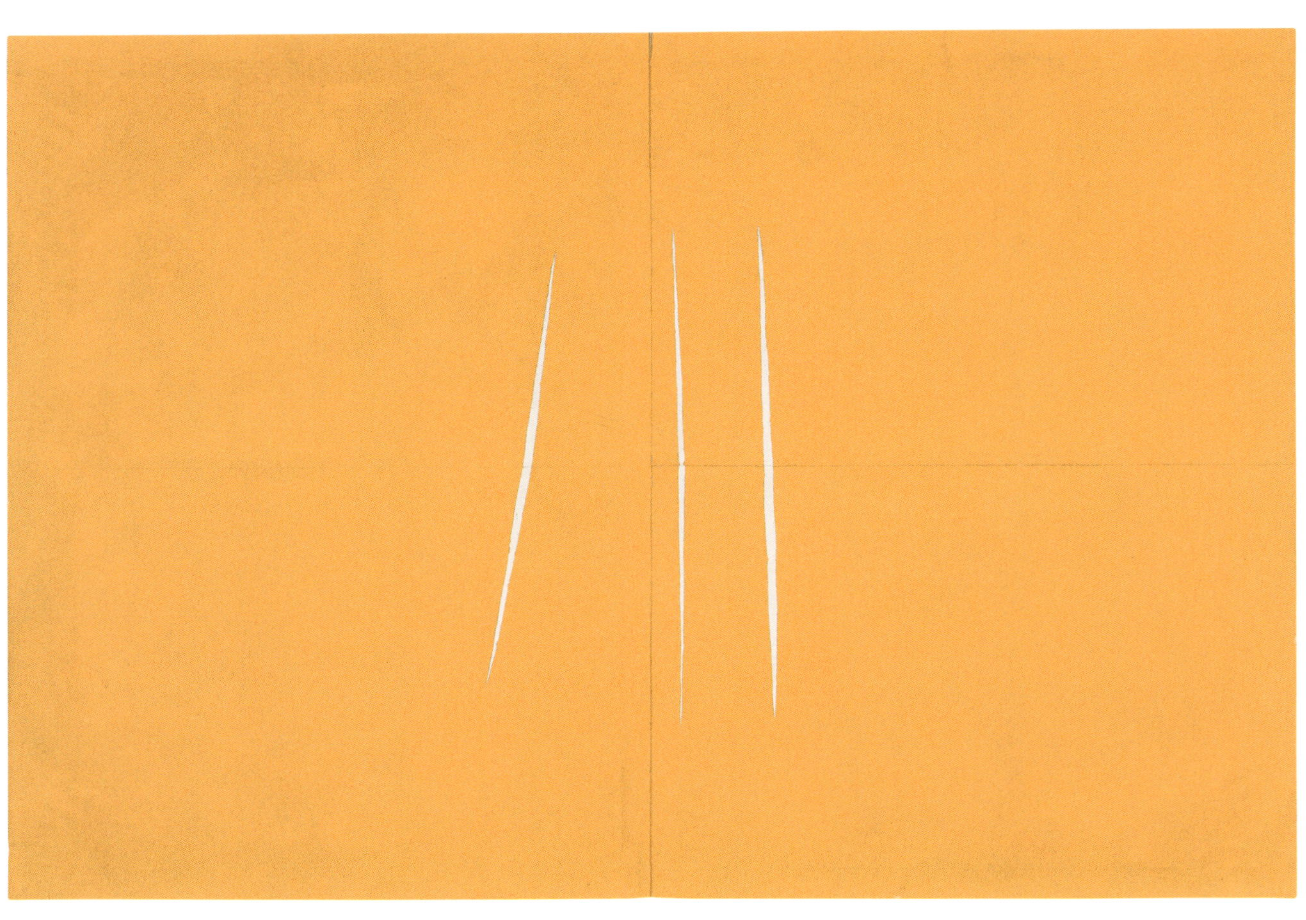

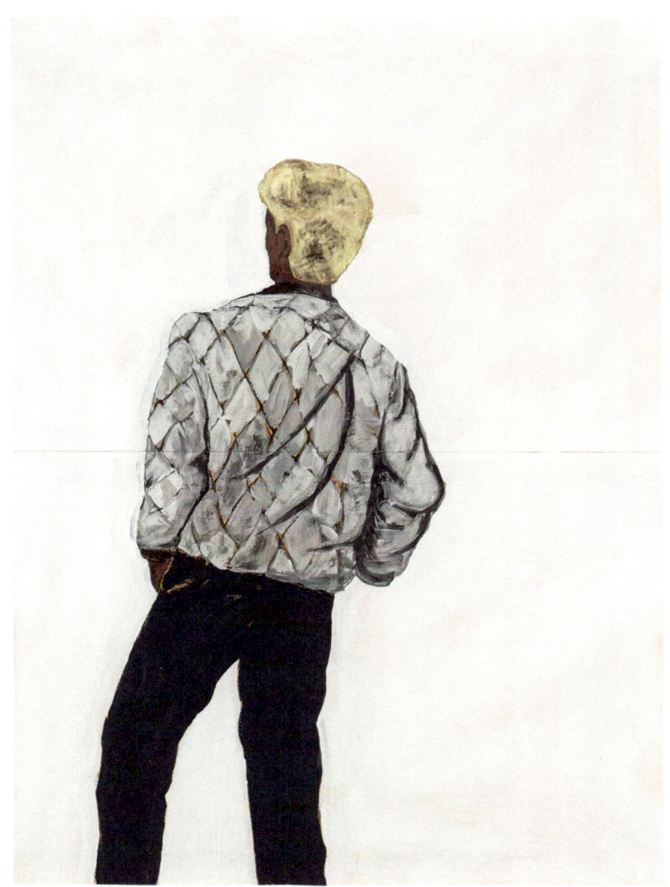

Concetto spaziale, 2021.

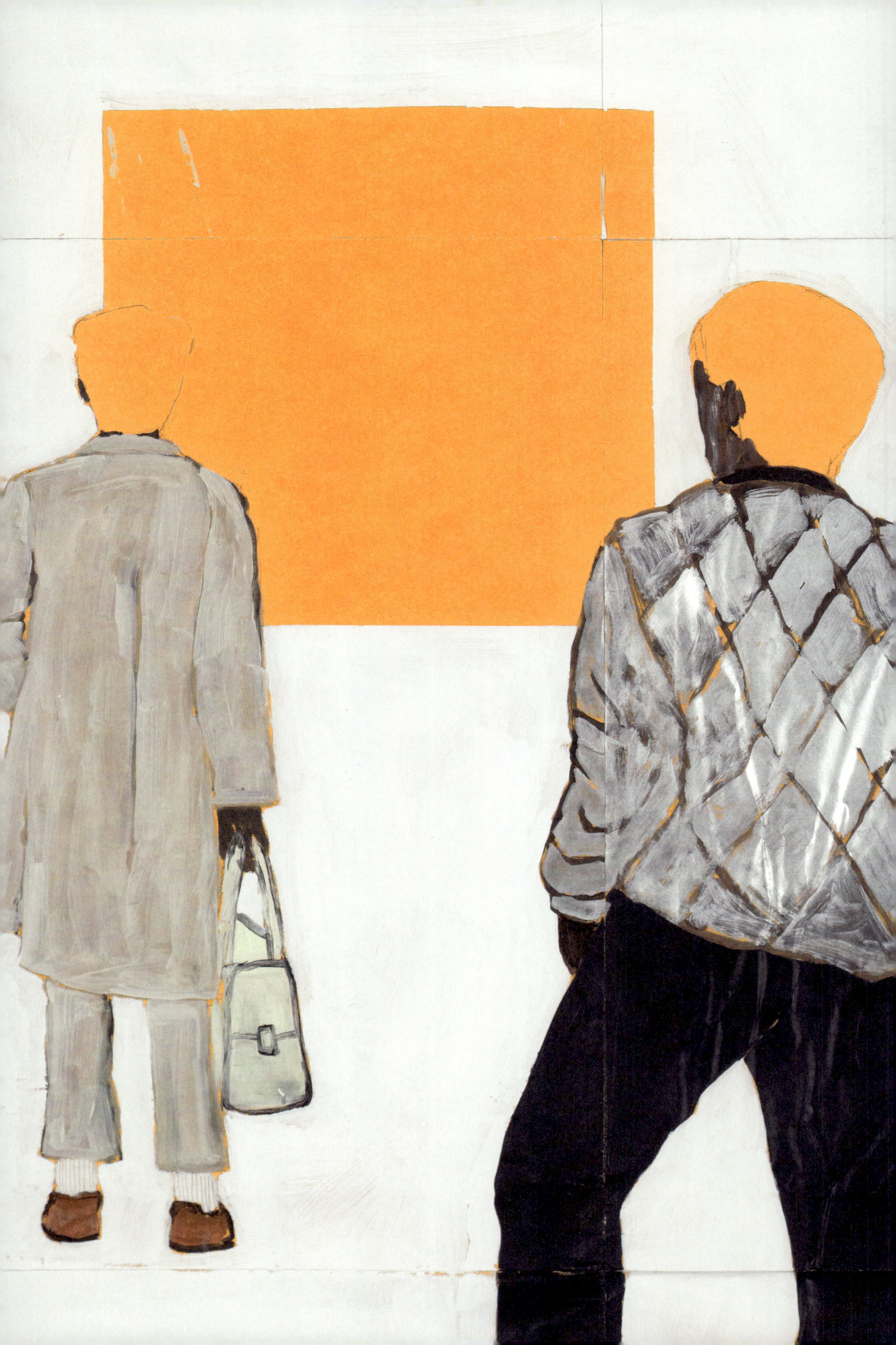

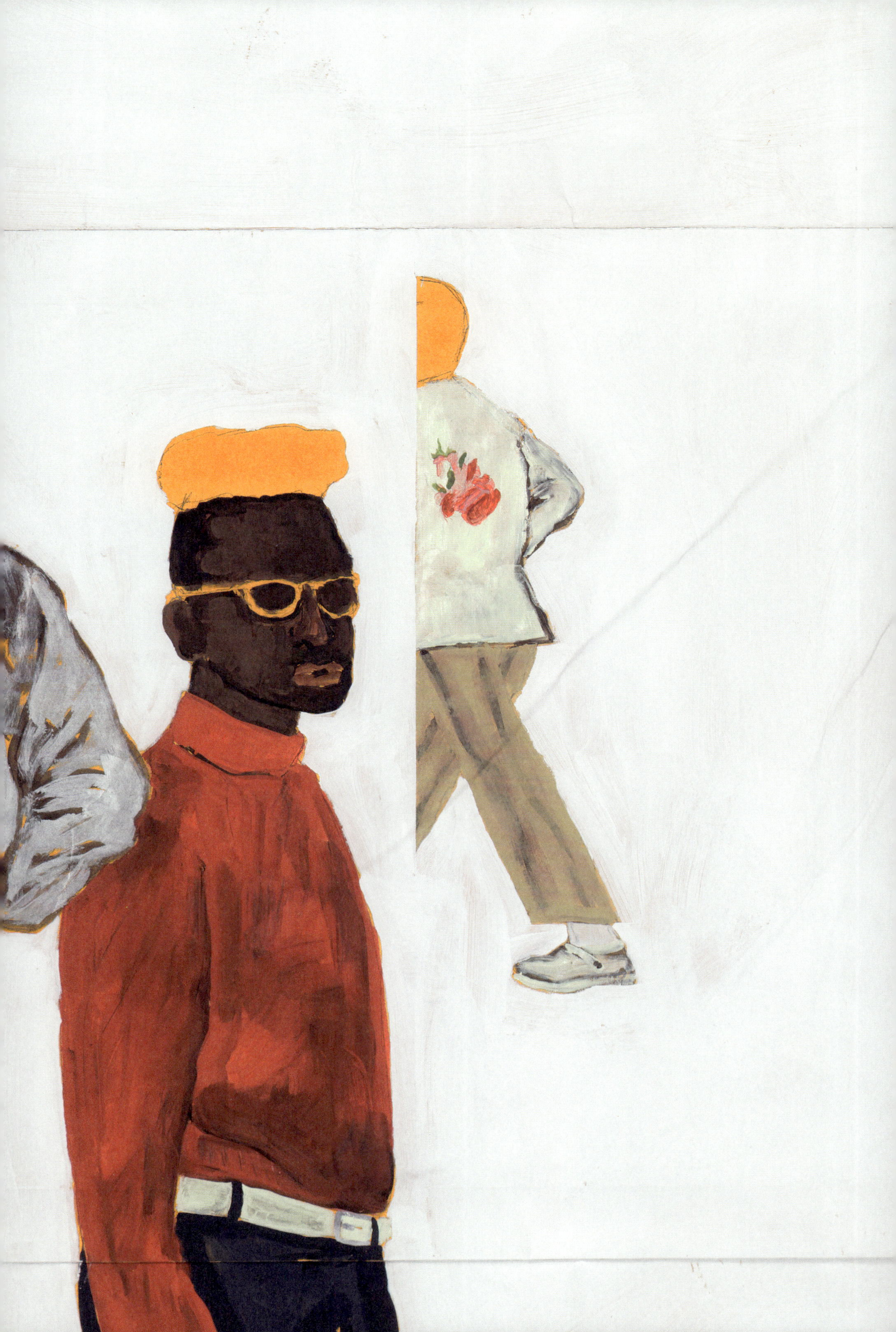

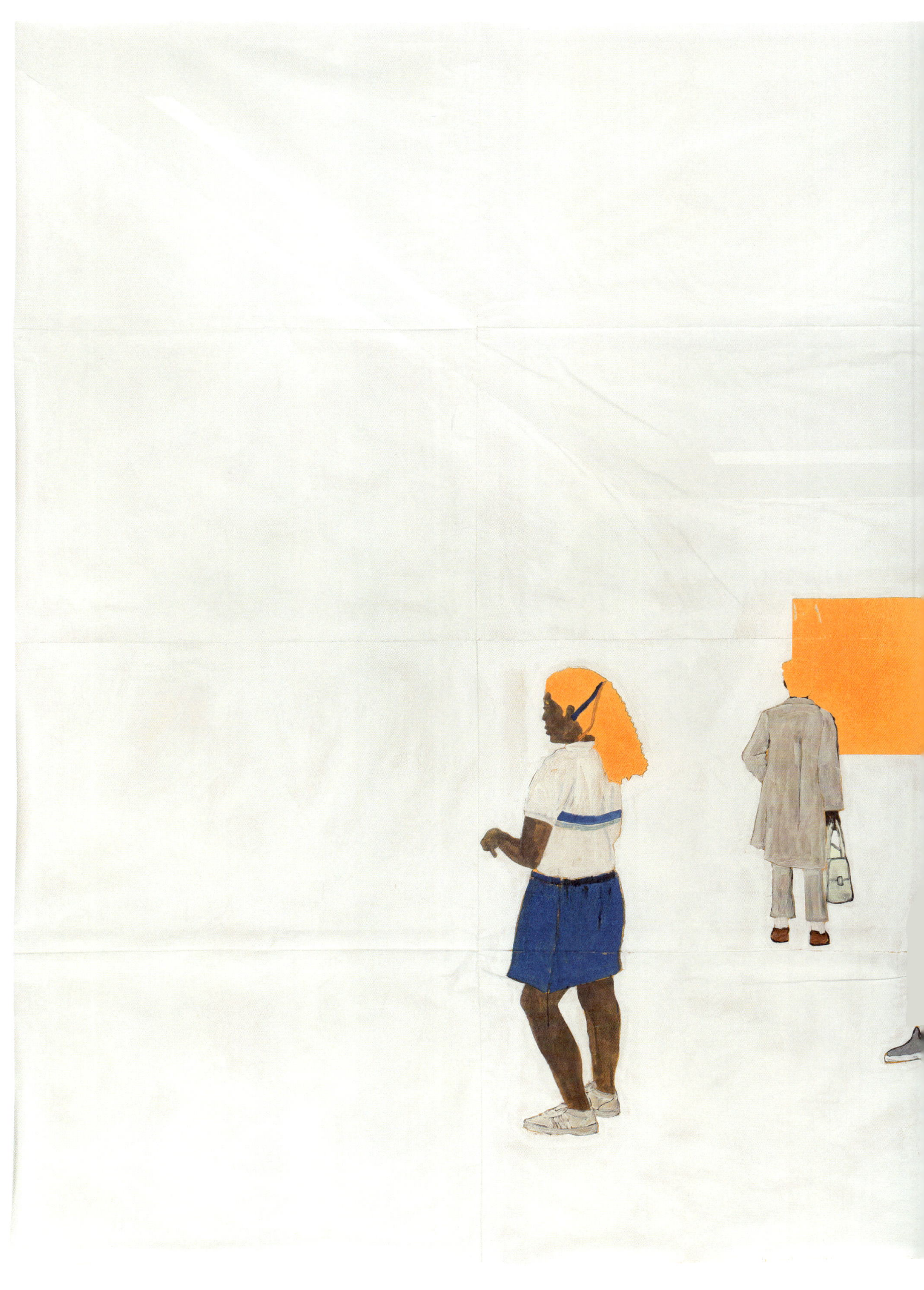

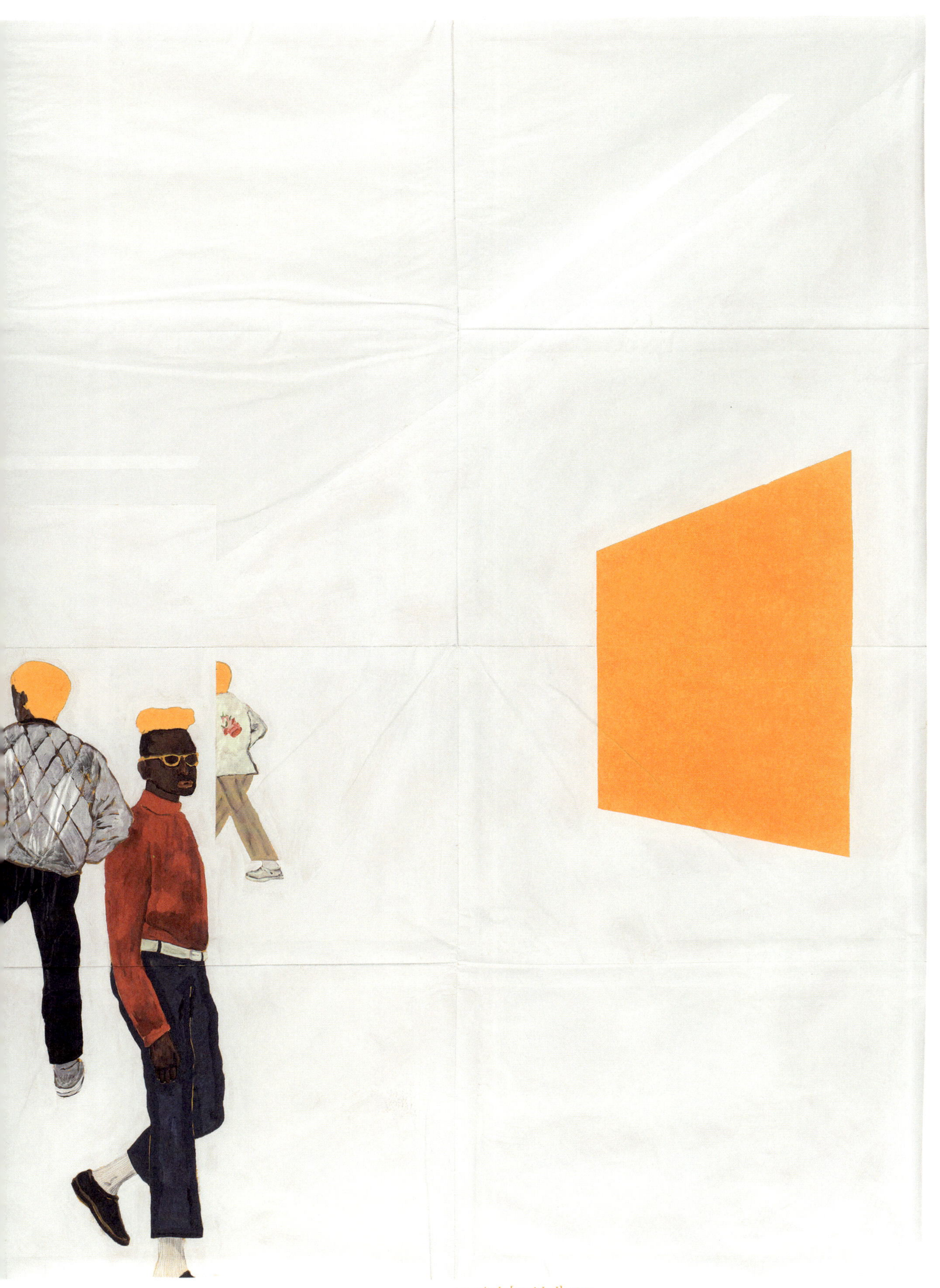

sem titulo [untitled], 2021.

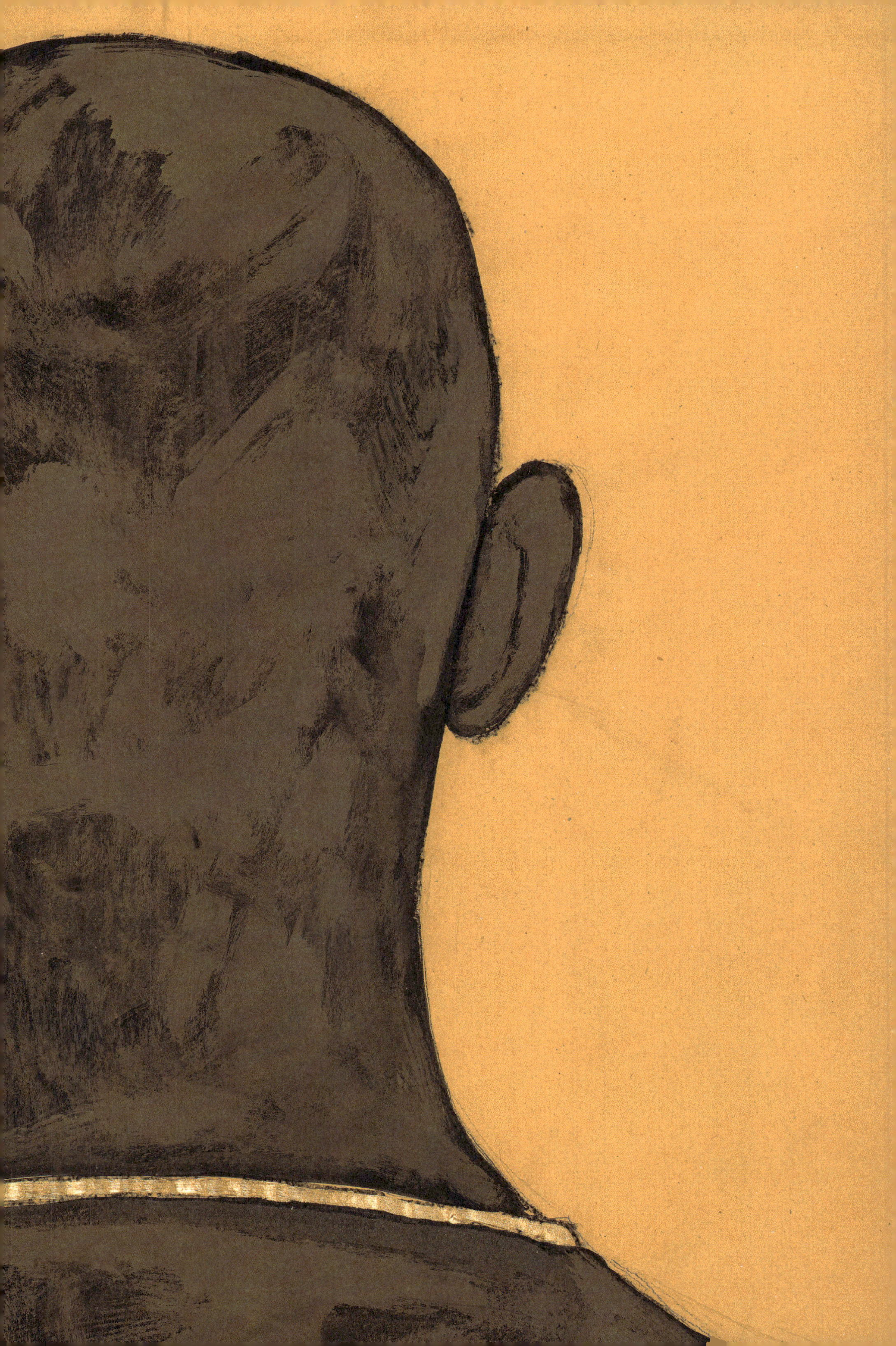

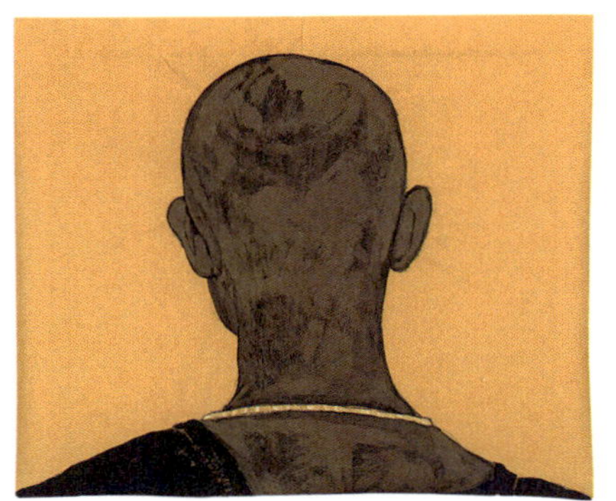
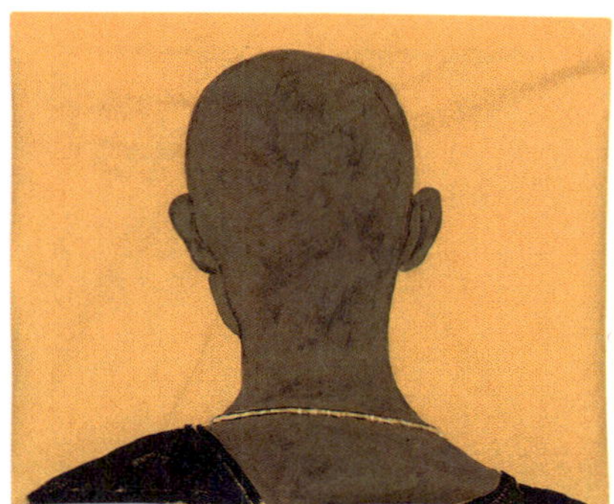
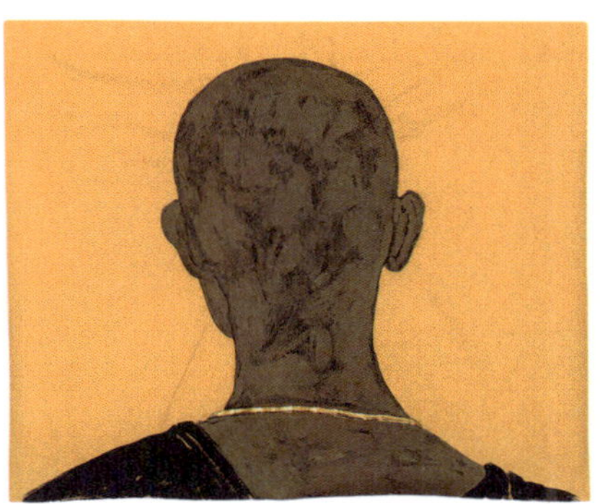

sem titulo [untitled], 2021.

sem título [untitled], 2021.

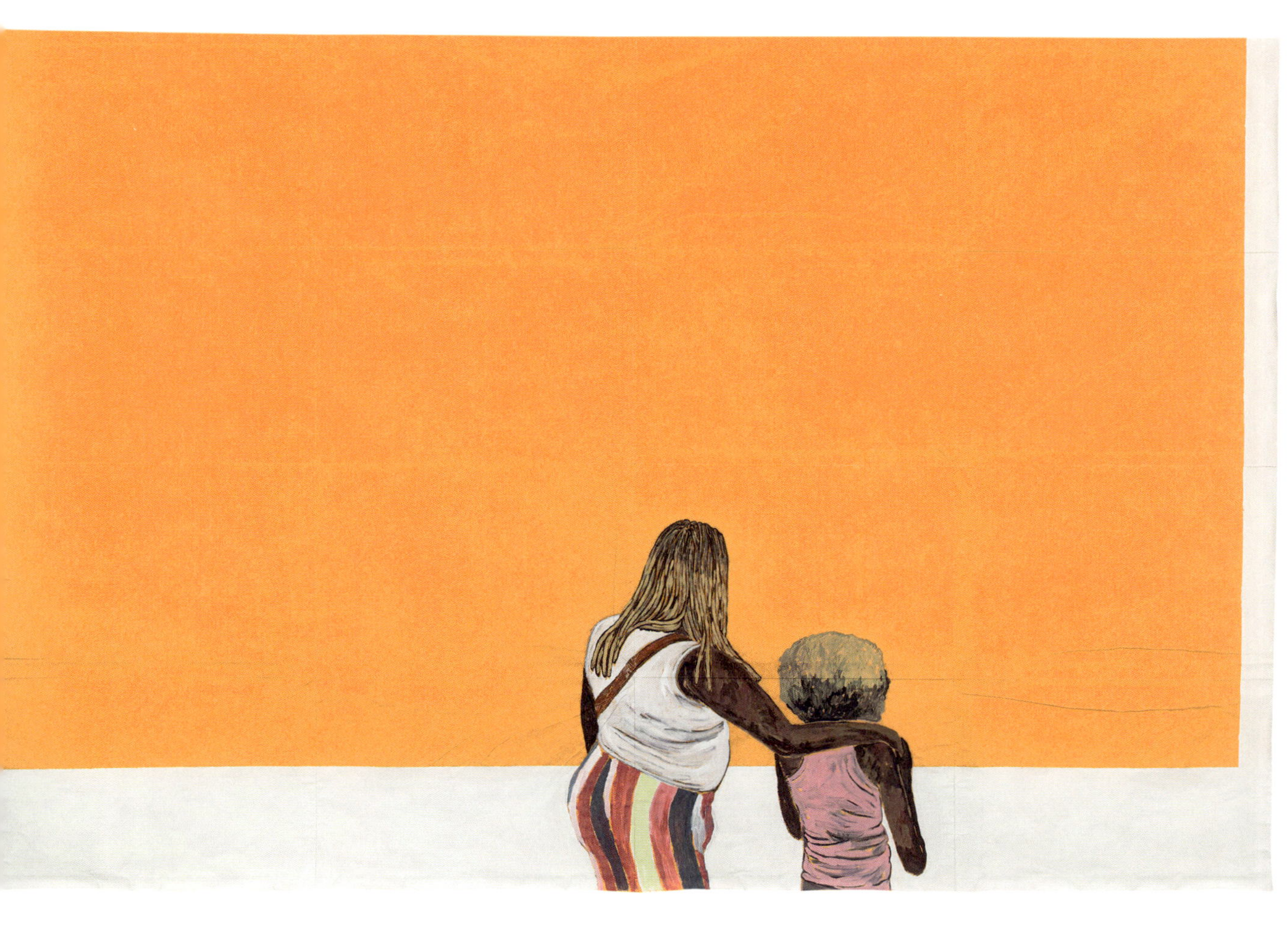

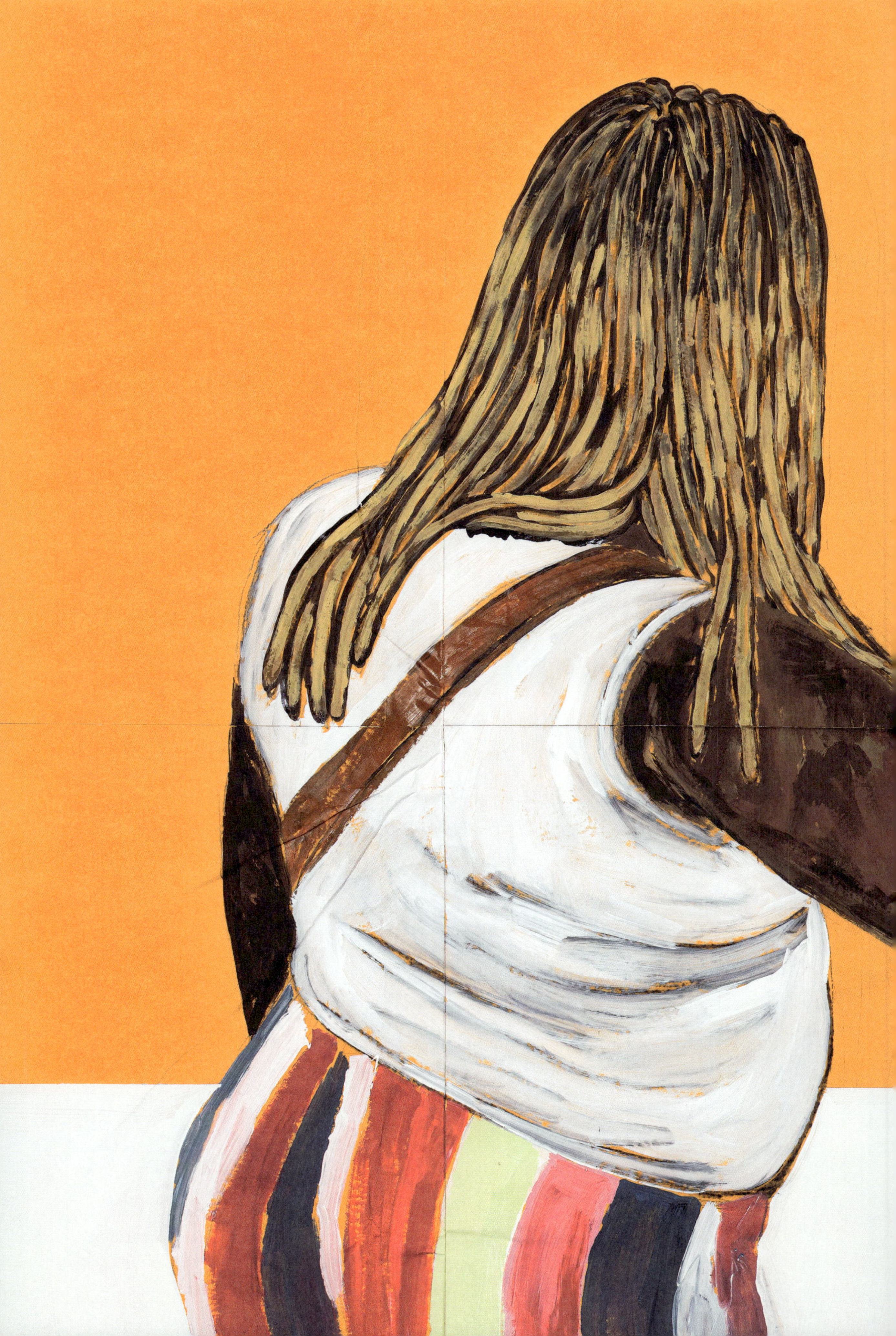

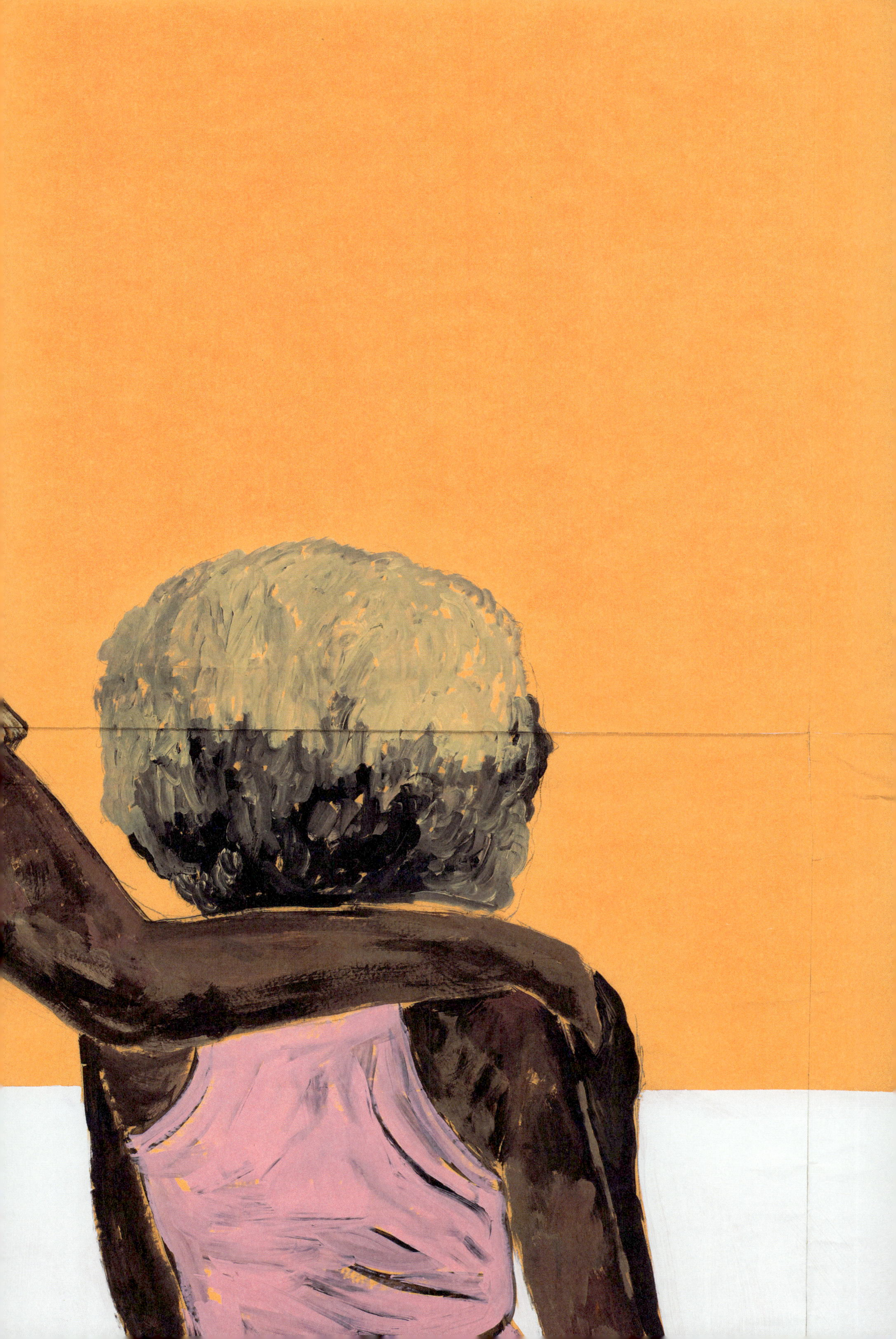

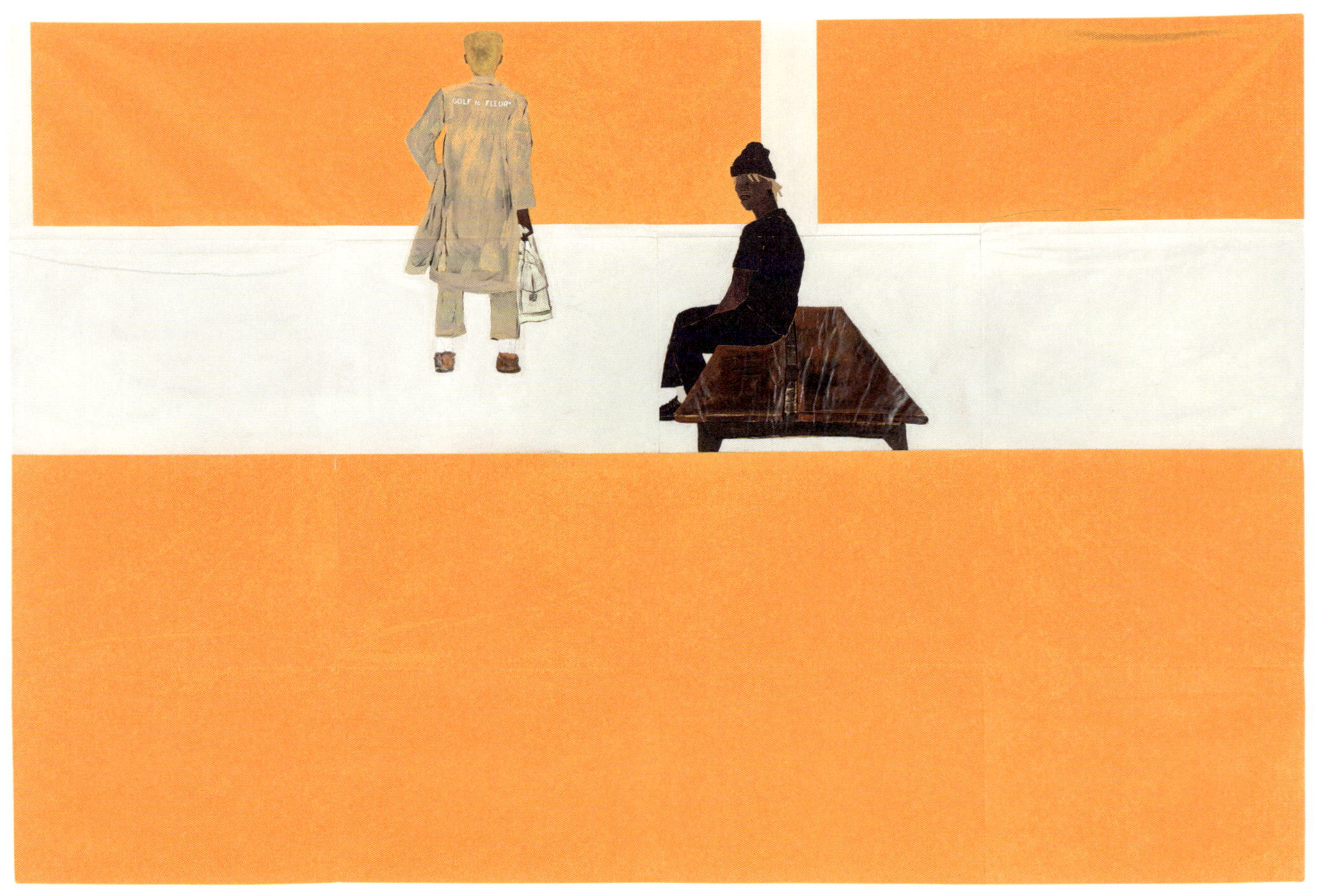

sem título [untitled], 2021.

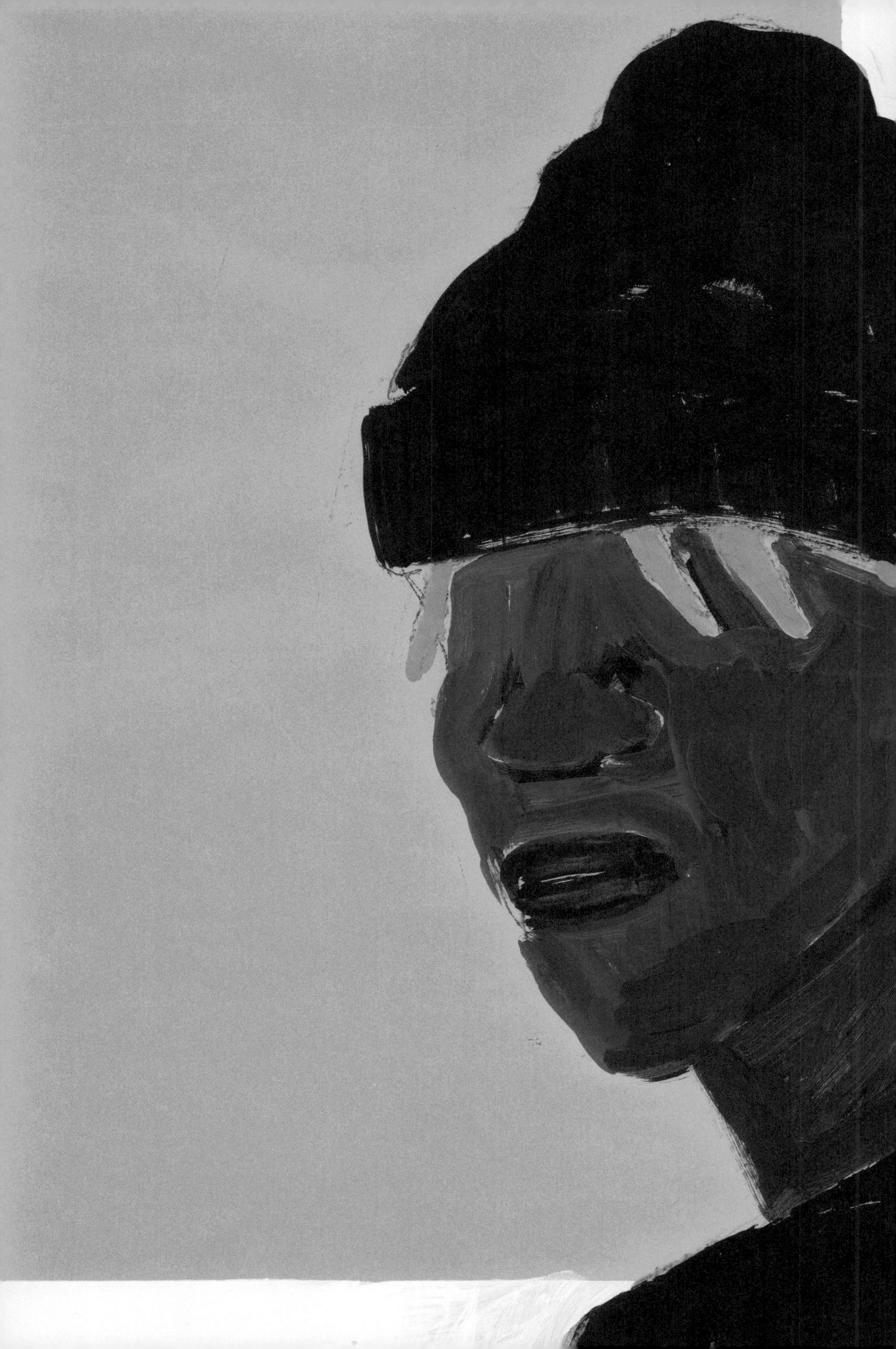

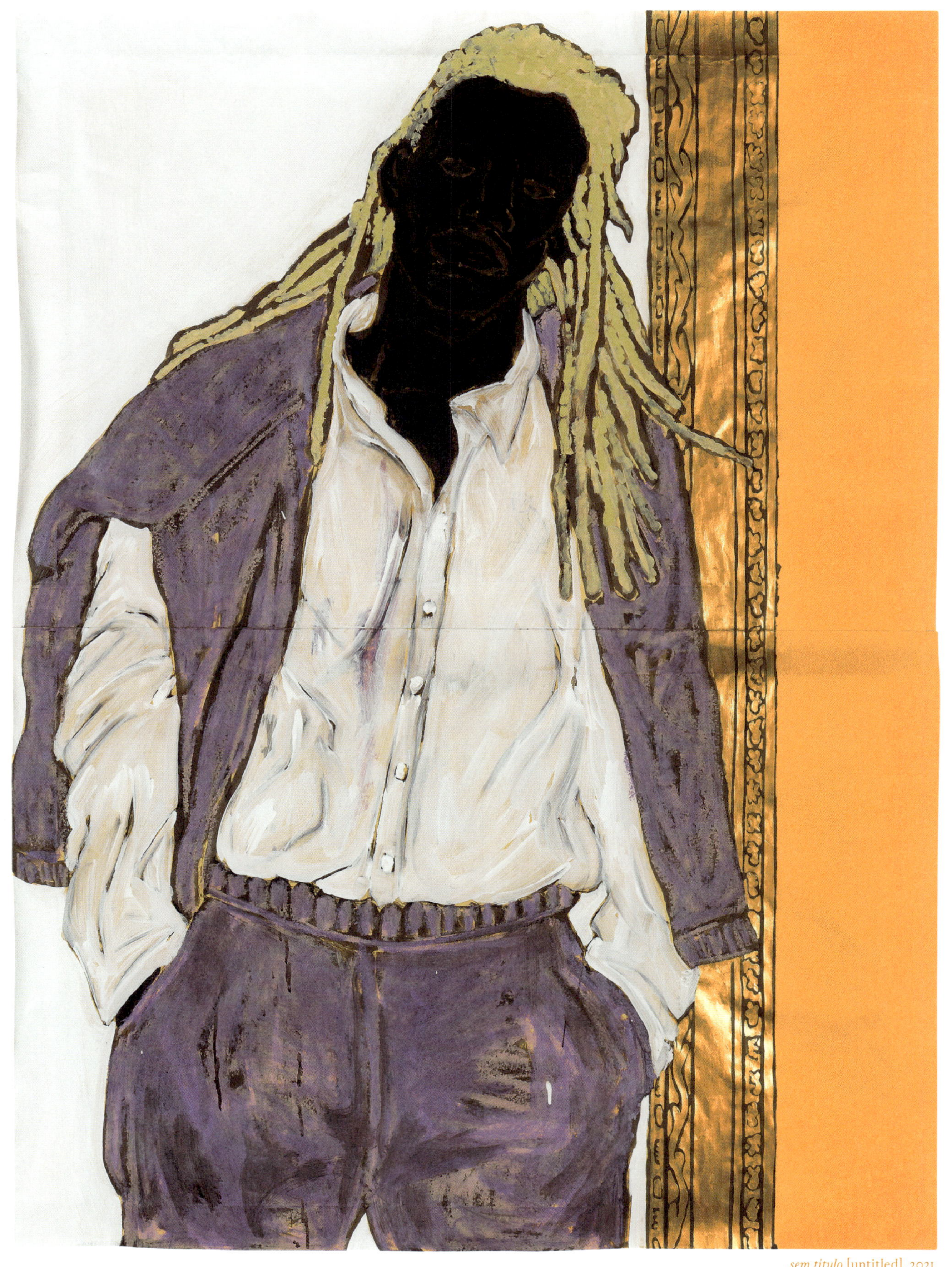

sem título [untitled], 2021.

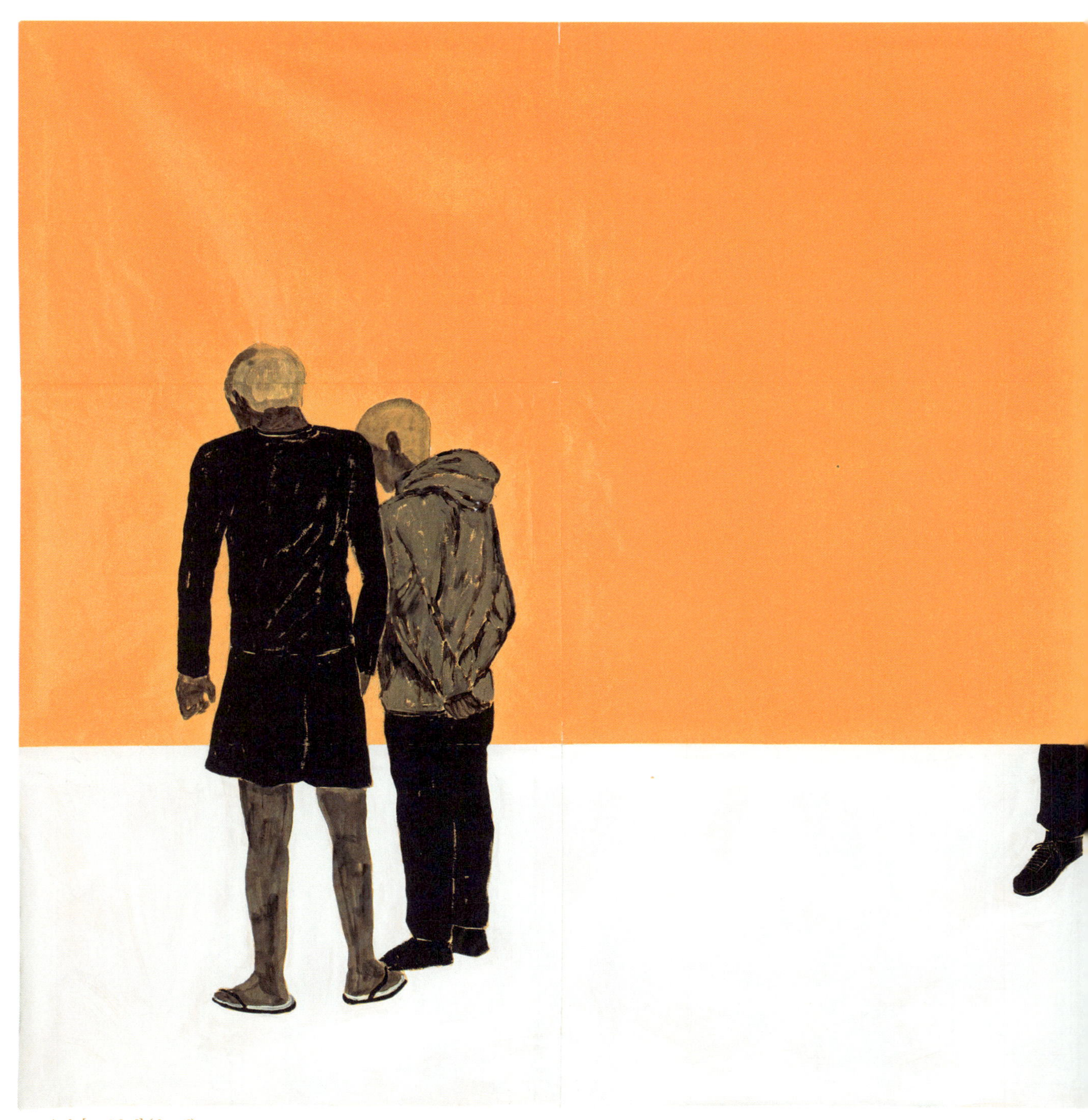

sem titulo [untitled] (detail), 2021.

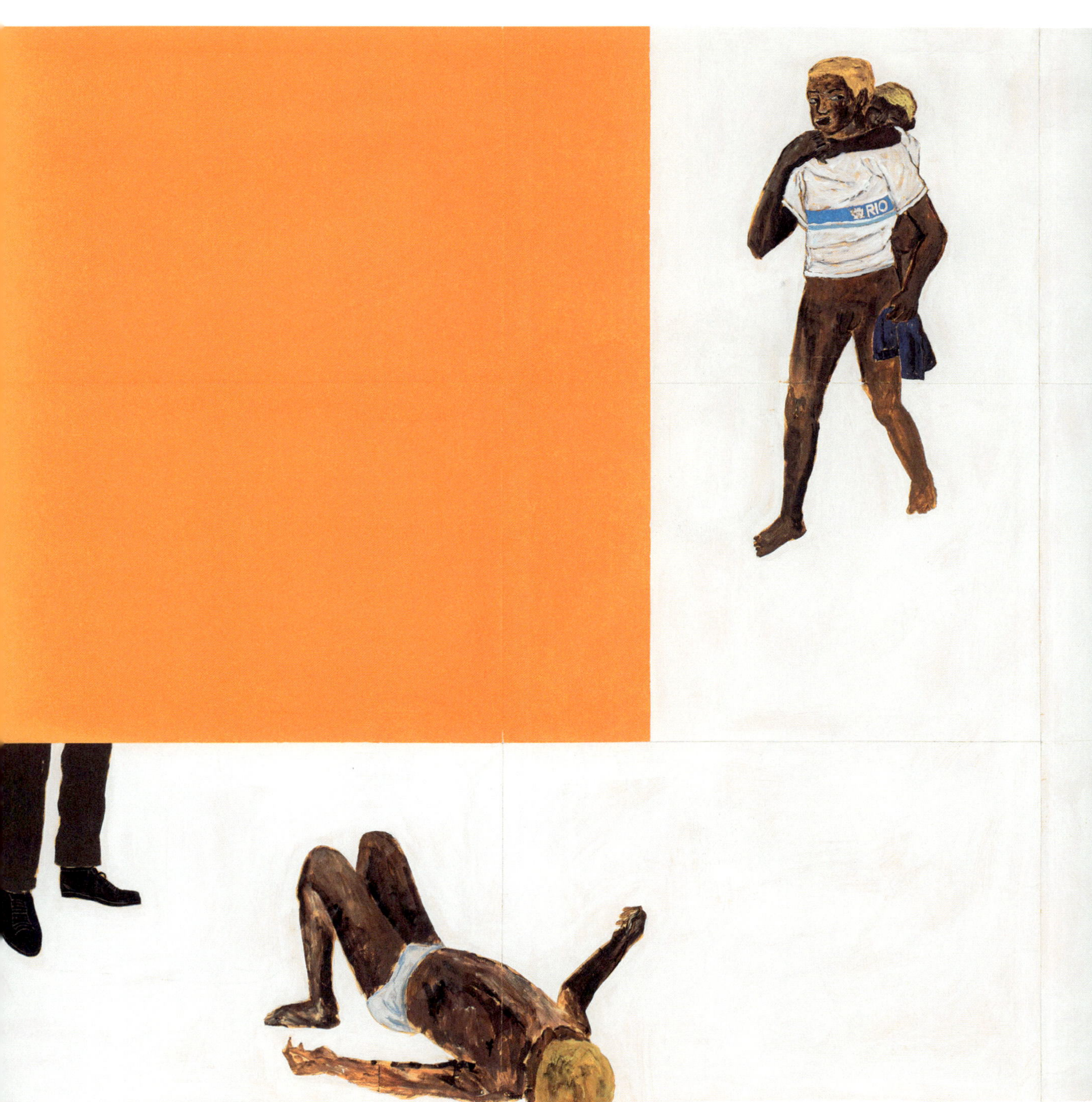
RIO

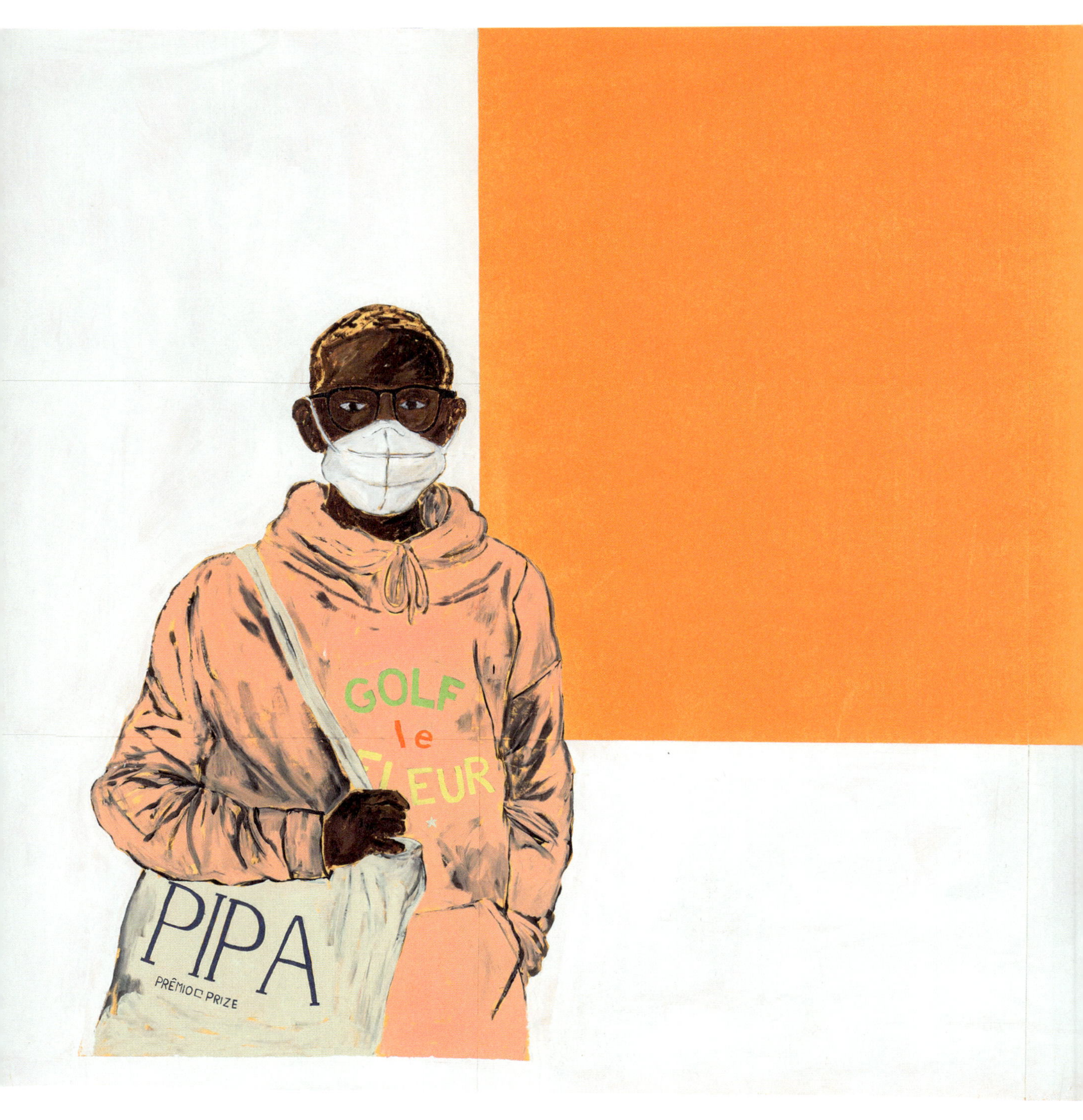
GOLF
le
FLEUR
PIPA
PRÊMIO PRIZE

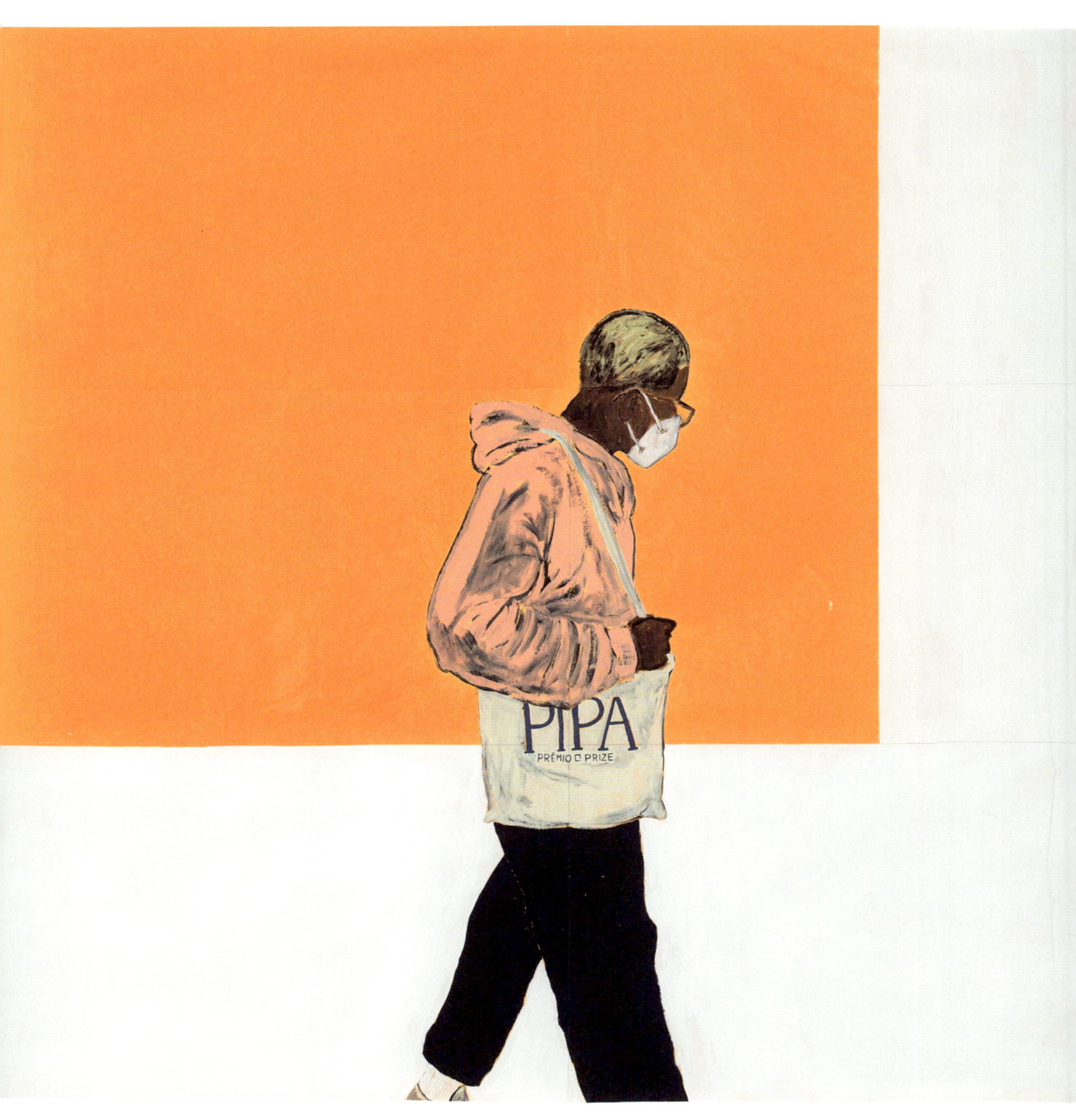
PIPA
PRÊMIO PRIZE

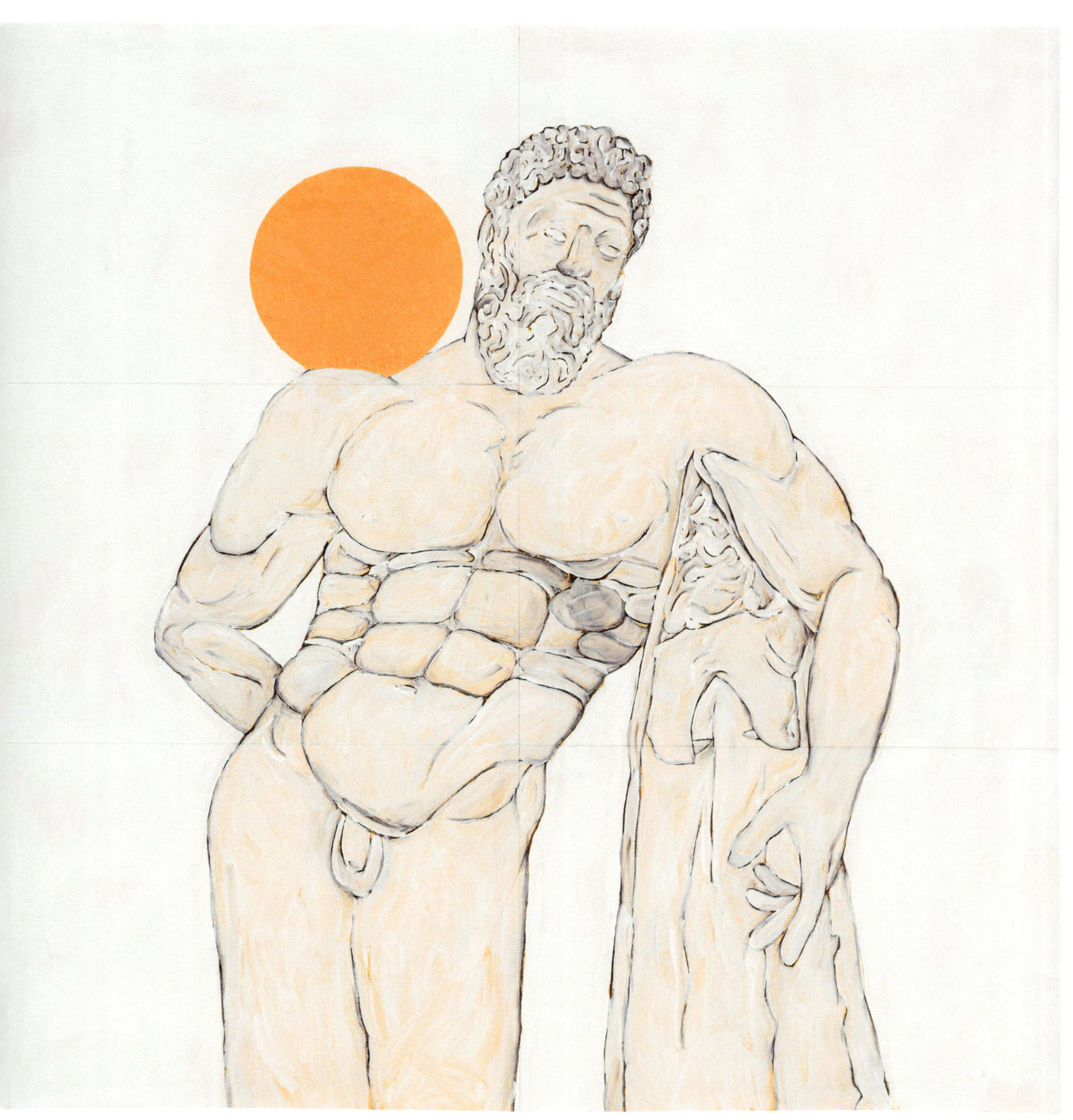

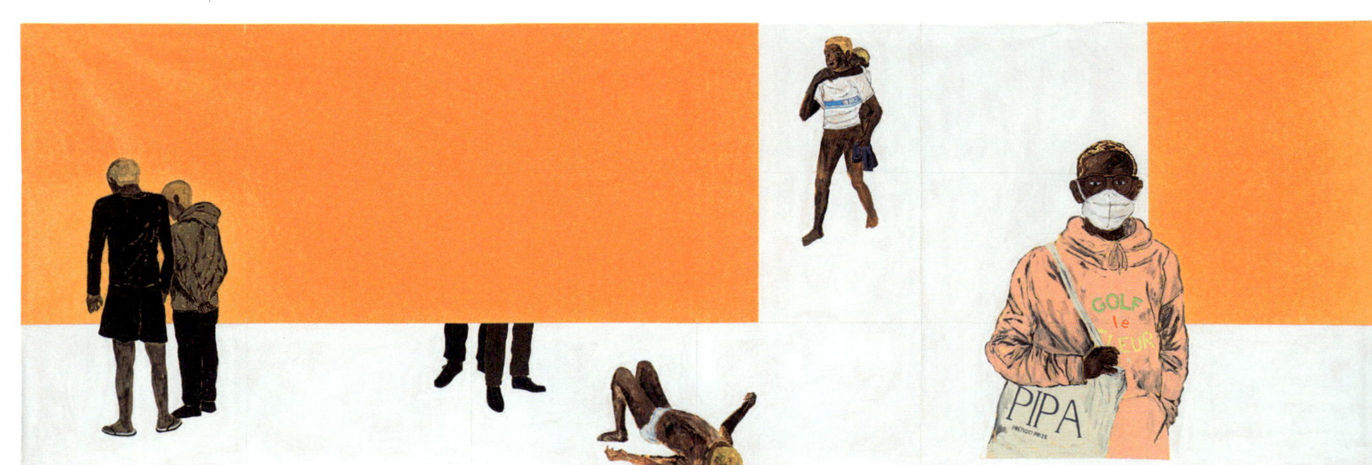

sem titulo [untitled], 2021.

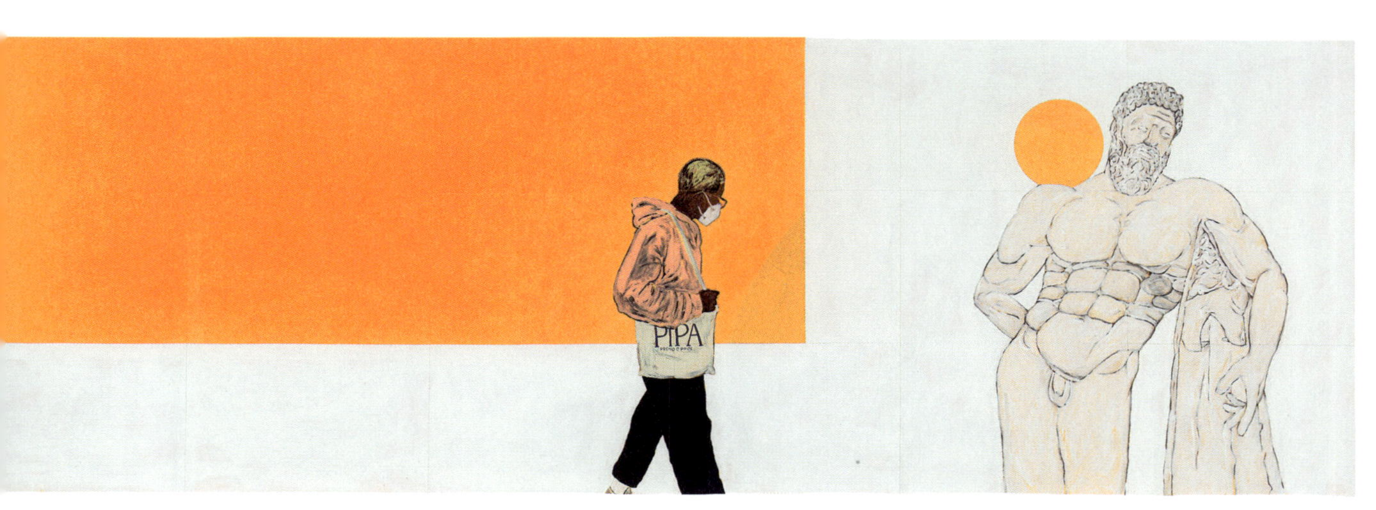
PIPA

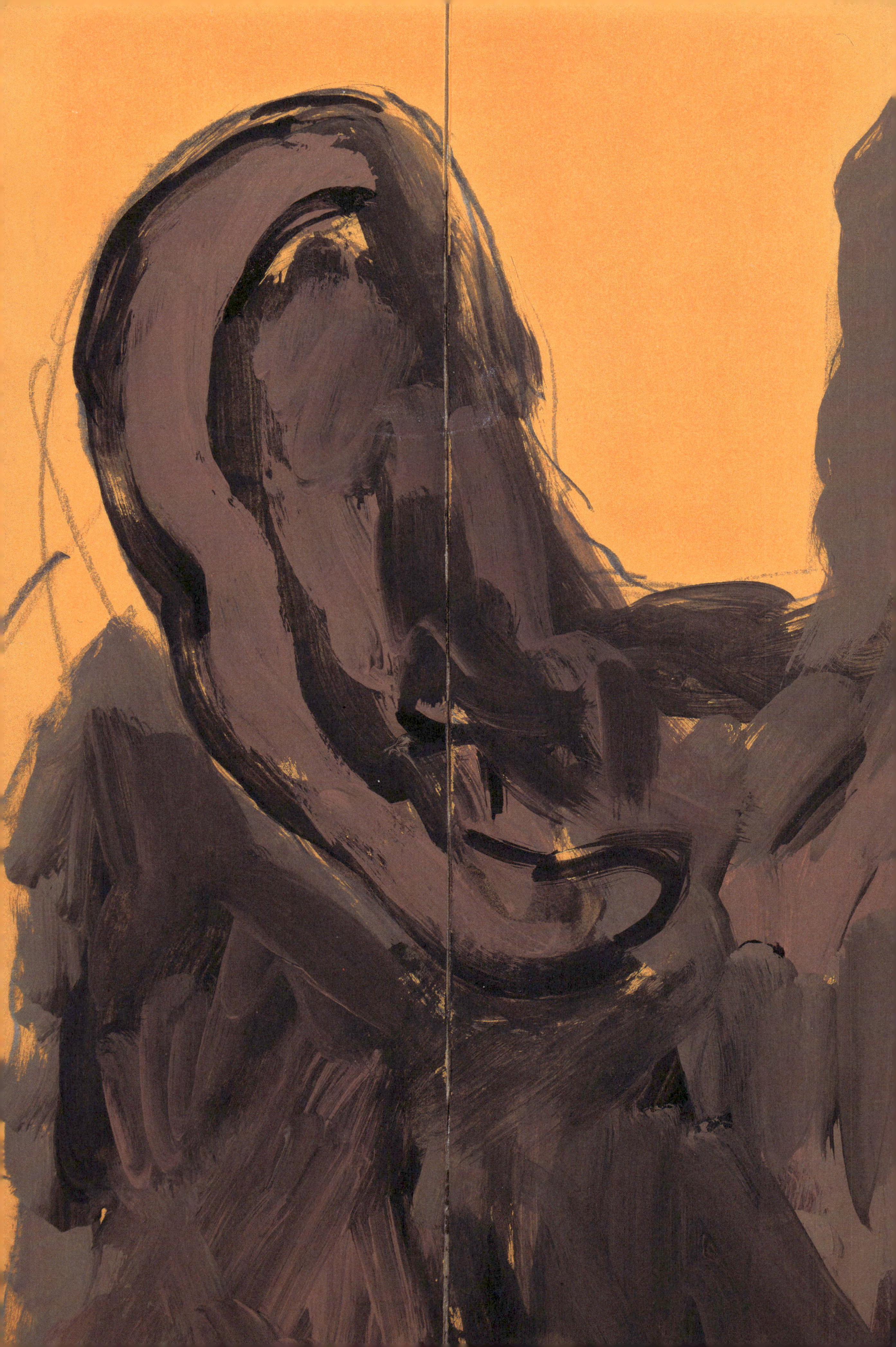

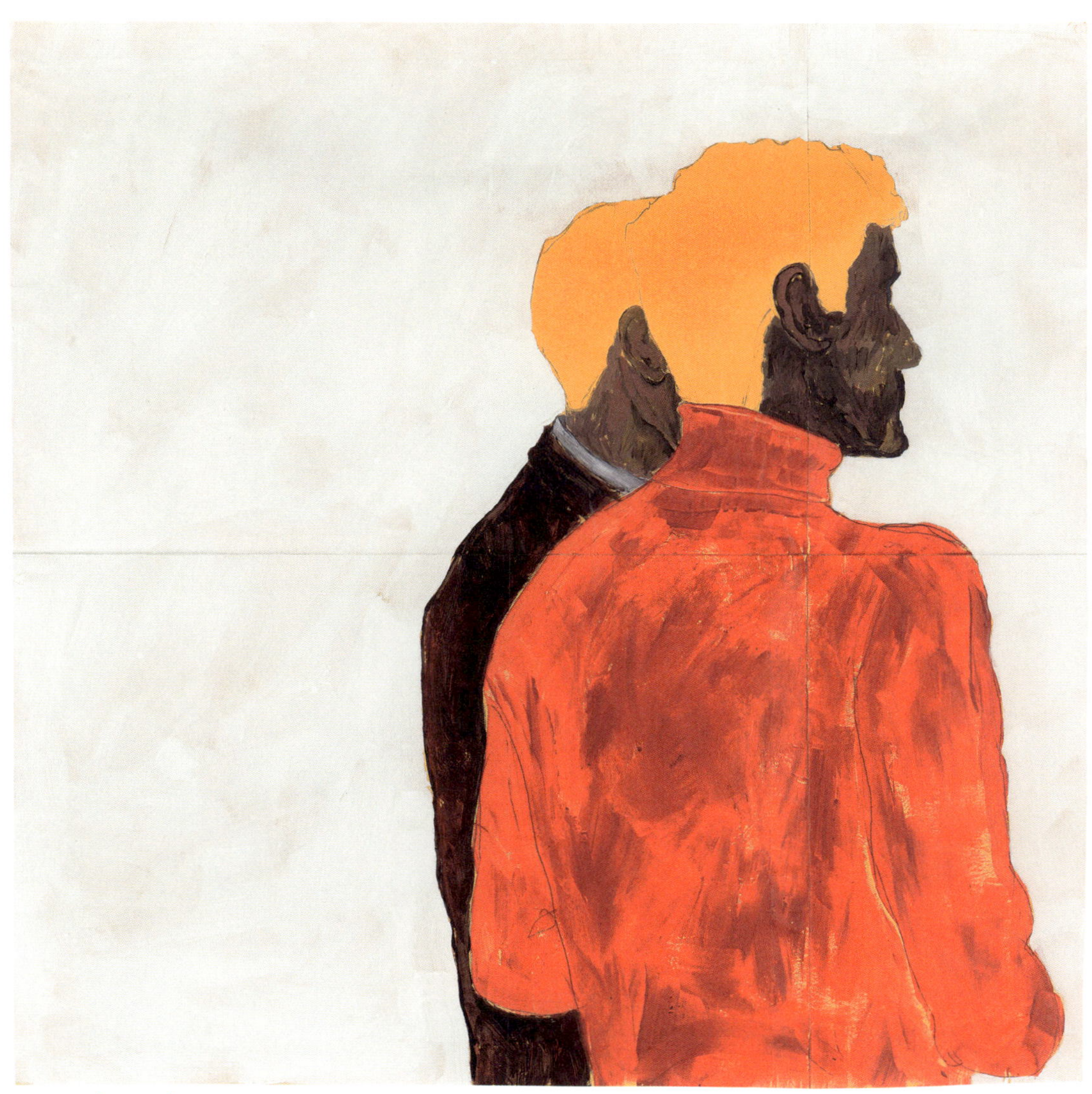

sem título [untitled], 2021.

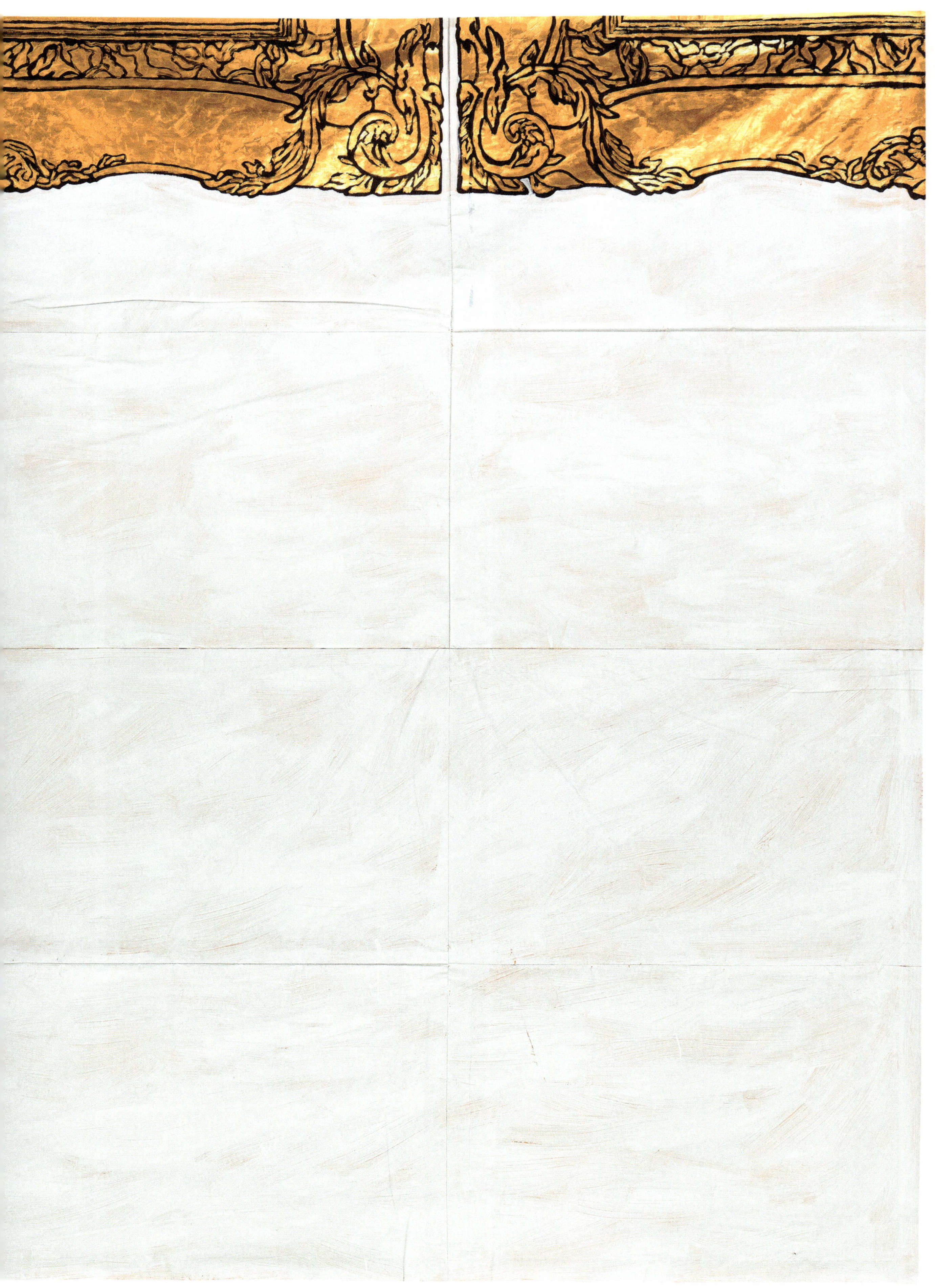

sem título [untitled], 2021.

Tina M. Campt

Mirror Effects: The Doubling Gaze of Maxwell Alexandre

Bold, expansive canvases dangle from taut wires.
They are canvases made not of cotton or linen, but paper.
Constructed of multiple squares of paper,
they compose mammoth tapestries that tell vivid stories and create vibrant encounters.
Suspended from high ceilings, they hang like sheets and towels from clotheslines;
clotheslines that symbolize the shared space of communities, impoverished but interwoven.
They line the walls of a white-cube space you will find in any gallery, in any city.
Here, they assume an architectural scale that creates multidimensional rooms of their own;
rooms peopled by those too often made invisible or seen as out of place in the exclusive space of the art gallery.

It is a slow space of observation and reflection that Maxwell Alexandre creates within the paper walls of the gallery within a gallery that is *New Power*, his 2021–22 installation-cum-exhibition at the Palais de Tokyo in Paris. Alexandre's reimagined gallery is also a quiet space, albeit one permeated by the ambient rumble of visitor conversations or the background noise of film soundtracks that bleed in from adjacent galleries. They are intermittent, sonic interjections that fail to disrupt the contemplative atmosphere of the installation. Yet, peaceful as it may be, the installation is nevertheless an occupation—one where the figures who populate Alexandre's paper canvases take center stage in ways that reconfigure the relationship between art and spectator, and challenge us to engage the space of the gallery from a markedly different vantage point (fig. 1).

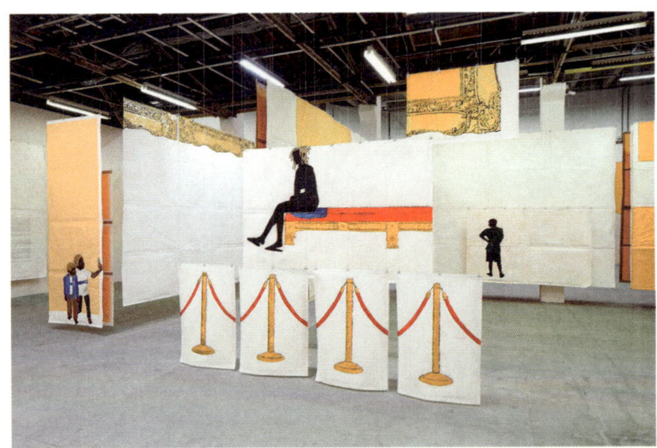

Fig. 1: Installation view: *New Power*, Palais de Tokyo, Paris, November 26, 2021–March 13, 2022.

The occupants of Alexandre's paper galleries are a diverse configuration of Black and brown figures with urban affect and stylization who stand and watch, ponder and reflect. They are depicted in scenes of reflection and repose, of swagger and celebration, of ambling and embracing. Some are seated on ornate benches, while others stand frozen or are relaxed in repose; still others engage each other, animated (figs. 2, 3). They express mundane and poignant gestures of everyday intimacies signified by subtle yet striking displays of embracing appendages: arms clasped behind backs; arms extended for a selfie; the arm of a mother draped around a child; the hands of an ambulating couple intertwined; the arms of nude lovers on a canvas within a canvas, grasping one another with expressions of longing and despair. Assembled on the walls of Alexandre's gallery rooms, their gestures are no longer mundane. They enact quotidian expressions of belonging and affirmation transposed into a gallery space that was not created for them to inhabit but which they claim as their own (fig. 4). In the hands of this gifted artist, the rooms become interactive spaces where they are depicted comfortable and at ease.

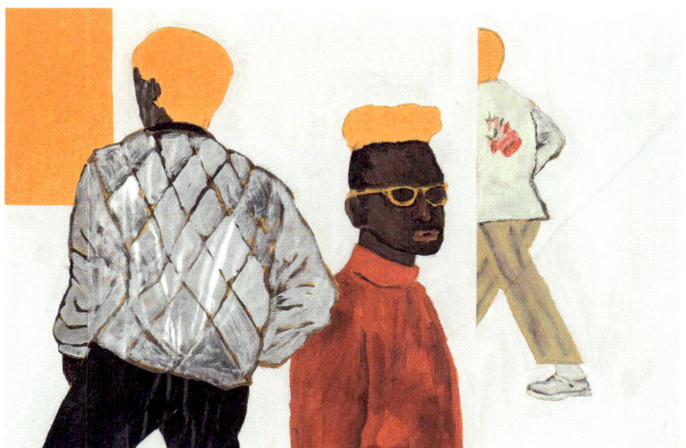

Fig. 2: *sem titulo* [untitled] (detail), 2021, from "Pardo é Papel: New Power," 2019–. Shoe polish, bitumen, charcoal, graphite, latex, and acrylic on brown kraft paper.

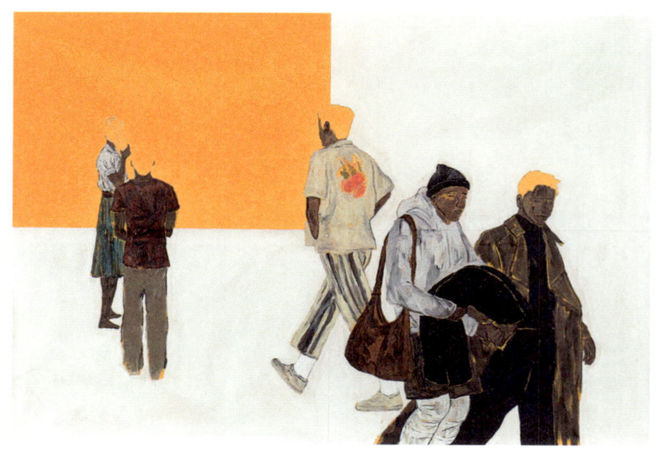

Fig. 3: *sem titulo* [untitled], 2021, from "Pardo é Papel: New Power," 2019–. Shoe polish, bitumen, charcoal, graphite, latex, and acrylic on brown kraft paper. 63 × 94 ½ inches.

Fig. 4 (opposite page): Installation view: *New Power*, Palais de Tokyo, Paris, November 26, 2021–March 13, 2022.

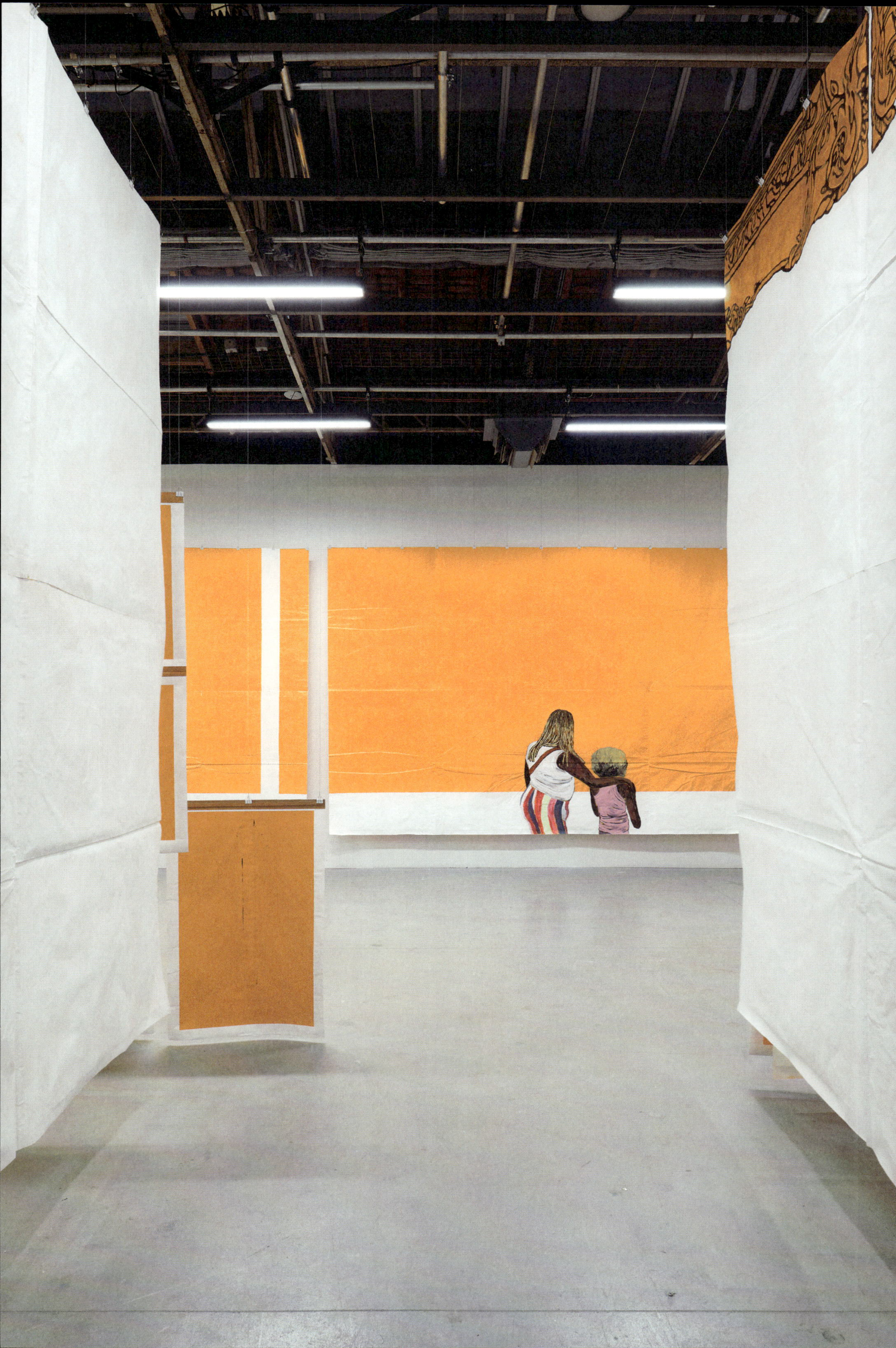

Schoolchildren in uniforms with backpacks or cell phones
wander across a paper tableau
or sit idle before other canvases displayed within them.
Some listen intently or distractedly to a docent narrating
the artwork.
In one scene, a gallery guard stands stoic yet intimidating in
his uniform, observing a child.
In another, a group assembles, some at a distance and some
close, to ponder a golden sphere.
In yet another, a cheerful couple hold hands.
Entering the room in the brick-and-mortar gallery,
we inhabit a liminal space that joins artwork and spectator.

It can be difficult to discern who is watching whom in Alexandre's artwork, and that is precisely his intention as I receive it. It is art that shifts our gaze away from passive viewing to active participation. In *New Power*, Alexandre creates an eerie encounter where visitors become participants in the narrative of the figures in his canvases, who often seem as animate as his viewers. These life-size simulacra create a disorienting doubling effect. They mimic us as viewer-visitors (fig. 5). As we linger before them, they seem to linger and take us in (fig. 6). Blurring the line between art and spectator, the gallery itself becomes a vehicle for the transformation of the gaze into a space of mutual interrogation. As we pause to contemplate the canvases and the figures that enliven them, they interrogate us in their own simulated gallery. Like them, we, too, are monitored and observed by the watchful eyes of guards in our respective galleries and exhibitions. But it is a doubling that reveals equally significant contrasts. For in their gallery, all the visitors are Black; in mine, I am the only non-white spectator for the two hours I spend in the space.

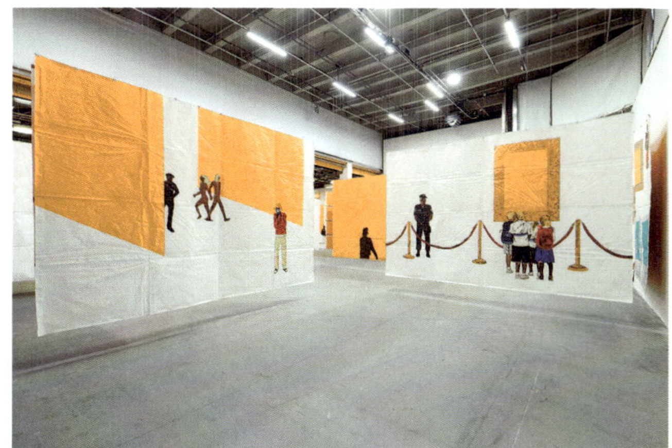

Fig. 5: Installation view: *New Power*, Palais de Tokyo, Paris, November 26, 2021–March 13, 2022.

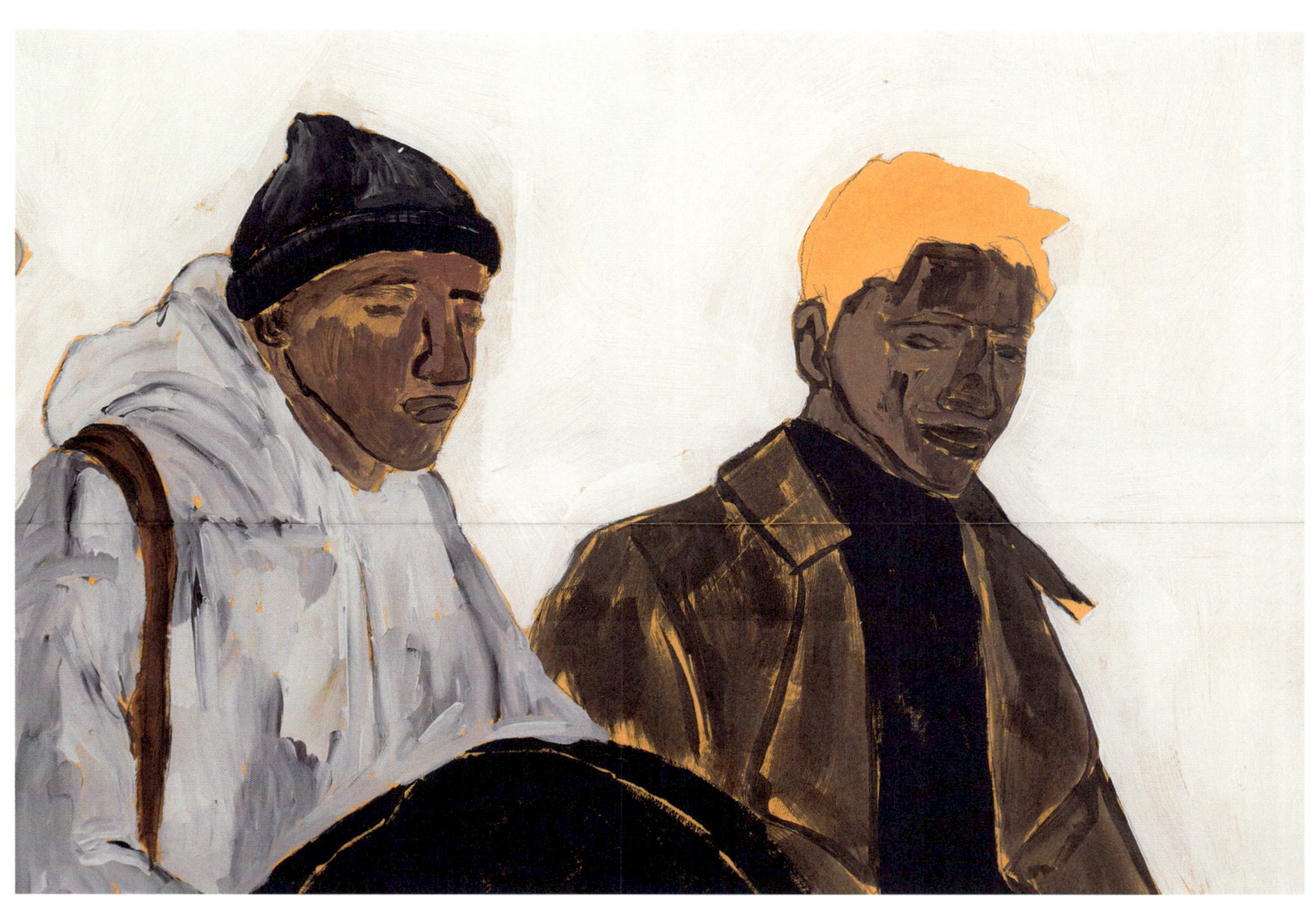

Fig. 6: *sem título* [untitled] (detail), 2021, from "Pardo é Papel: New Power," 2019–. Shoe polish, charcoal, graphite, latex, and acrylic on brown kraft paper.

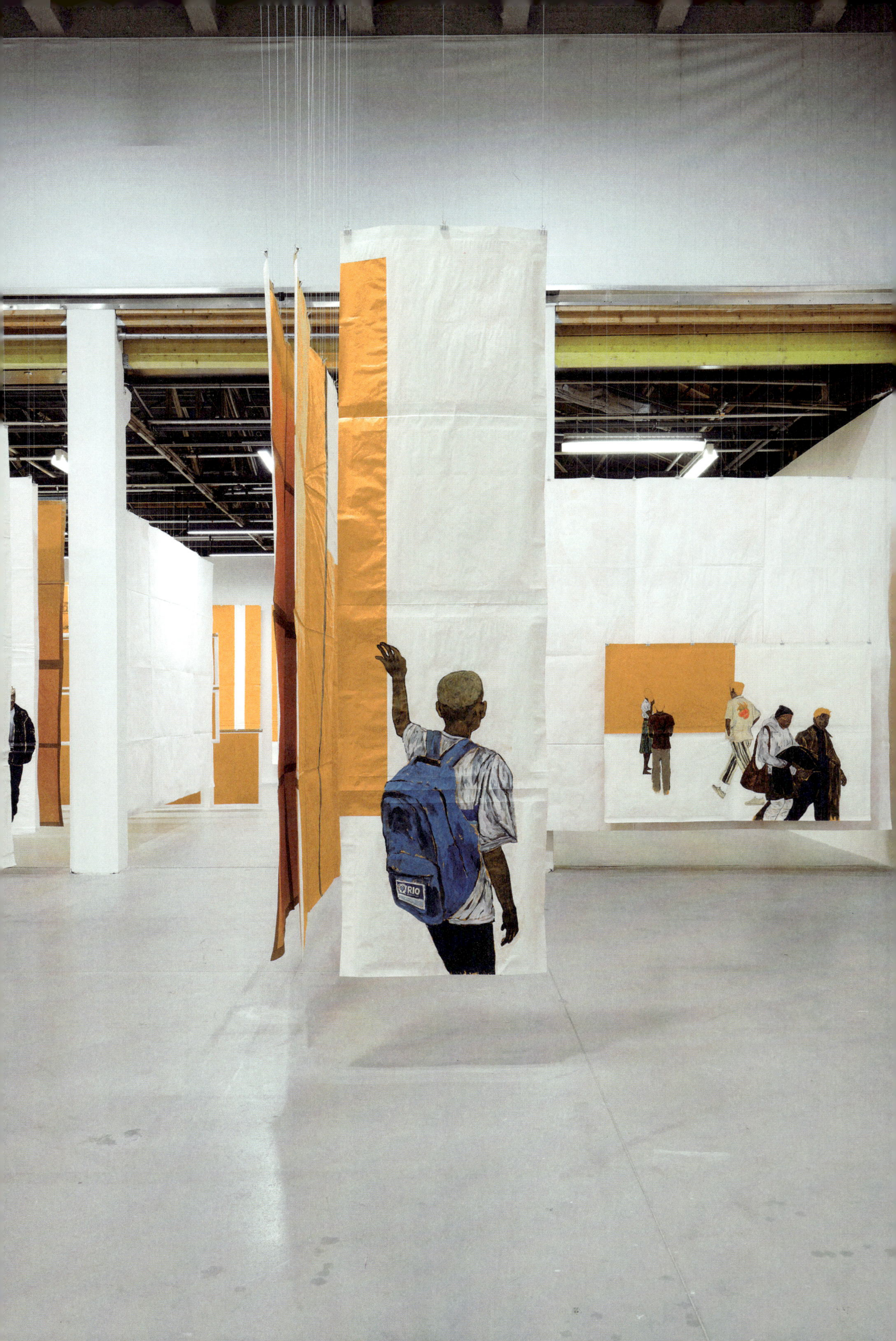
RIO

It is a contrast I have long internalized as normal: an expectation of being out of place that usually overtakes me as I approach the ticket counter of a museum. It is equally palpable when I pass the threshold of a gallery and am met with blank stares or a lack of acknowledgment from blasé gallery staff who fail to look up from their computers. *New Power* upends the dynamics of being out of place by recentering those often relegated to this position. The installation reconfigures those relations visually, spatially, and sonically. Like many of Alexandre's works, it demands a three-dimensional engagement that exceeds the visual (fig. 7). They are works that require us to navigate them as bodies in space.

On the first of two visits to the exhibition, I walked the gallery, gazing at the wall panels in slow wonder, then retraced my steps, filming them on my mobile to capture the spatial and sonic experience of the installation. *New Power* pushes us to attend to how the narratives that unfold on the walls of the paper gallery position us in relation to the real bodies that inhabit the space with us. What emerges in this complex interplay between figures and bodies is an experience of distortion akin to a hall of mirrors that, in its distorting effect, provides important insights into the whiteness of the white spaces of the art world. The architecture of Alexandre's installation forces us to navigate these encounters physically by requiring us to move within them, to take in their magnitude and scale, to be unsettled by our spatial relations, and to confront the discomfort of where and how we encounter ourselves and our reflections within them (fig. 8).

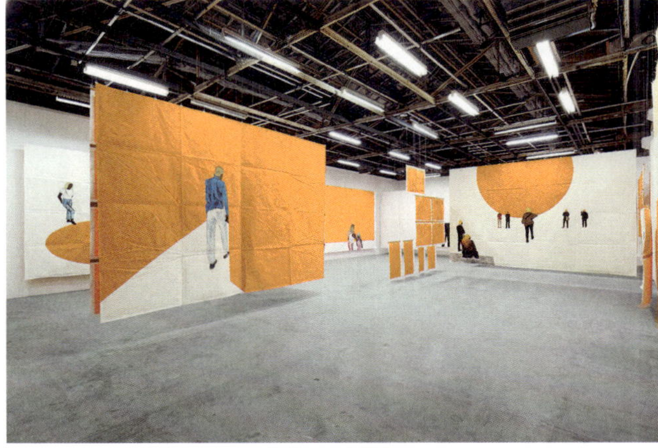

Figs. 7 (opposite page), 8: Installation views: *New Power*, Palais de Tokyo, Paris, November 26, 2021–March 13, 2022.

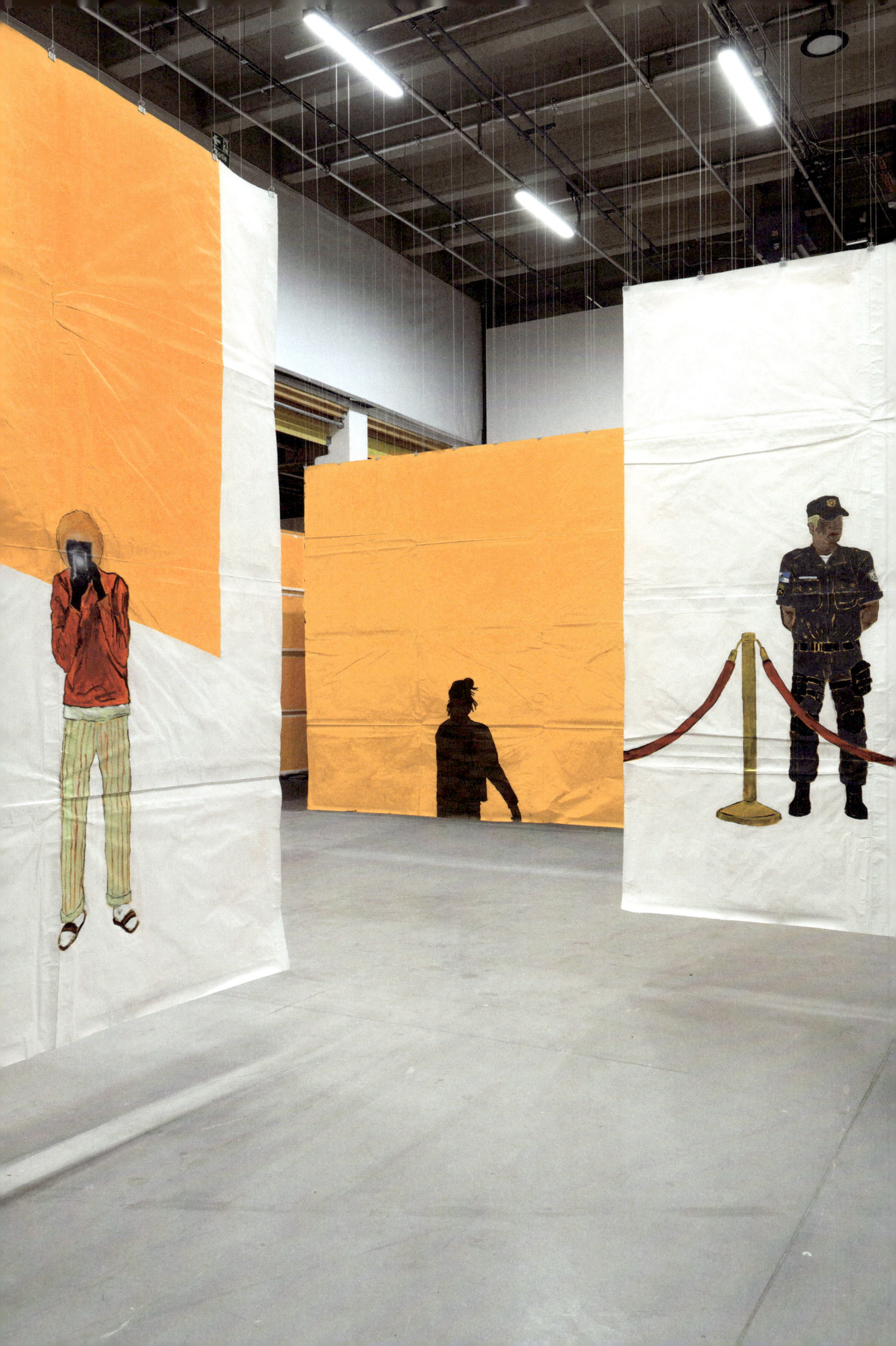

A blond brown girl greets me on a canvas opposite the entrance to a room in the paper gallery.
She hovers, dipping a toe into a golden sphere that rests at her feet.
She interrogates it alongside a tie-clad man and a Black officer in uniform.
This painted officer mirrors a similarly implacable real-life guard,
who sizes me up as I move through the gallery in silent conversation with the wall tableaux.
Raised to greet any Black person regardless of context, I wave when I pass, though he never seems to thaw.
His dark-skinned colleague is more lighthearted, and I smile when he greets me with a polite "Bonjour, Madame."

Sound plays an unlikely, invigorating role in this work. As someone who cannot help but attend to the sonic dimensions of visual art, my attention immediately fixed on the impact of one particularly striking sound in the space—one that intentionally or unintentionally amplifies the doubling dynamic so central to the installation. It is a sonic disruption that might be overlooked as a regular occurrence in any visit to a gallery or museum: the penetrating, unexpected bursts of scratchy speech emanating from the always-too-loud walkie-talkies of security guards monitoring the gallery. Mirroring the gallery scenes Alexandre creates on his paper canvases, uniformed Black security guards, who all too frequently go unnoticed by visitors, are ubiquitous in both the real and simulated galleries. But the guards do double duty not only as arbiters of order but also as unwitting protagonists in the encounter Alexandre stages in the installation.

When a lively group of young people arrive to attract his attention, a Black security guard follows discreetly at a distance, keeping them in full view and observing them attentively. Watching the guard as he shadows them moving through the gallery, I am struck by the fact that the art gallery is one of the few places where Black folks (often armed) are permitted to actively surveil white people (figs. 9–11). I watch this scene unfold over and over again in real time while standing in front of a canvas in which an armed guard pursues a young boy making his way toward the red velvet rope that cordons off a space in the paper gallery (fig. 12). Toggling back and forth between real and paper galleries, I found myself straddling the two when the real-life Black guard entered my view alongside

Fig. 9: Installation view: *New Power*, Palais de Tokyo, Paris, November 26, 2021–March 13, 2022.

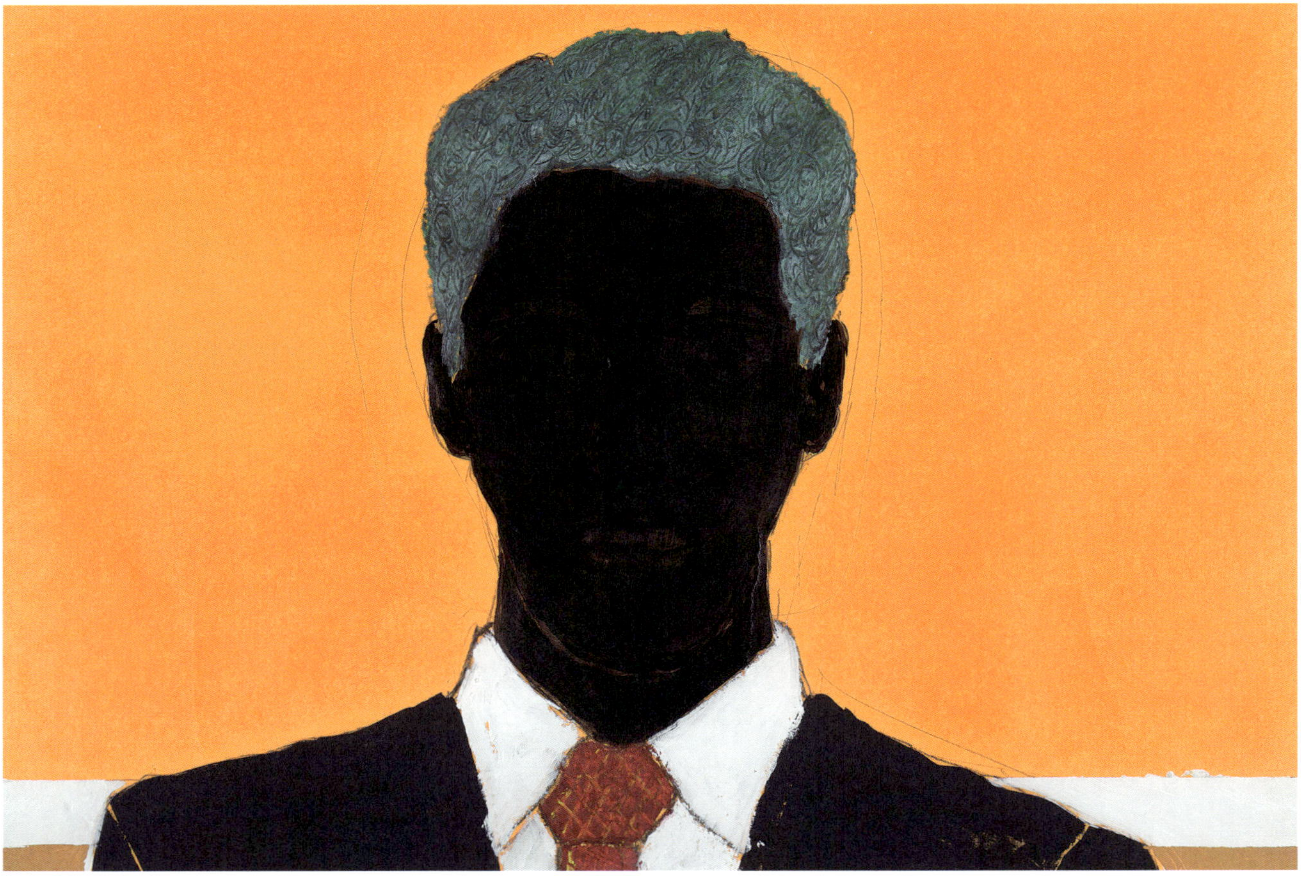

Fig. 10: *sem titulo* [untitled] (detail), 2021, from "Pardo é Papel: New Power," 2019–. Shoe polish, bitumen, charcoal, graphite, latex, acrylic, and oil stick on brown kraft paper.

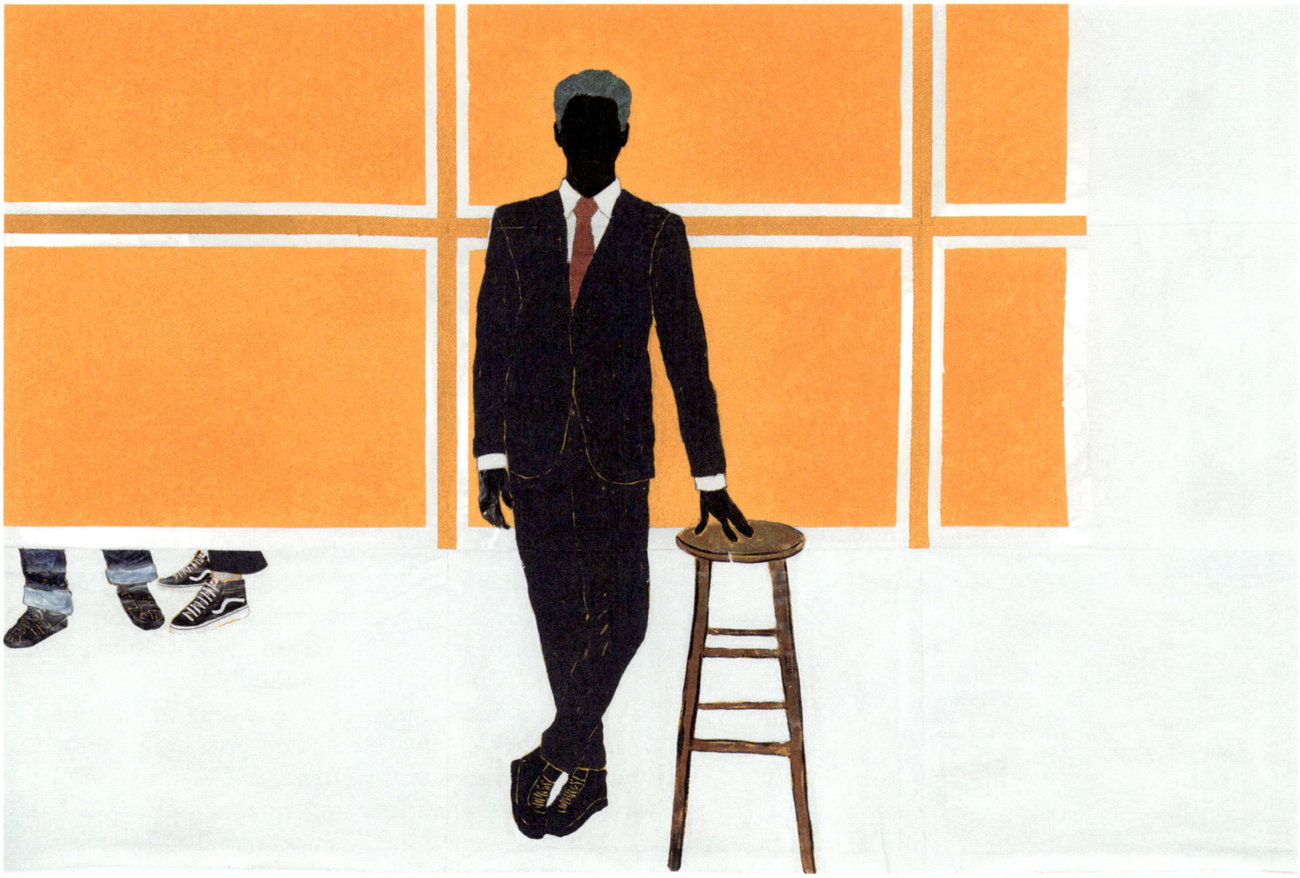

Fig. 11: *sem titulo* [untitled] (detail), 2021, from "Pardo é Papel: New Power," 2019–. Shoe polish, bitumen, charcoal, graphite, latex, acrylic, and oil stick on brown kraft paper.

his double in the paper gallery. What do the guards think of encountering their painted simulacra in spaces where they are usually innocuous or invisible? What do they make of the scenes depicted on Alexandre's canvases of white-cube spaces occupied by Black publics, policed by their mirror doubles? Sadly, both my French and my nerve failed me: I didn't pose these questions. It is nevertheless the central question posed by Alexandre and articulated unequivocally in *New Power*. In the dual gallery spaces of the installation, the artist takes us on a slow, reflective journey that stages a complex, triangulated encounter between artwork, viewer, and the space of the gallery itself. It is a journey that raises the stakes of what it means to see art and to see the gallery itself, differently.

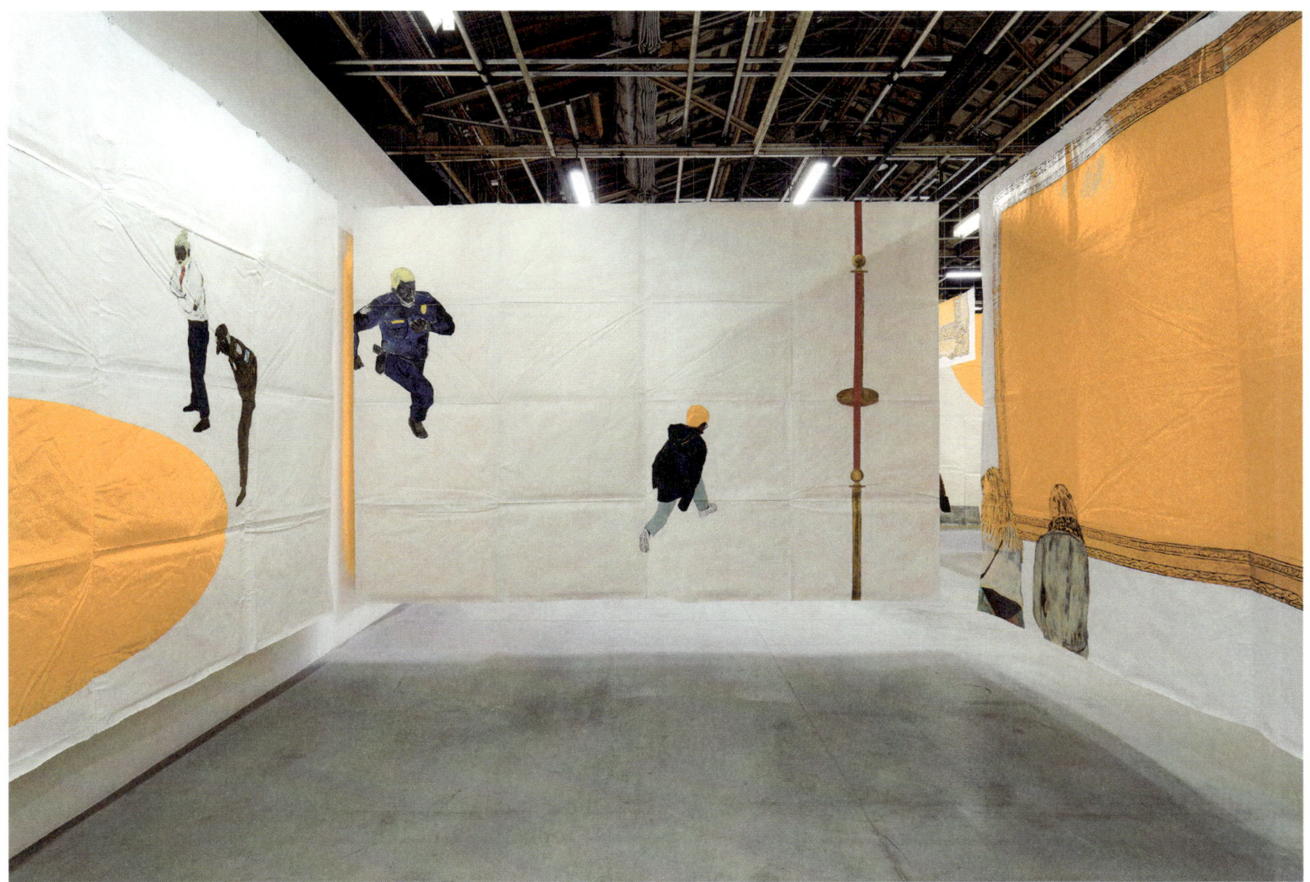

Fig. 12: Installation view: *New Power*, Palais de Tokyo, Paris, November 26, 2021–March 13, 2022.

Hans Ulrich Obrist
in Conversation with Maxwell Alexandre

The Name of the Religion Is Art

Translated by
Matthew Rinaldi

In 2020, Hans Ulrich Obrist interviewed Maxwell Alexandre in anticipation of his solo exhibition at David Zwirner Gallery in London called *Pardo é Papel: Close a door to open a window*. Alexandre conceived the show as the second "album" of his "Pardo é Papel" series in which each painting pays tribute to Black musicians from Brazil and beyond. Many of his influences for these works take inspiration from songs by Solange, Frank Ocean, and Tyler, the Creator. Alexandre, who borrowed the exhibition's title from Tyler, the Creator's song "New Magic Wand," interpreted these artists' lyrics into paintings to celebrate Black identity and express feelings of prosperity, self-esteem, and empowerment.

Alexandre's show reflected on the window as a metaphorical source of hope and connection to the outside world in a time of collective physical isolation brought on by the Covid-19 pandemic. As a result of this global crisis, Obrist in London and Alexandre in Rio de Janeiro were separated by nearly 6,000 miles. In addition to discussing Alexandre's plans for his forthcoming exhibition in London, they touched on aspects of his personal and artistic life: his background as a professional in-line skater, his interest in comics, the founding of A Igreja do Reino da Arte, A Noiva [The Church of the Kingdom of Art—The Bride], as a meeting place for young artists, and the ongoing development of "Pardo é Papel." Alexandre's Shed exhibition is the culmination of his artistic development over the years and includes "Pardo é Papel" artworks that preceded and followed *Close a door to open a window*, including his first album, "The Glorious Victory," and his most recent subseries, "New Power."

HANS ULRICH OBRIST
I'd like to start at the beginning. How did you come to art?

MAXWELL ALEXANDRE
I've been drawing since I was little. And my dream was to work with Mauricio de Sousa, the cartoonist who created *Turma da Mônica*.[1] I was a kid when I first became interested in the world of comic books. I used to watch anime on TV and play video games. It was part of my childhood.

HUO
Can you tell me about your childhood in the favela and your contact with these comics?

1
A Brazilian comic strip that has been popular among children since the 1960s.

MA

I grew up in Rocinha in Rio de Janeiro, the largest favela in Latin America. And comics are accessible to children in the favela. Since I was always drawing, people used to say, "Wow, you're an artist. An artist." And I thought art was *Turma da Mônica*. I started drawing my own comic books to sell at school. My fear was having a normal life—growing up, having a regular job, getting married, you know? Stuff like that. So I tried to turn my life into an adventure. And I started playing video games.

HUO

So you wanted your life to be an adventure and that's why you took an interest in video games?

MA

Yes. I fell in love with this character from [the video game franchise *Sonic the Hedgehog*] and I started skating. I skated for 12 years. I was a professional skater. I had sponsors. I used to participate in competitions. All this because I discovered this character from *Sonic Adventure* who wore futuristic skates.

HUO

Which video game inspired you the most?

MA

That one. *Sonic Adventure* on Dreamcast, the last video-game console from Sega. I found out about this character who was a futuristic hedgehog that skated. Sonic is blue, but this character is black. And for the first time, I saw a Black hero, this hedgehog. I wanted to be that character, Shadow. And in order to be Shadow, I had to learn how to skate.

HUO

I didn't know about this video-game influence. The interesting thing is that all this ended up in your paintings later. It was the skates that led you to painting. Do you still skate?

MA

No. But this was the way I found to turn my life into an adventure. This kind of market is not sustainable, so I tried to create a market. I had to work for the in-line skating industry and I tried to create some things, to create prints for T-shirts, for example. I needed to produce my videos to get sponsorship, to travel to competitions. I decided that I would go to university to improve my situation.

HUO

You started painting in an abandoned building, is that right?

MA

Yes, an abandoned 16-story hotel.[2] It was completely empty. I occupied this building for almost two years with various other artists. There, I was able to experiment with different types of work and I did my first painting with skates. I found a way to combine my old practice of skating with my new practice as an artist.

HUO

Where are you now?

MA

I'm in my studio in Rocinha, in Rio de Janeiro, working on an exhibition that I'm going to have at the David Zwirner Gallery in London.

HUO

And what are you going to show?

MA

Nine paintings, the second part of the series "Pardo é Papel."

HUO

And could you tell us about these paintings?

MA

These paintings, this second part of "Pardo é Papel," I'm calling it "Close a door to open a window." This second phase of "Pardo é Papel" is pretty intense, and I felt the need to catalog the paintings by making an analogy with music. While in painting distinctions are often made by series and themes, there's something in music that allows you to create collections and bring songs together with more precision. Like in the organization of albums, EPs, mixtapes, and so on. Starting with this exhibition, I began to retroactively look at the group of previous paintings from "Pardo é Papel." I'm calling this group of paintings "The Glorious Victory," which is the title of one of the paintings. This painting is going to be the cover of what I am calling the first "album," which is this old album, the first part of the series. The album I'm calling "Close a door to open a window" is the moment when I start inserting three international poets: Frank Ocean, Solange Knowles, and Tyler, the Creator. On the first album, I was working with three Brazilian rappers: BK', Baco Exu do Blues, and Djonga. For this international context, I saw an opportunity to bring these poets to this new show. The name "Close a door to open a window" comes from the lyrics of a song called "New Magic Wand," off of Tyler, the Creator's new album.

2
Gávea Tourist Hotel, located in São Conrado, Rio de Janeiro. There, Alexandre presented the performance *Sangue Preto* [Black blood], which can be seen in the video: https://www.youtube.com/watch?v=yDo814GDE5s

HUO
One thing that also made me curious was the connection to music. You already talked a little about it today and when we first met. The titles of your works are very political and some are inspired by rap. *Não foi pedindo licença que chegamos até aqui* [We didn't get here by apologizing] is a direct reference to "Abre caminho" by Baco Exu do Blues, who is famous for his political lyrics.[3] Can you talk a little bit about this connection to politics, activism, and rap?

MA
I don't consider myself an activist, but my existence alone already ends up incorporating activist notions and attitudes because I am who I am, and because I was born here, in the favela of Rocinha, and because I'm now occupying a prestigious space as an artist. This is going to reinforce this activist side on some level. But I also don't want to raise that flag or carry that weight that an activist sometimes carries. I really like the space of art as a space for vagrancy.

When I was doing abstract painting, or doing a work to talk about the spirit or the soul, I had no voice. But from the moment I begin to talk about the political Black body, it starts to become a relevant voice. That bothers me. The Black man's place is still very much predetermined in these matters. If you're Black, and you're from the favela, and you're an artist, your art has to be political. Somehow this role, or this reading, is a place where they must try to fit in the Black artist. The Black artist has less room to talk about sublime subject matter, about the spirit. Your place is much safer when you talk about the Black political body. And my work is subjected to this interpretation. But I also deliver excellent work that is resolved in terms of visual and poetic issues. I can hold my own in these matters.

Incidentally, rap is subjected to this a lot. It's an art form that was born in this context of the political, but these days it's already starting to move more toward a place of social disengagement too. Trap, for example, which is a subgenre of rap, goes through these issues. I actually make this analogy: trap is to rap what abstract painting is to figurative painting. Trap rappers are much more concerned about sound. Take [rapper] Playboi Carti, for example. He keeps repeating the same word. He's almost taking his voice out and only throwing noise in there. That's moving away from this commitment and flirting with matters inherent to the field of the artistic language itself. The work of visual artists is mostly made based on white European poetry. So they're going to read Nietzsche, Italo Calvino, whatever. When I paint based on Baco Exu do Blues, BK', and Djonga, it's a statement that I'm making. It means establishing a production in the fine arts based on Black poetry from the slums by artists who are Brazilian, who have experiences congruent to mine.

For my exhibition at Palais de Tokyo opening June 11, 2021, I'm going to present a subseries and extension of "Pardo é Papel" called "New Power."[4] I consider contemporary art like a new power in that it's a field where there is a significant amount of financial capital, symbolic capital, social capital, but above all intellectual capital. This exhibition will be focused only on one theme, which is the Black community in spaces for the contemplation of works of art, which are museums and galleries. Why am I talking about this? Because one of my interests is to draw my community's attention to these spaces that legitimize narratives and histories, which are galleries and museums. To allocate what is in the place of oblivion to a place of permanence and reverence.

But, at the same time, this is it. I'm here in my studio. I live on Travessa Mesopotâmia in Rocinha, which is one of the busier alleys, and, at the same time, painting here is not valued. I'm making a life for myself, opening up spaces of power, prestige, making money from this, but that is not a value, because it's not part of the values here. When I open an exhibition at the museum, the community doesn't go there. The ones who deliver this experience of the sublime and the transcendent to the community are the neo-Pentecostal churches. This notion of crying before a work of art or being moved in front of a Rothko, this whole thing is part of another ritual, of other temples of another faith, which is not the faith here.

When I paint a rap verse, because rap is an artistic expression that is seen as one of the voices of the urban poor, it is a way to bridge this gap. Because the kids on the street here, the minors on the street here, they listen to BK', they listen to Djonga, they listen to rap, they listen to Brazilian funk. These are the arts that are more assimilated here. It's when I get close to this field of rap, trying to make this approximation between the world of art and the world of the favela.

HUO
So you created your own religion. Do you think art replaces religion? Is art the new religion?

MA
If you analyze the word *religion*, it means "reconnection with the divine," with the idea of the divine. The name of the religion is Art.

3
"Abre caminho," from the album *Esú*, 2017

4
As a result of changes brought on by the pandemic, this exhibition opened later than originally planned, running from November 26, 2021, to March 13, 2022.

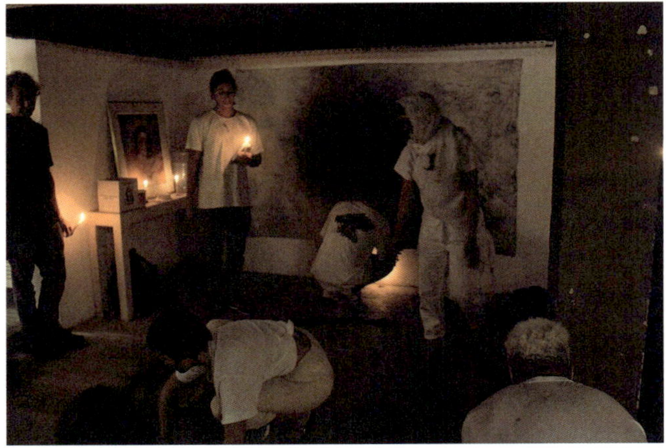

Fig. 1: Culto de Confraternização [Fellowship service] at Espaço Saracura, January 11, 2017.

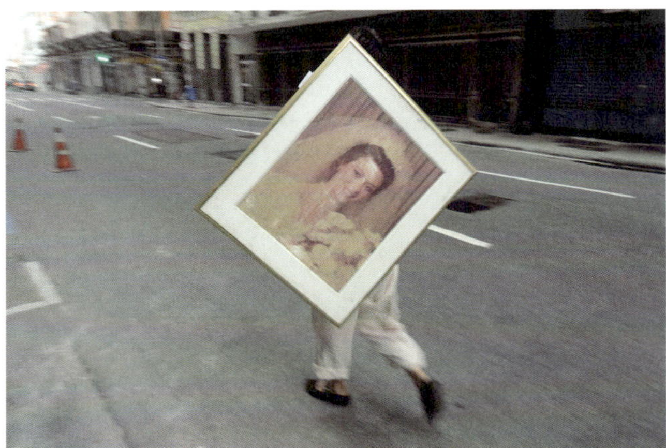

Fig. 2: Quarta peregrinação, do Centro à Saracura [Fourth pilgrimage, from Downtown to Saracura], January 11, 2017.

HUO
In Rio de Janeiro, a group of artists founded an art scene that you're a part of, which you helped to conceive: the Church of the Kingdom of Art—The Bride. This church is based in Rocinha and it's a meeting place for young artists. It's amazing that this art scene has formed so quickly. I'd like you to talk about how this scene came about and what it means to you. And also about the name you gave it. I'm also very interested in knowing about these works that are a procession, these rituals. Could you tell us a bit about the genesis of this church? I wonder if any miracles happened.

MA
The Church of the Kingdom of Art, also known as The Bride, is basically a church for artists that was born in 2017 out of a meeting of some friends there at PUC [Pontifical Catholic University of Rio de Janeiro] (figs. 1, 2). Raoni Azevedo and Edu de Barros are some of the founding members. We started to meet as a congregation as a way to create an outlet for what we were doing (fig. 3). At that time, I wasn't a full-fledged artist yet. We were flirting with the art world, but we still didn't know how to find the way in. And these ways into the arts often come [about] because of relationships, not necessarily because of the quality of the work. And since we were not well connected to the agents in the field, we decided to create this congregation (fig. 4). And we knew that we couldn't create an art collective because art collectives were already... I don't know if "outdated" is the word, but it carried this connotation that was not what we wanted. The idea of a collective also has to do with the collective practice, whereas church is a meeting that happens collectively, but the practices are individual. We have the idea of "one's own gospel." At the same time that we're creating, we're outlining a collective narrative, but we all have a point of view and can choose our own gospels, our own bibles.

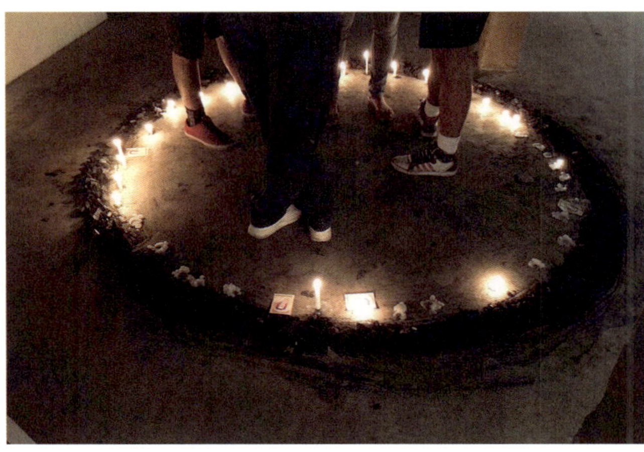

Fig. 3: Culto de Confraternização [Fellowship service] at Espaço Saracura, January 11, 2017.

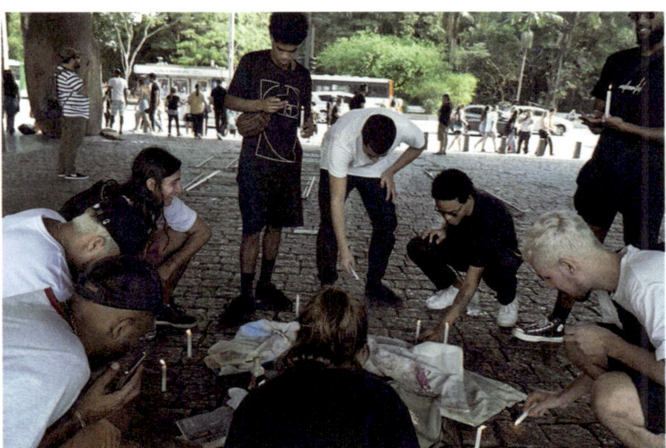

Fig. 4: Quarta oferenda [Fourth offering] at Museu de Arte Moderna de São Paulo, January 9, 2018.

HUO
You said that everything is faith, that the same faith that leads a person to a church of any religion also leads a person to art. What is your definition of art?

MA
Defining art always seems pretentious to me. And when you name something, when you start to delineate something, it loses its potency. For me, art is a mental, internal phenomenon, something in the spirit that can become everything in materiality. I think it's something close to that.

A longer version of this interview originally appeared in Portuguese in the book *Hans Ulrich Obrist: Entrevistas brasileiras vol. 2*, published by Editora Cobogó.

Opposite page: *Crianças atrás de telas* [Kids behind canvases], 2018.

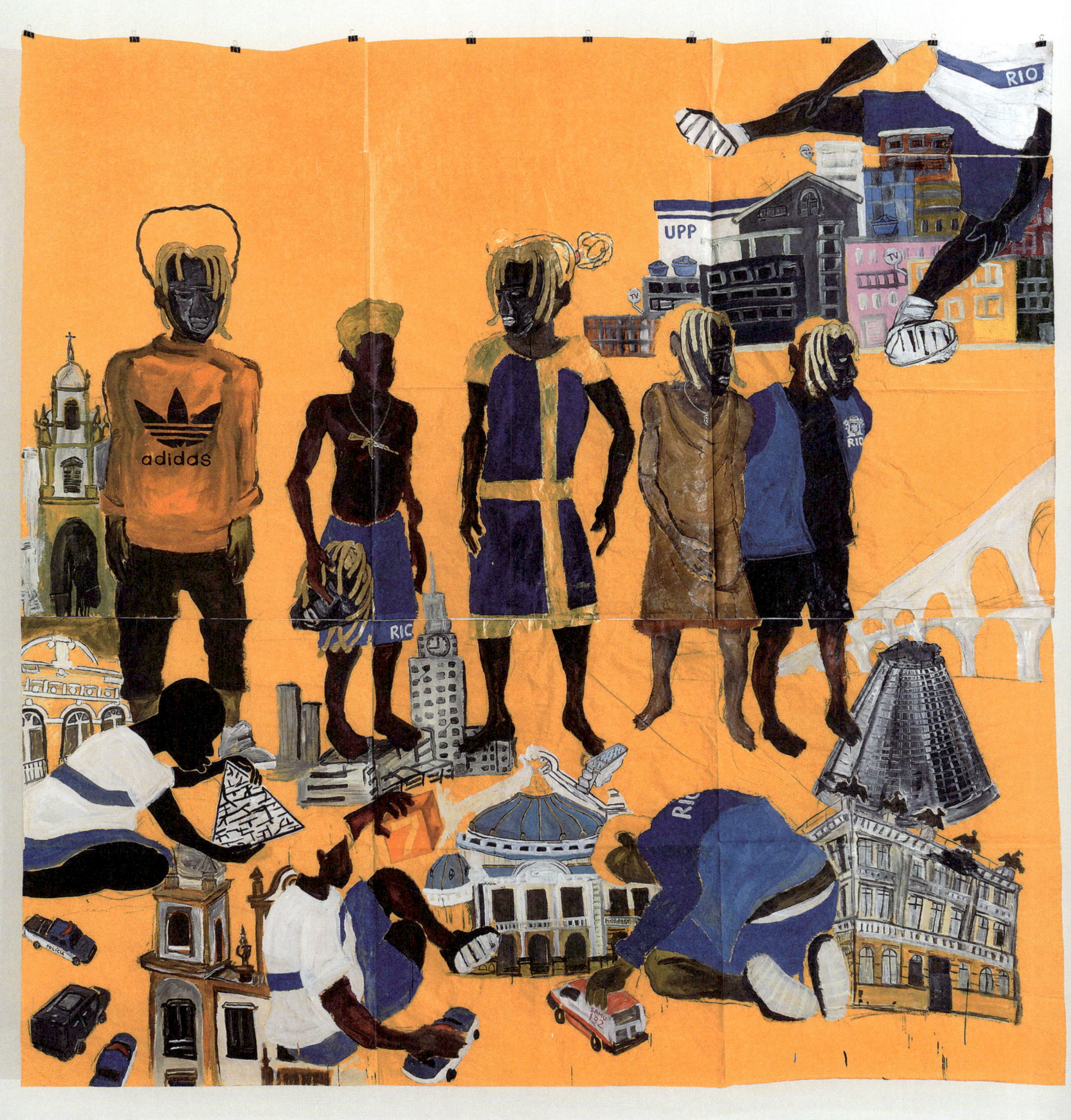
RIO
UPP
adidas
RIO
RIO

Opposite page: *A lua quer ser preta, se pinta no eclipse (diss)* [The moon wants to be black, it paints itself in the eclipse (diss)] (detail), 2019.

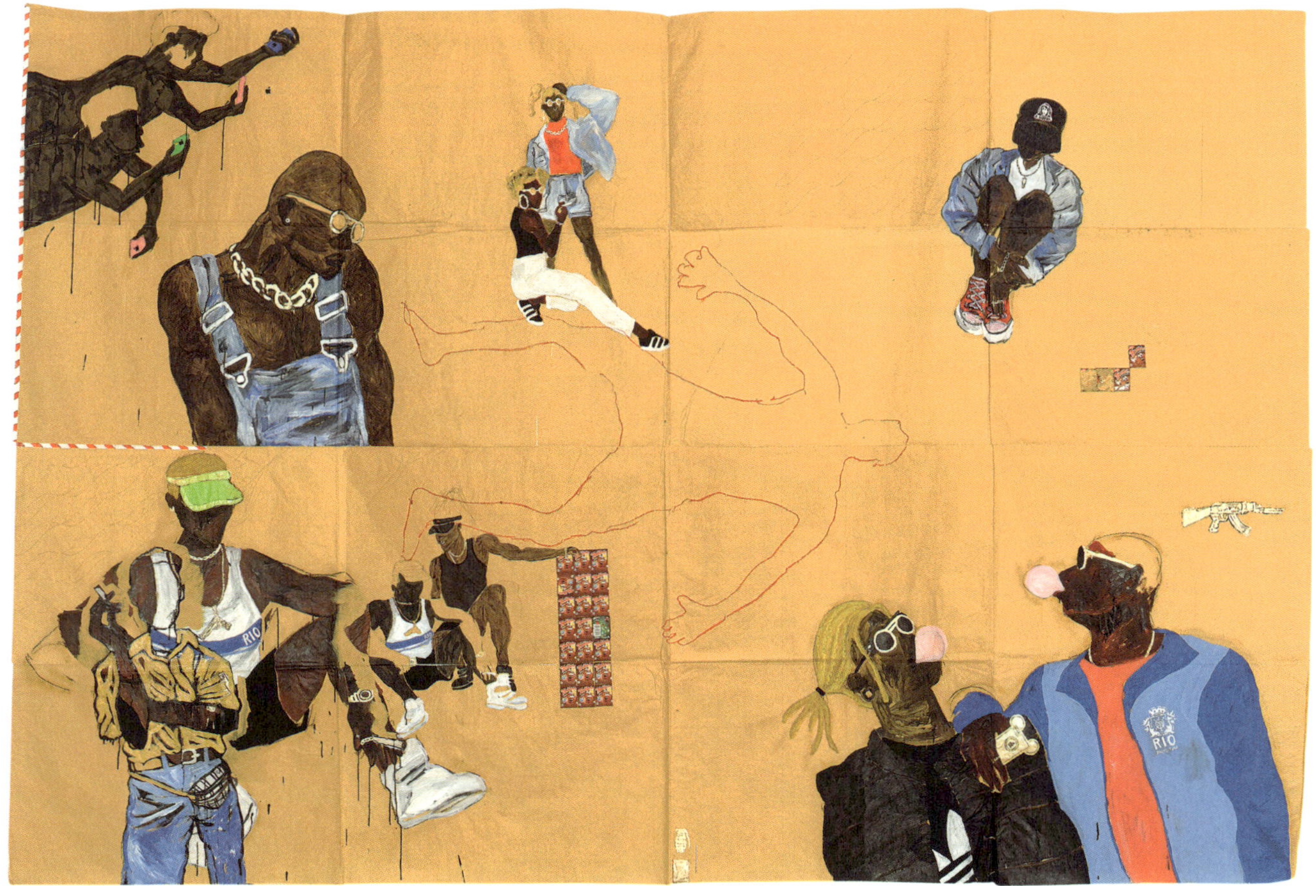

Bilionário escuro [Dark Billionaire], 2018.

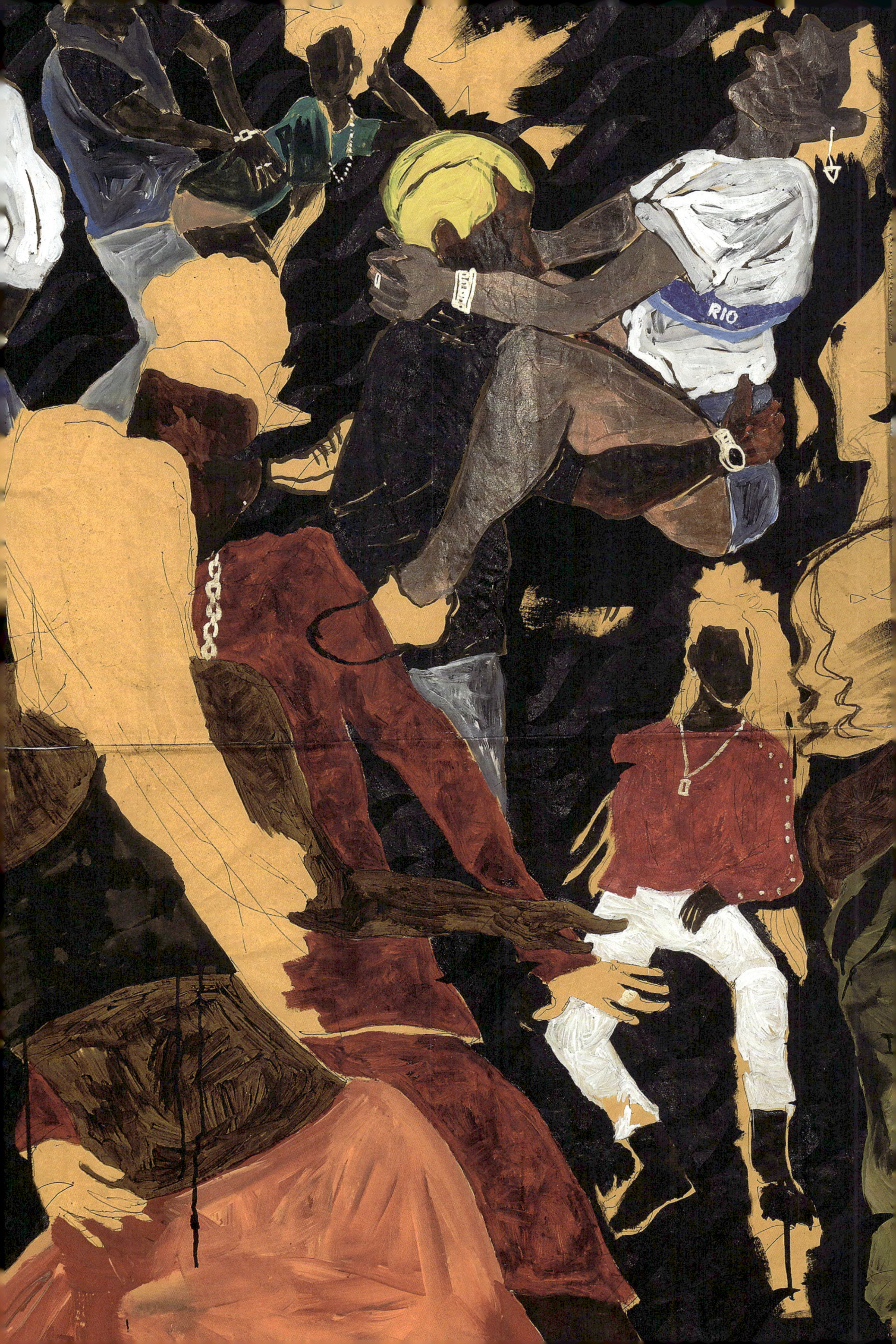
RIO

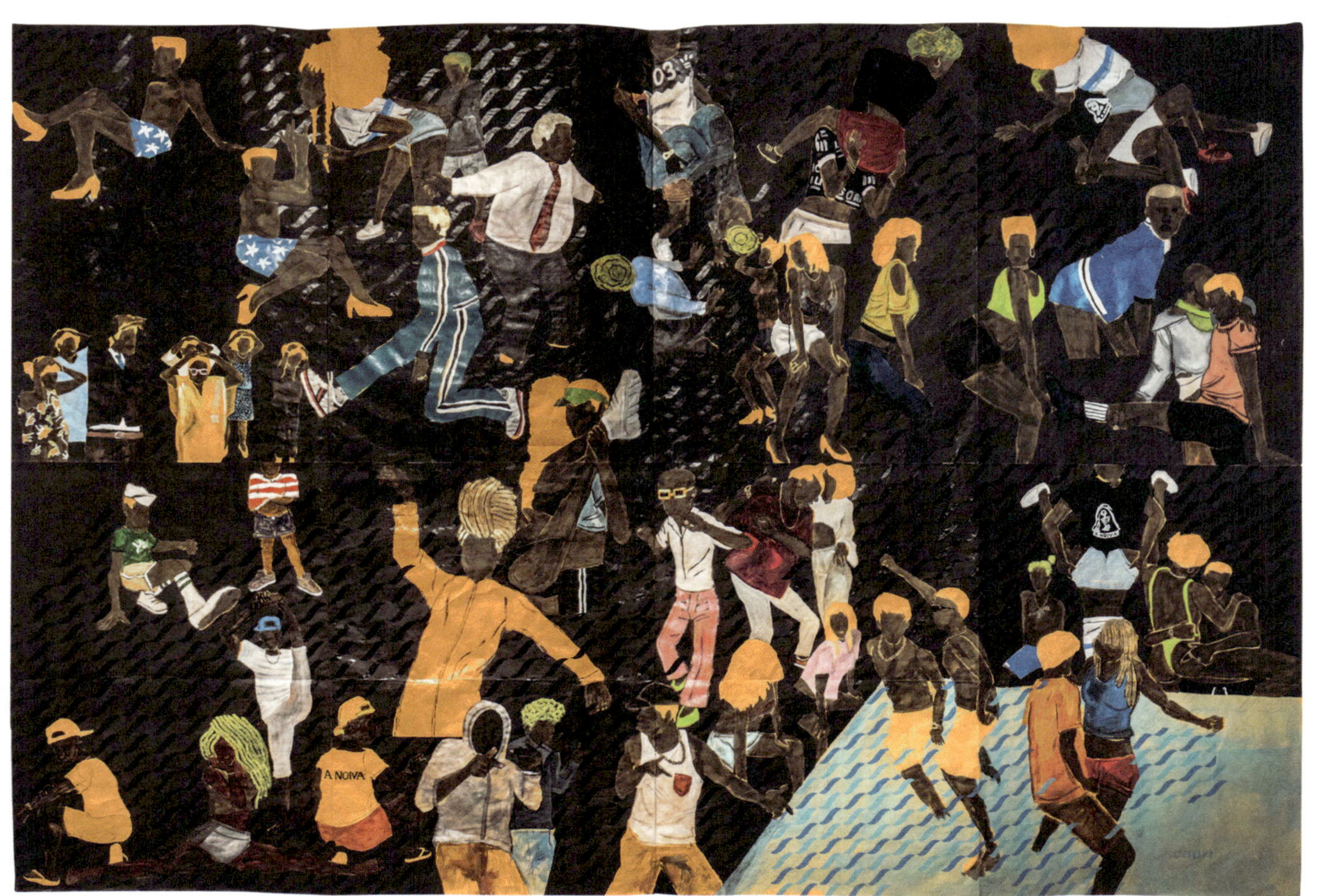

A lua quer ser preta, se pinta no eclipse (diss) [The moon wants to be black, it paints itself in the eclipse (diss)], 2019.

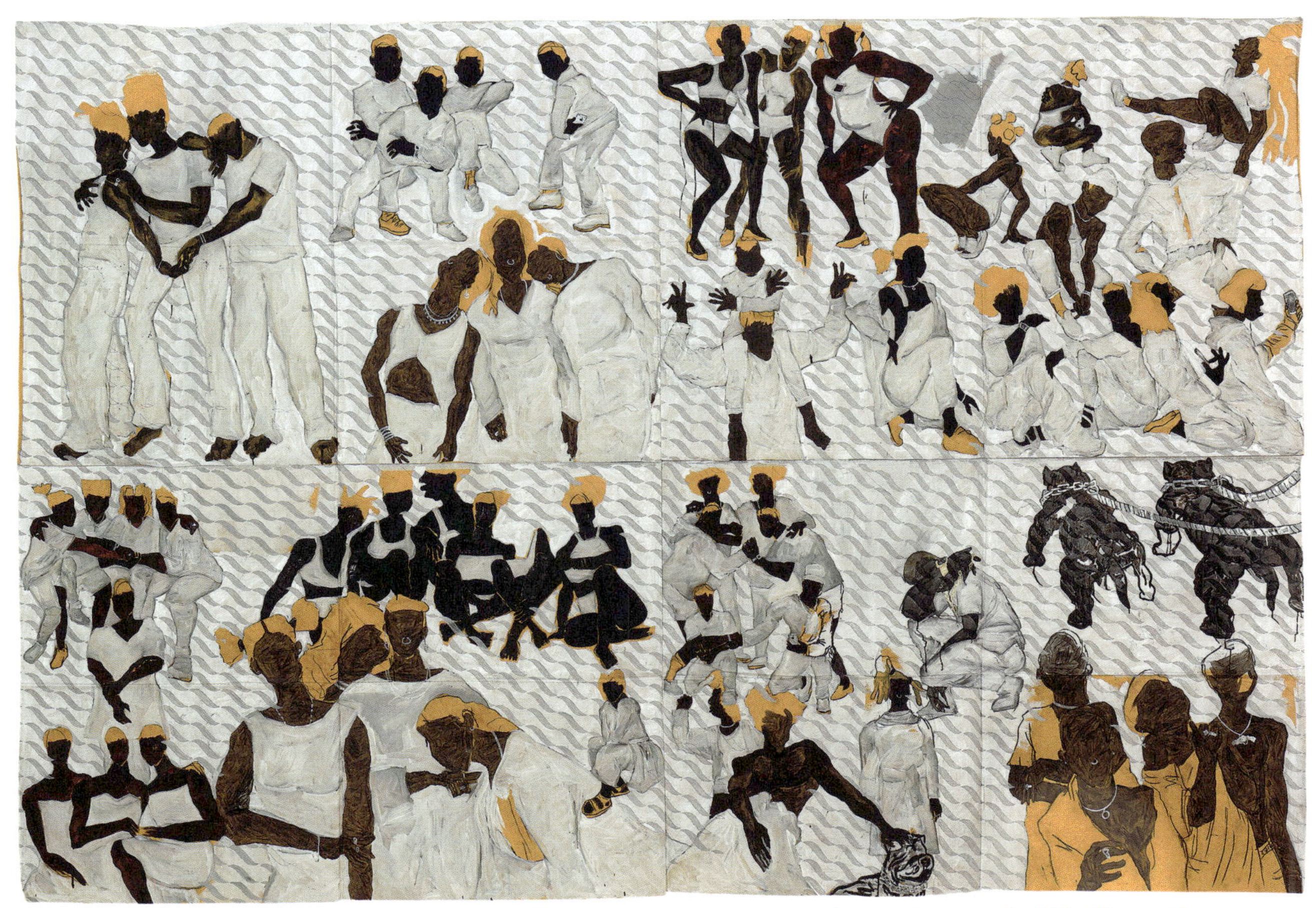

Meus manos, minhas minas, meus irmãos, minhas irmãs e meus cães [My homies, my homegirls, my brothers, my sisters, my dogs] (detail), 2017–18.

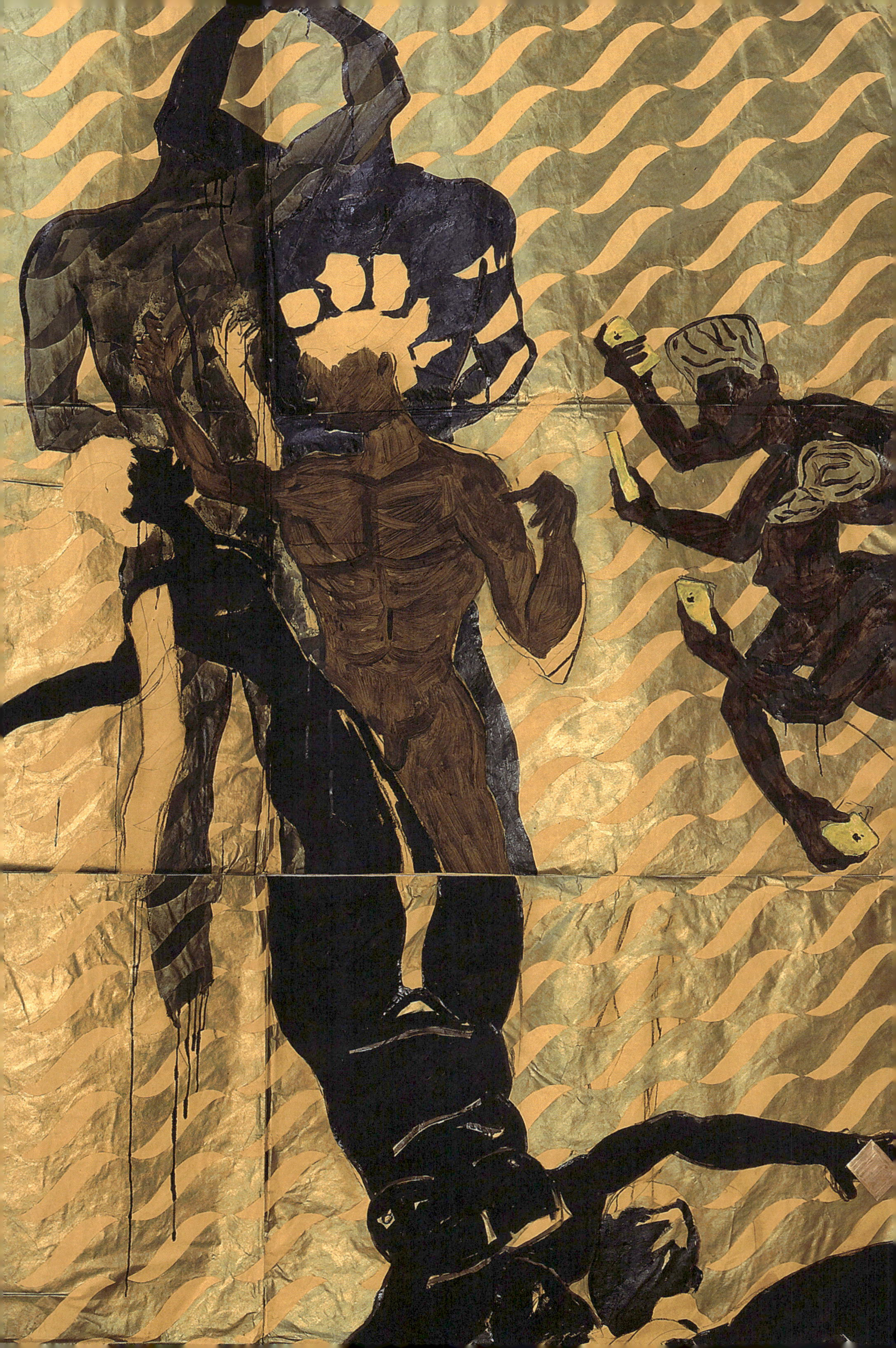

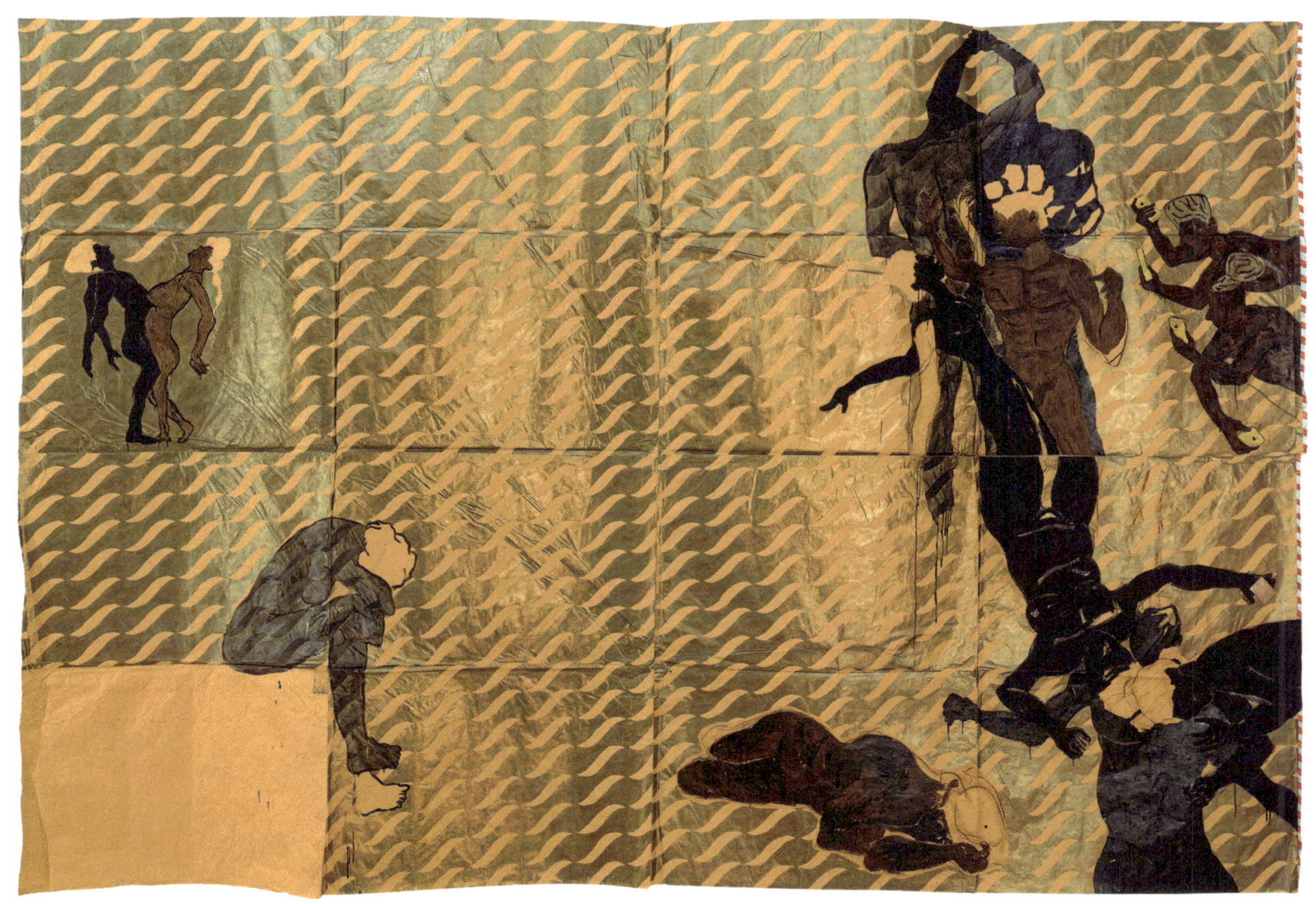

Olhar embriagado no espelho [Drunk look in the mirror], 2018.

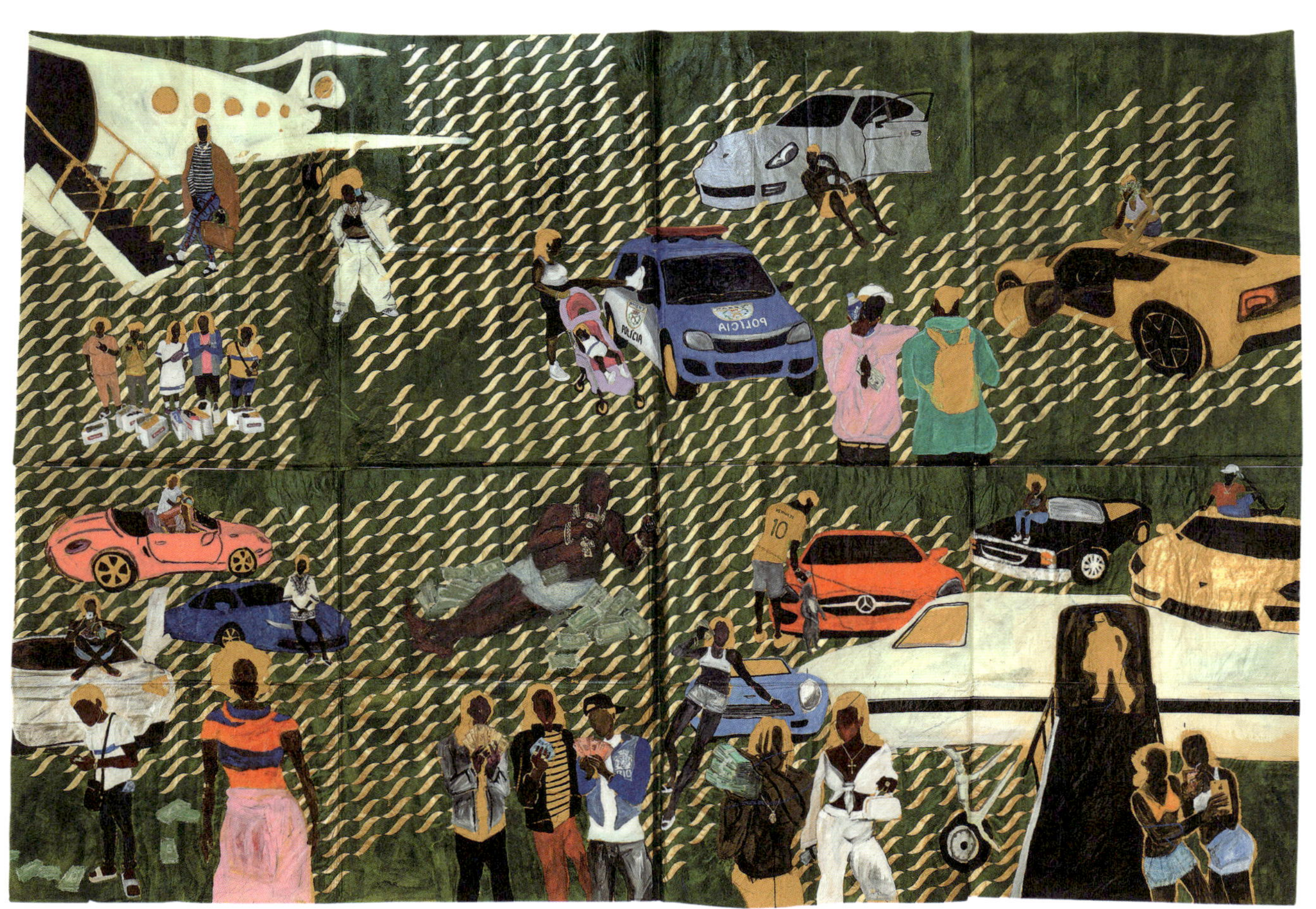

Só quando tu tá com as folhas geral gosta de salada [Only when you're with leaves do people like salad], 2018.

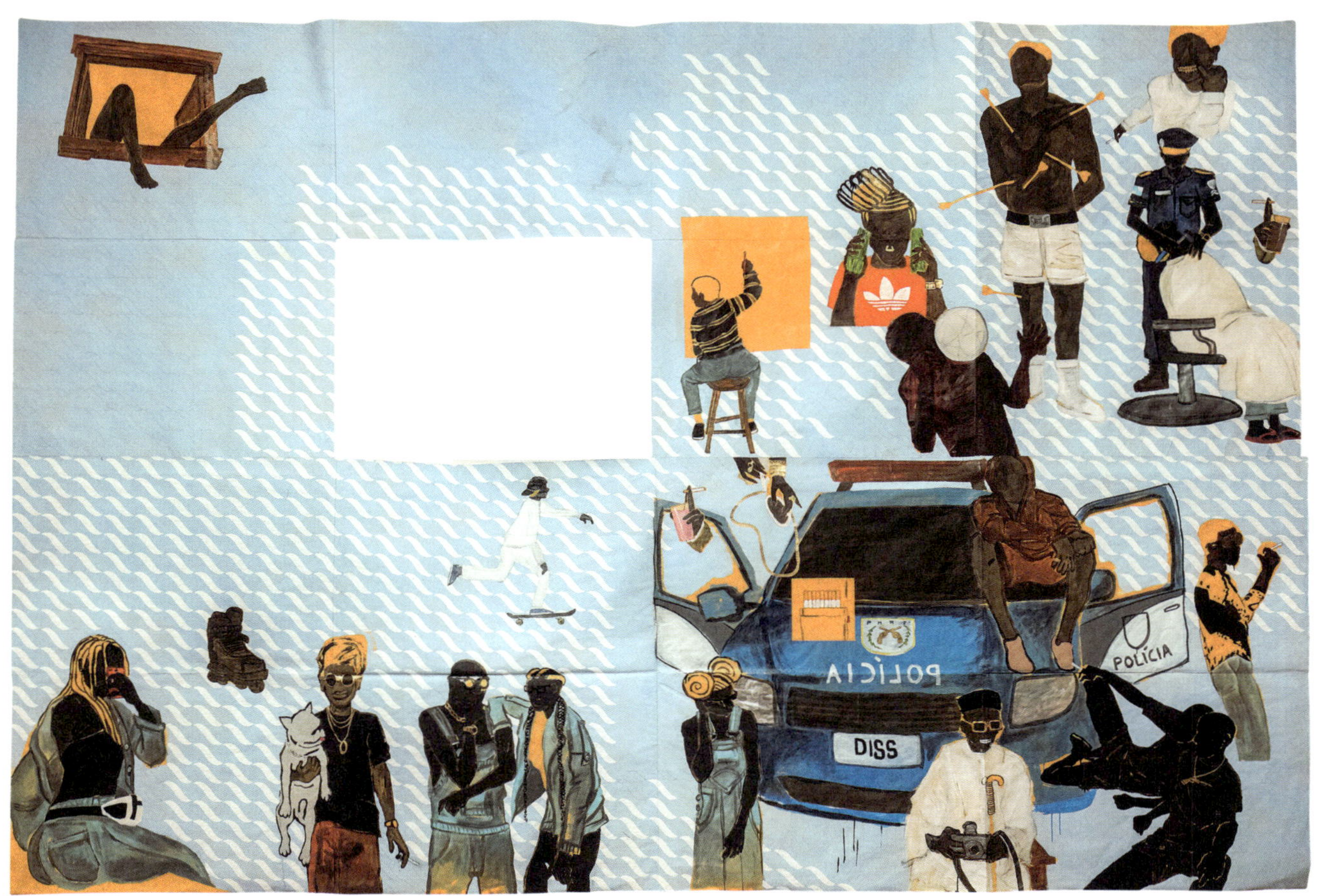

Um cigarro e a vida pela janela (diss) [A cigarette and life through the window (diss)], 2019.

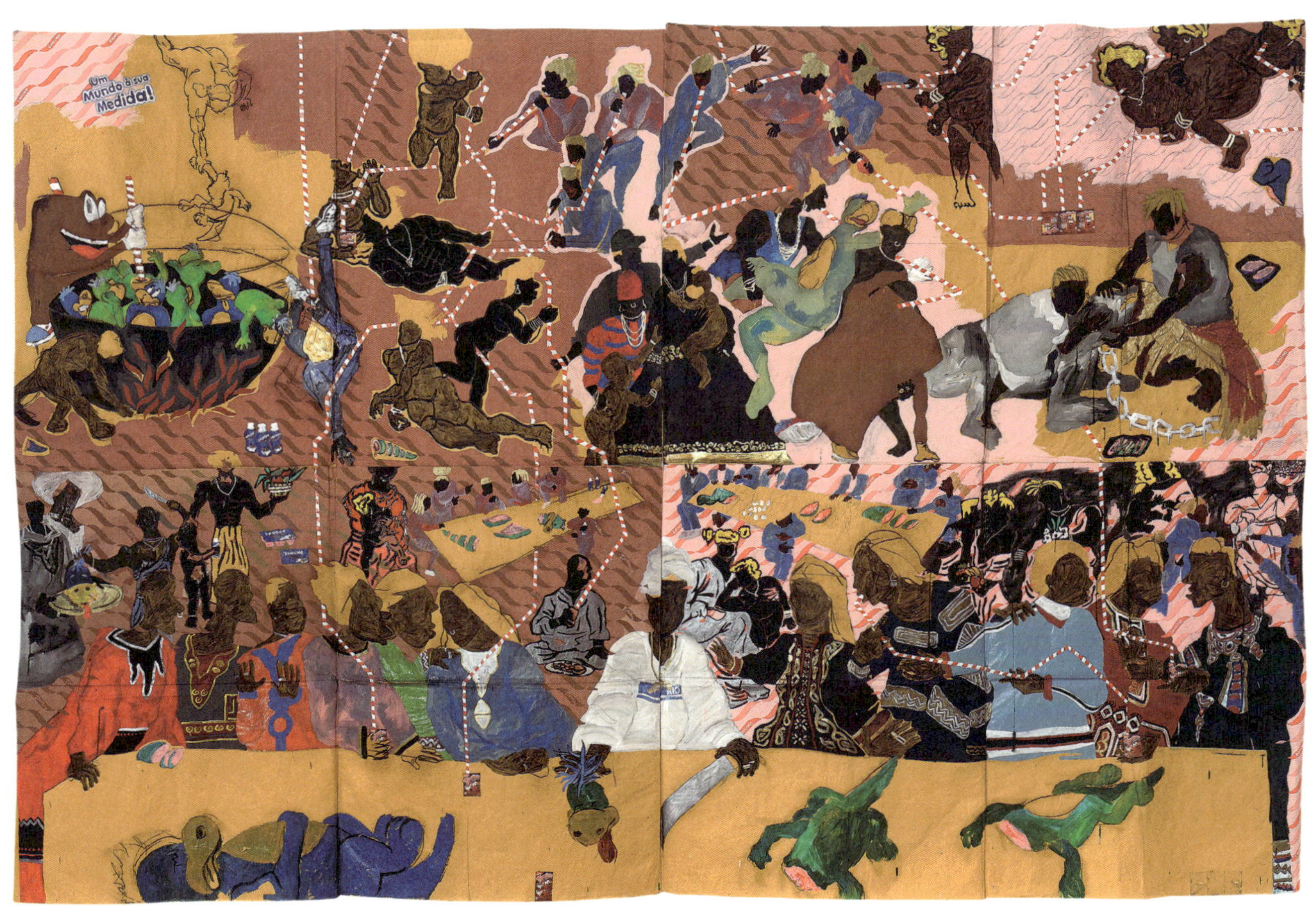

Não foi pedindo licença que chegamos até aqui [We didn't get here by apologizing], 2018.

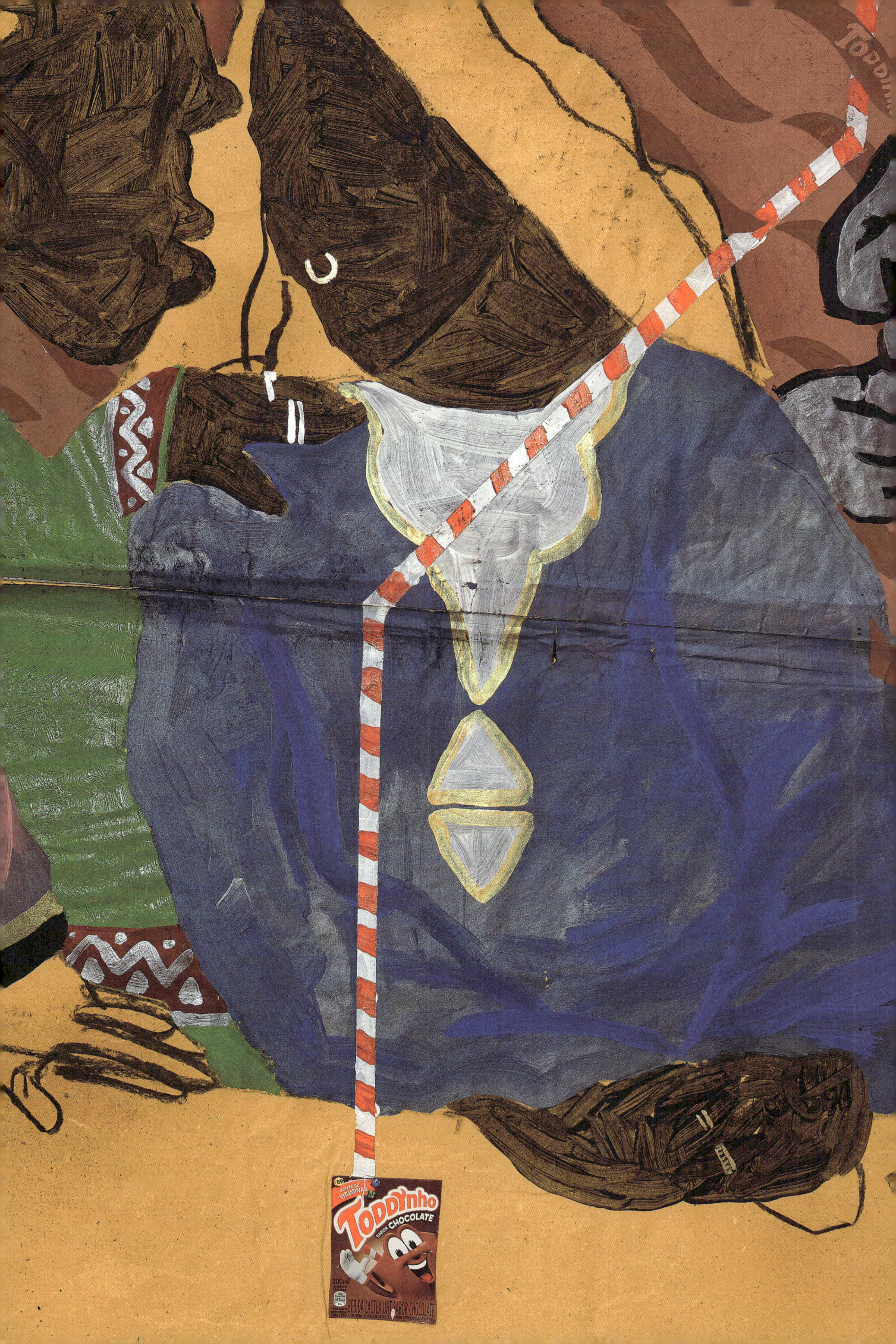
B9
FONTE DE VITAMINAS
Toddynho
SABOR CHOCOLATE
200ml
BEBIDA LACTEA UHT SABOR CHOCOLATE

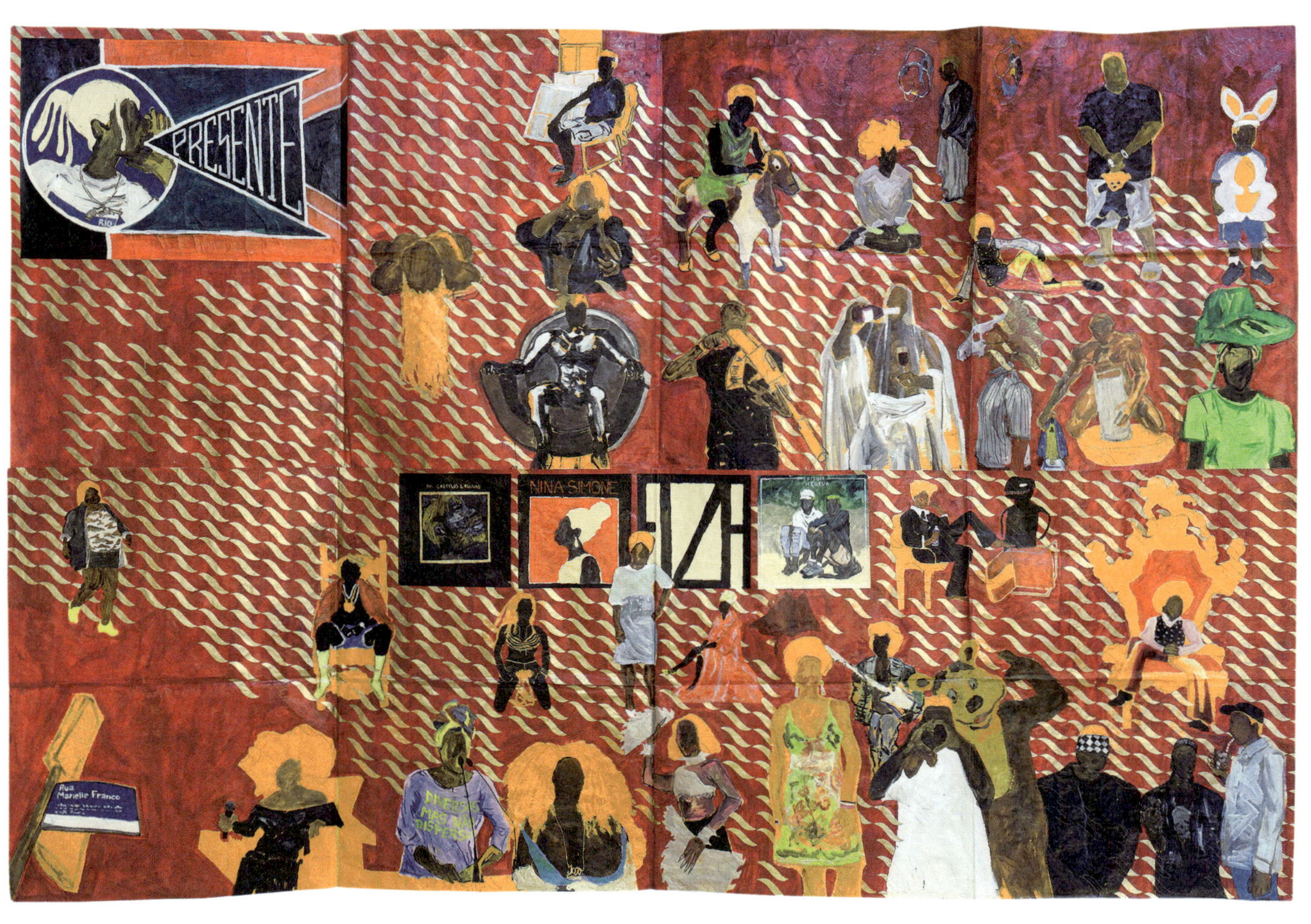
PRESENTE
RIO
NINA SIMONE
Rua
Marielle Franco

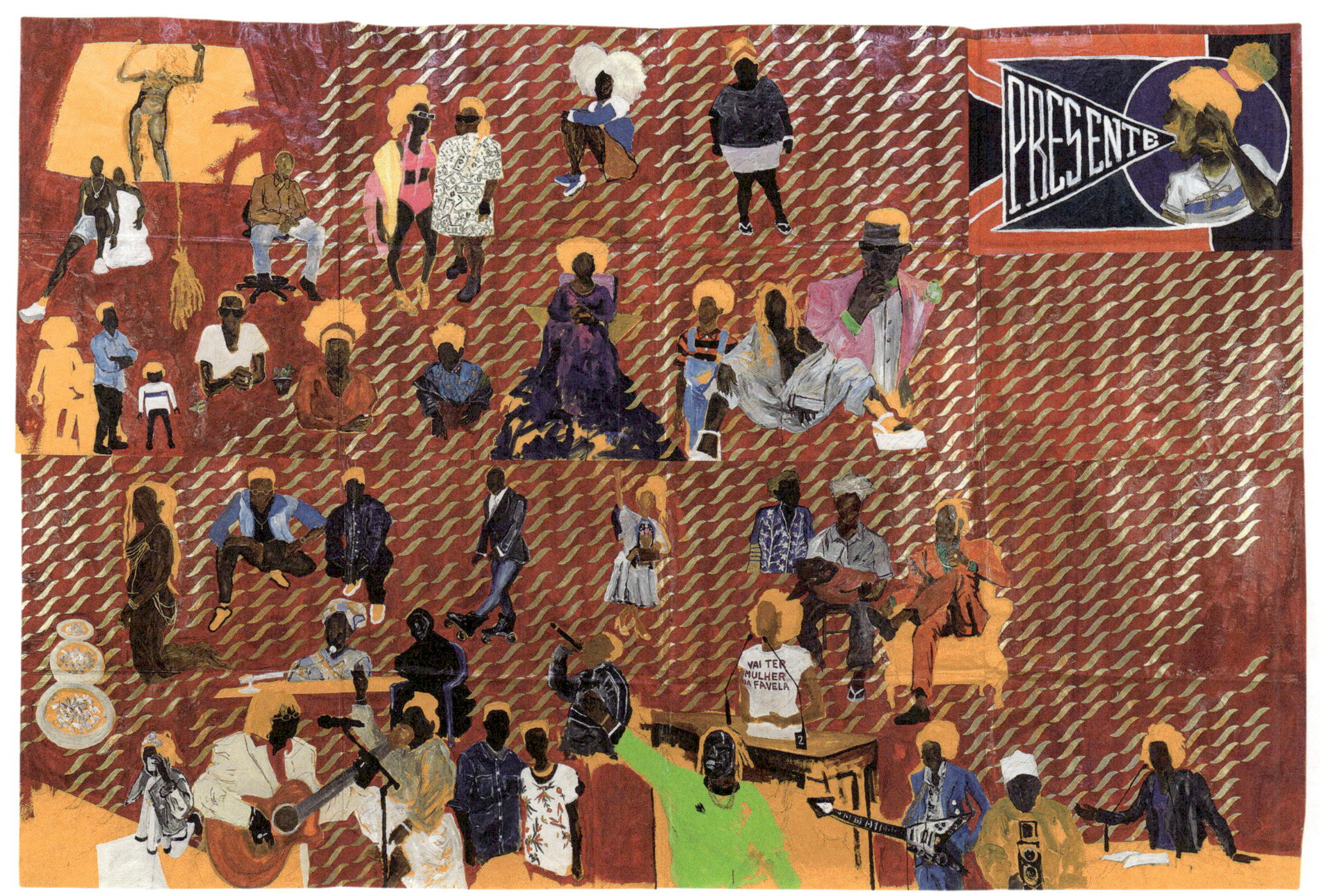

Cantos de esquinas [Street corner songs], 2019.

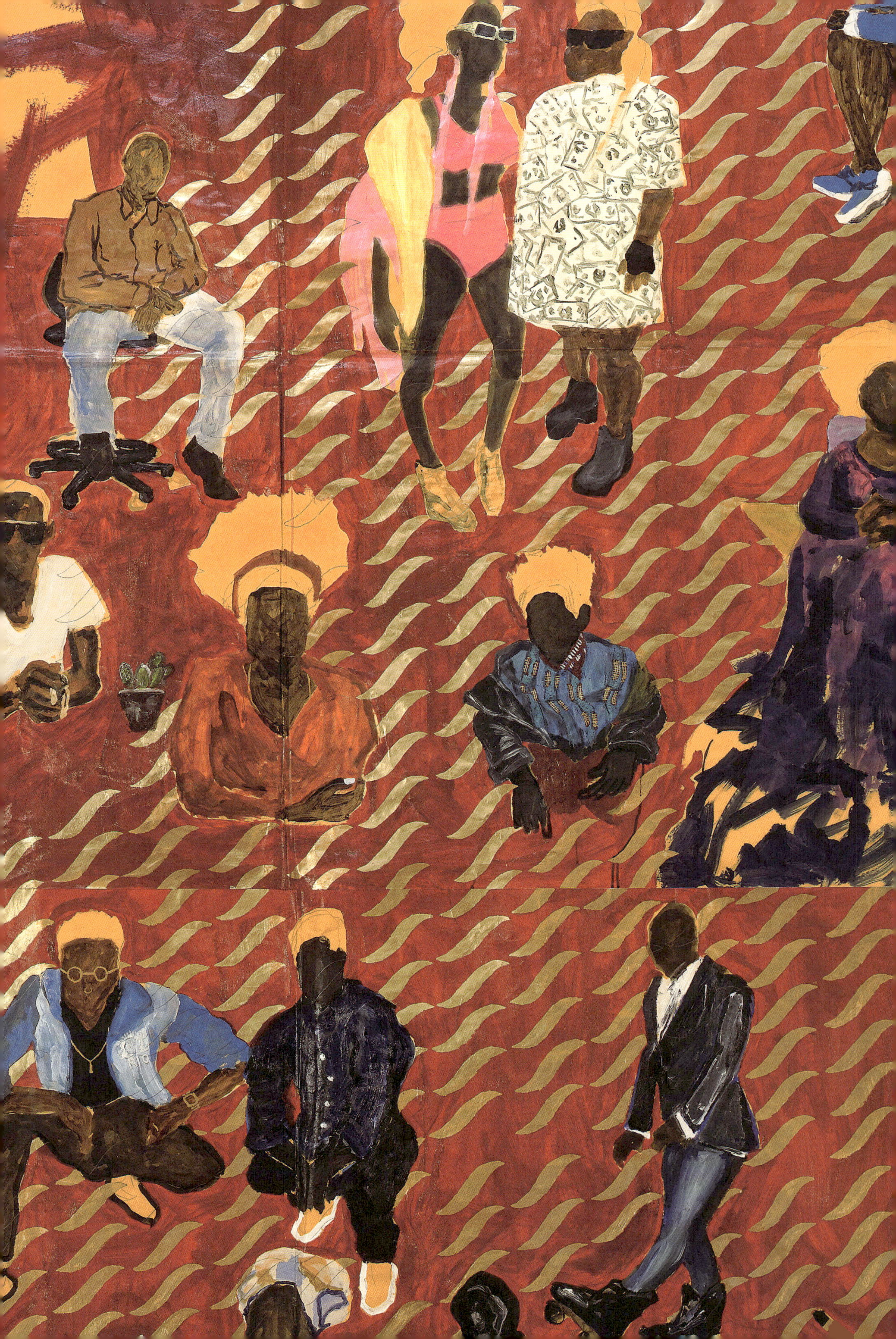

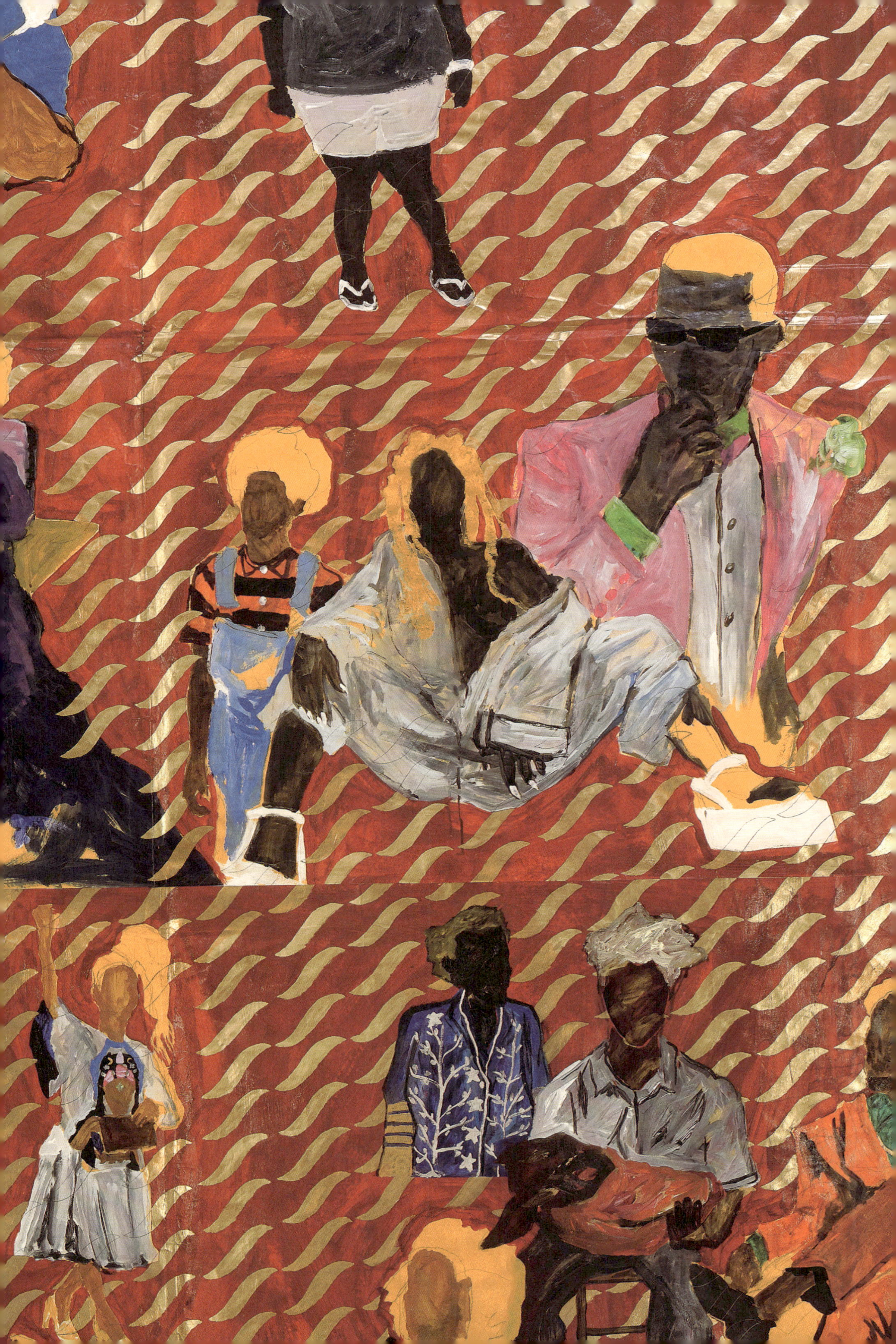

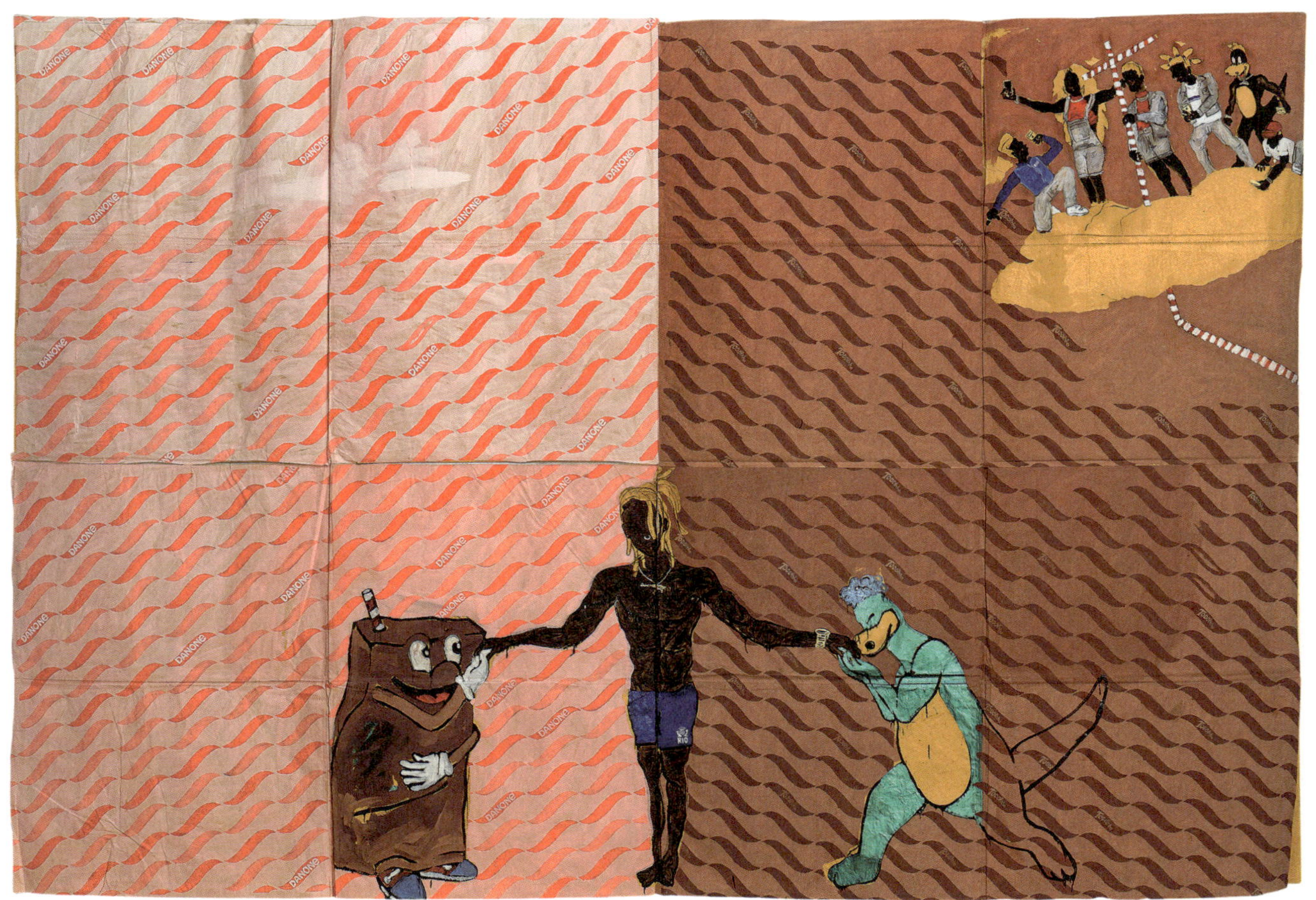

A vitória gloriosa [The glorious victory], 2018.

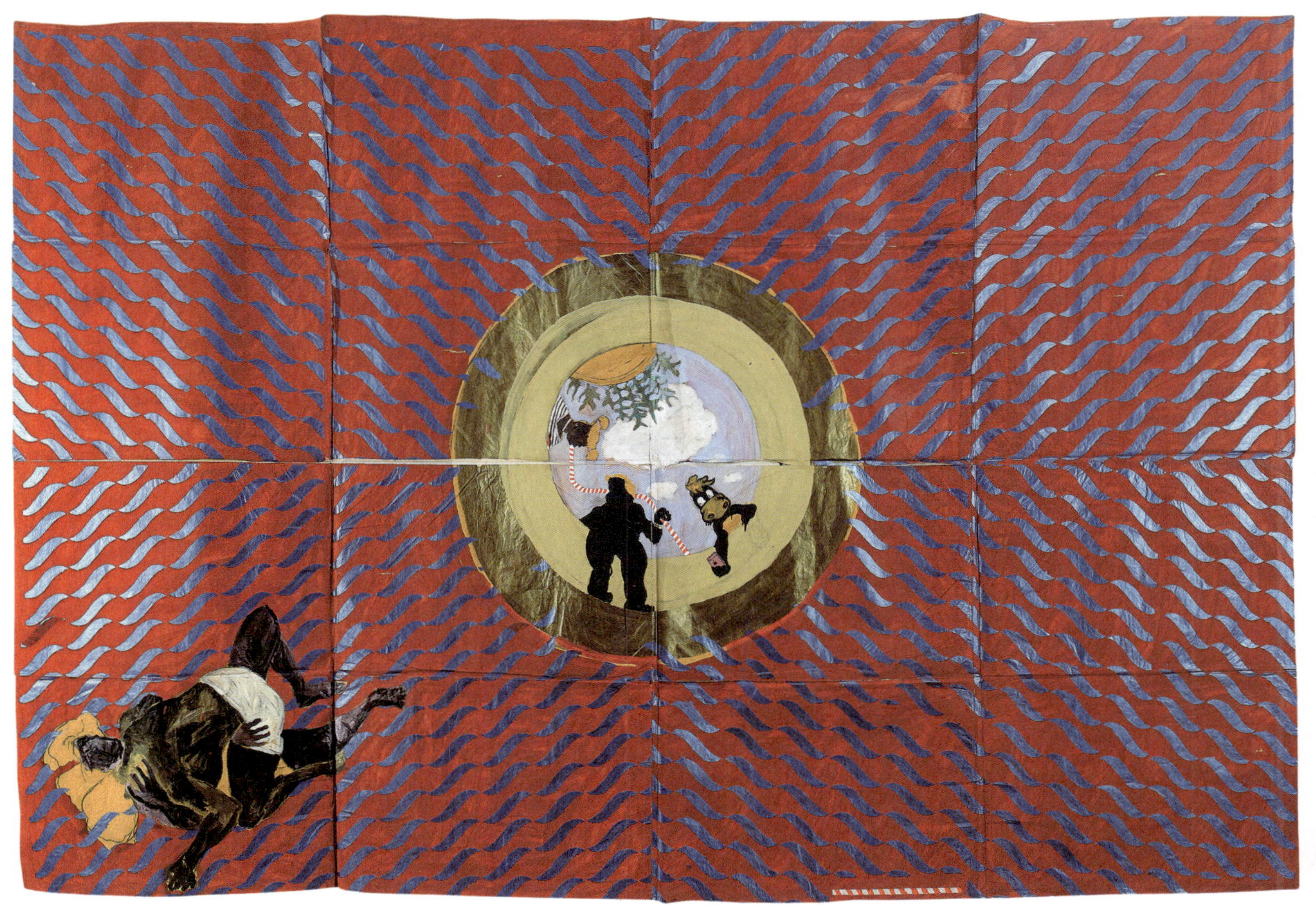

Insatisfeito com o tamanho do mundo [Displeased with the size of the world], 2018.

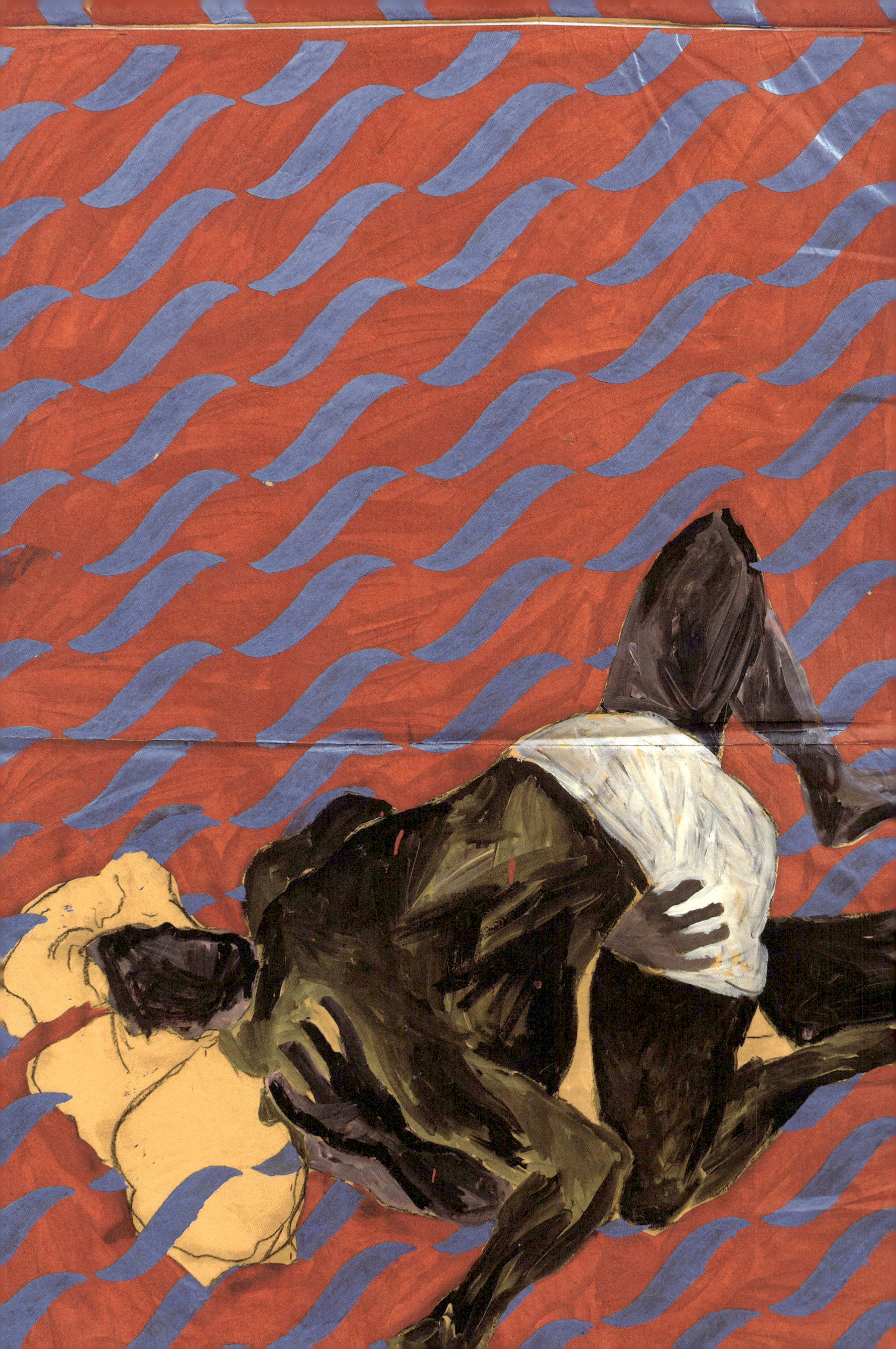

Até Deus inveja o homem preto [Even God envies the Black man], 2018.

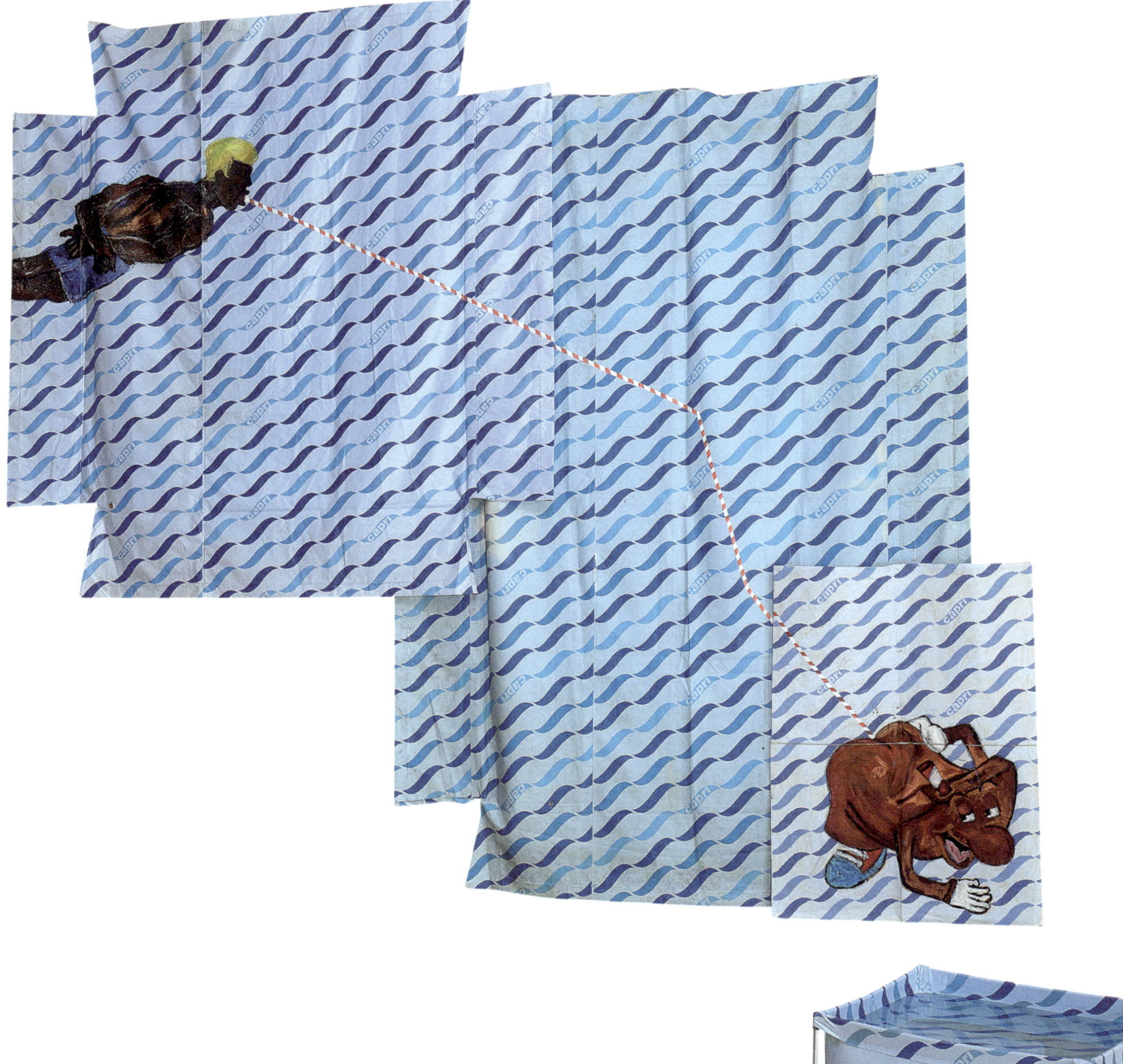

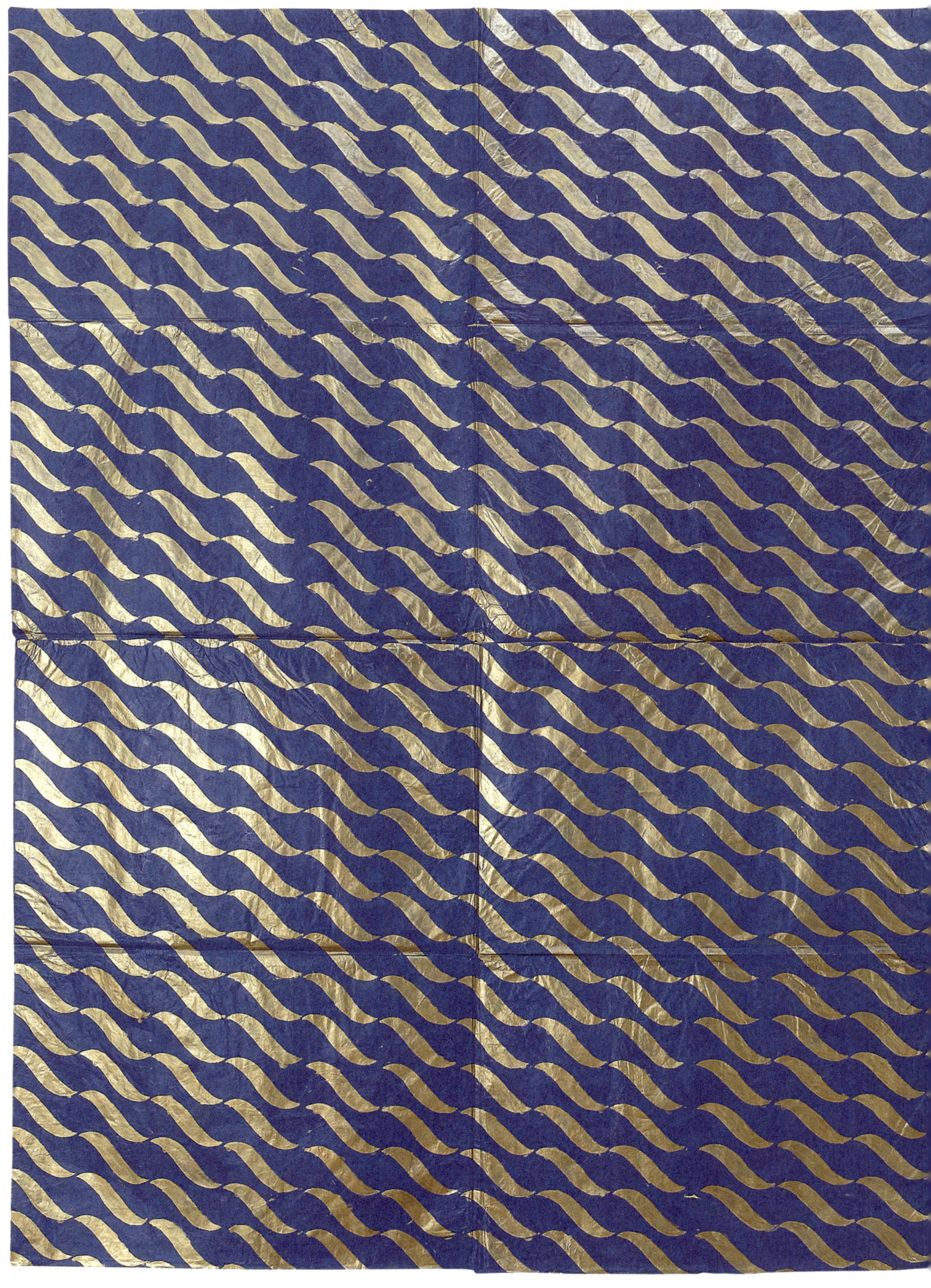

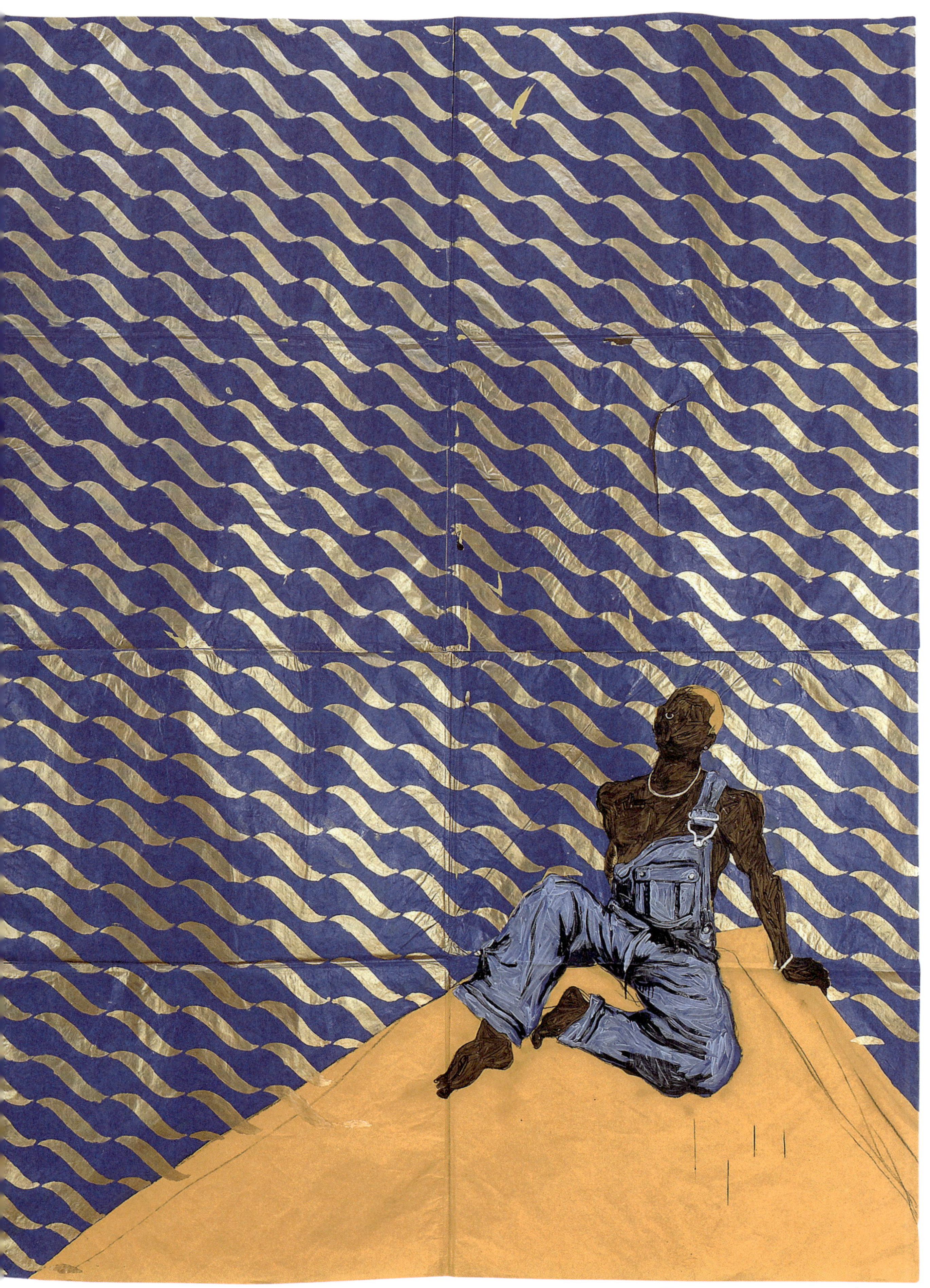

Se eu fosse vocês olhava pra mim de novo [If I were you I'd look at me again], 2018.

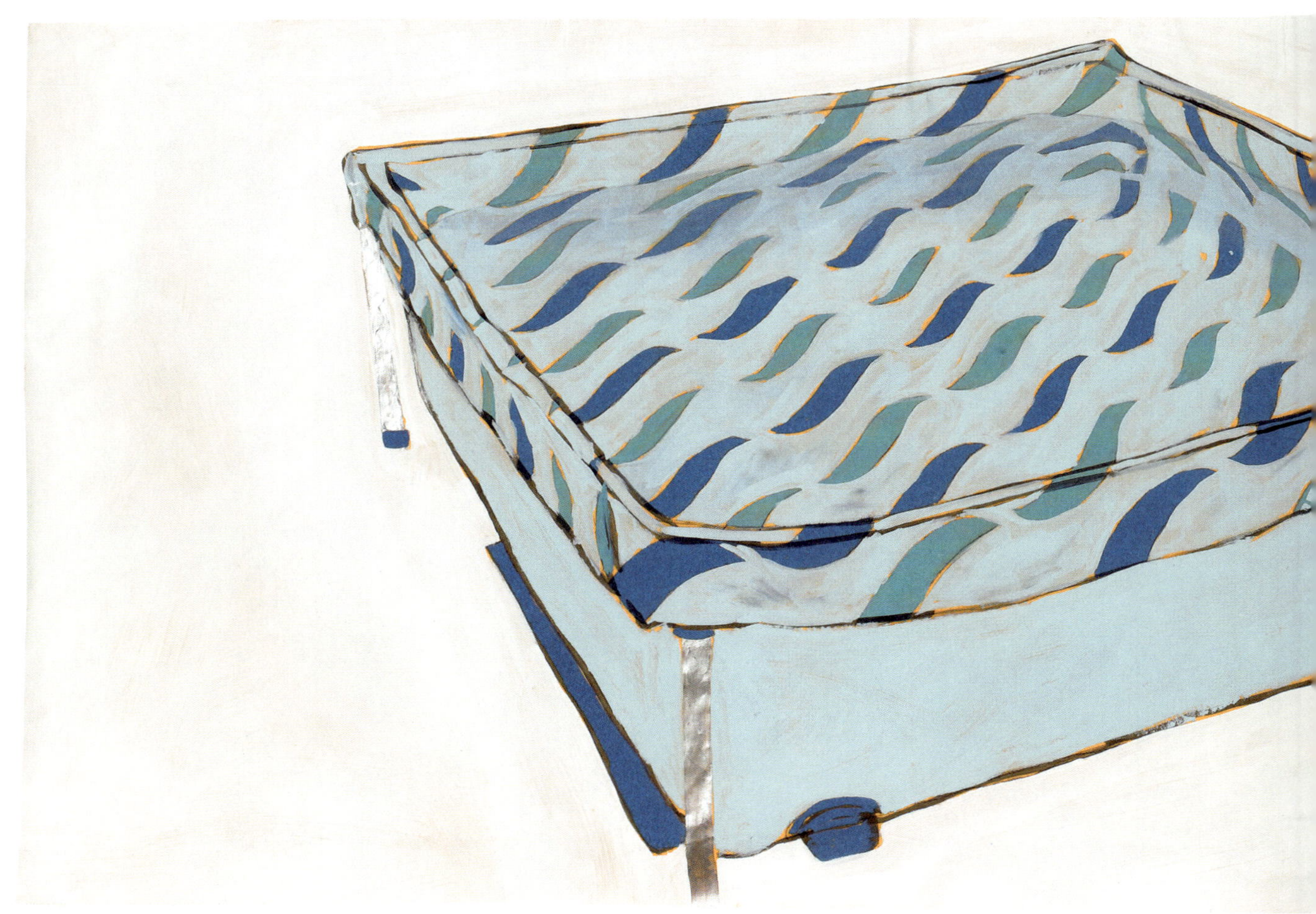

sem titulo [untitled], 2021.

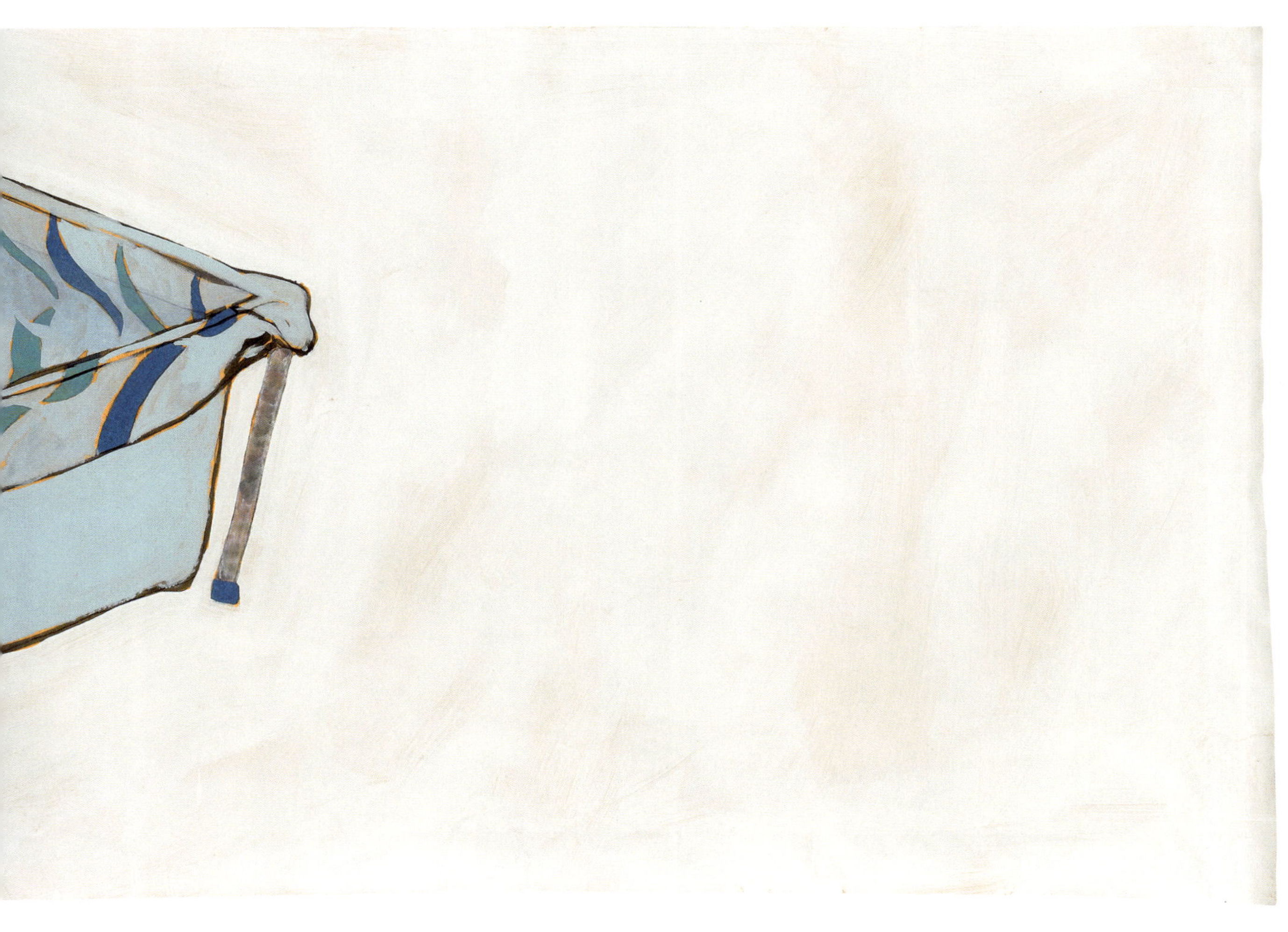

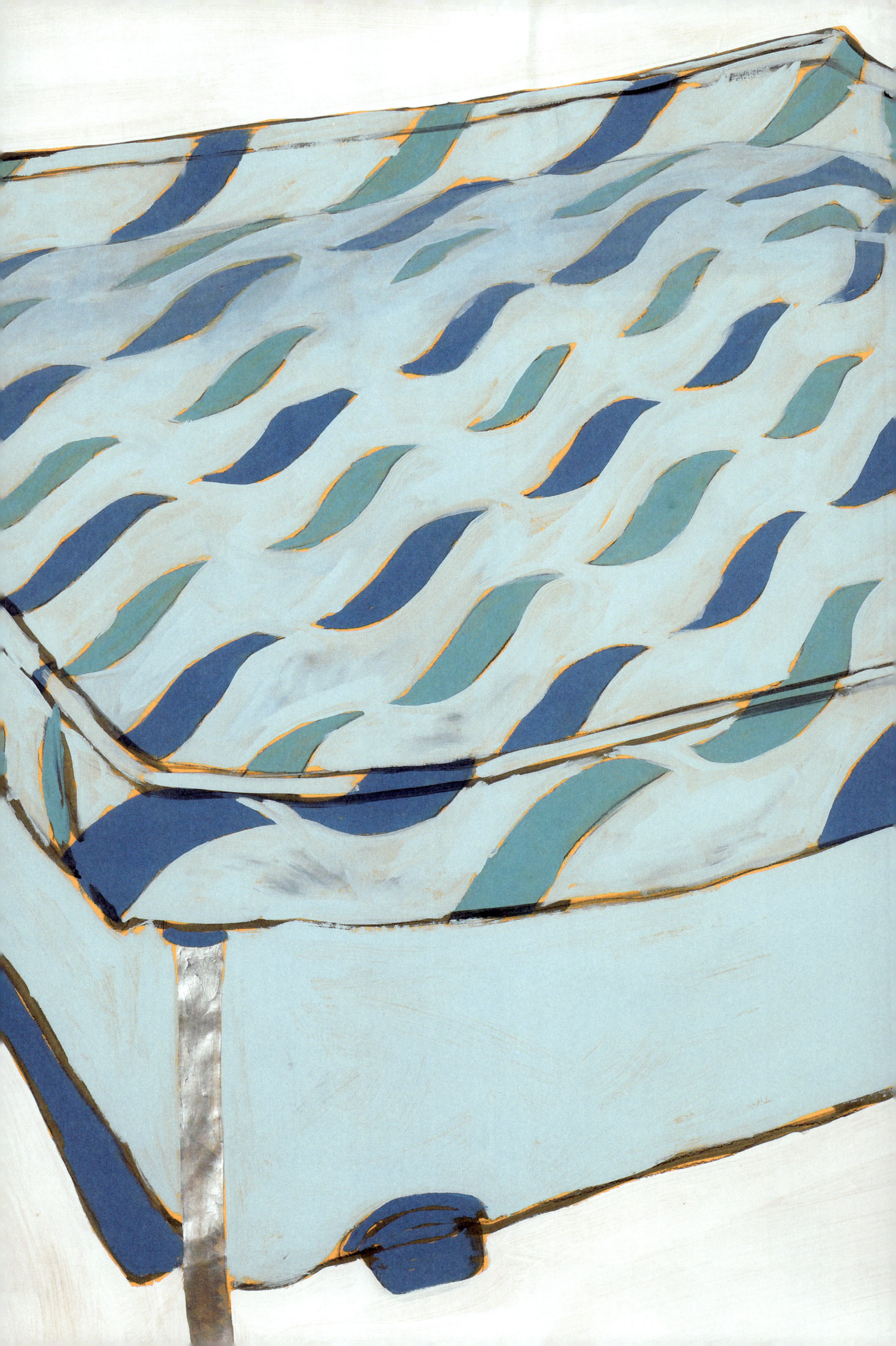

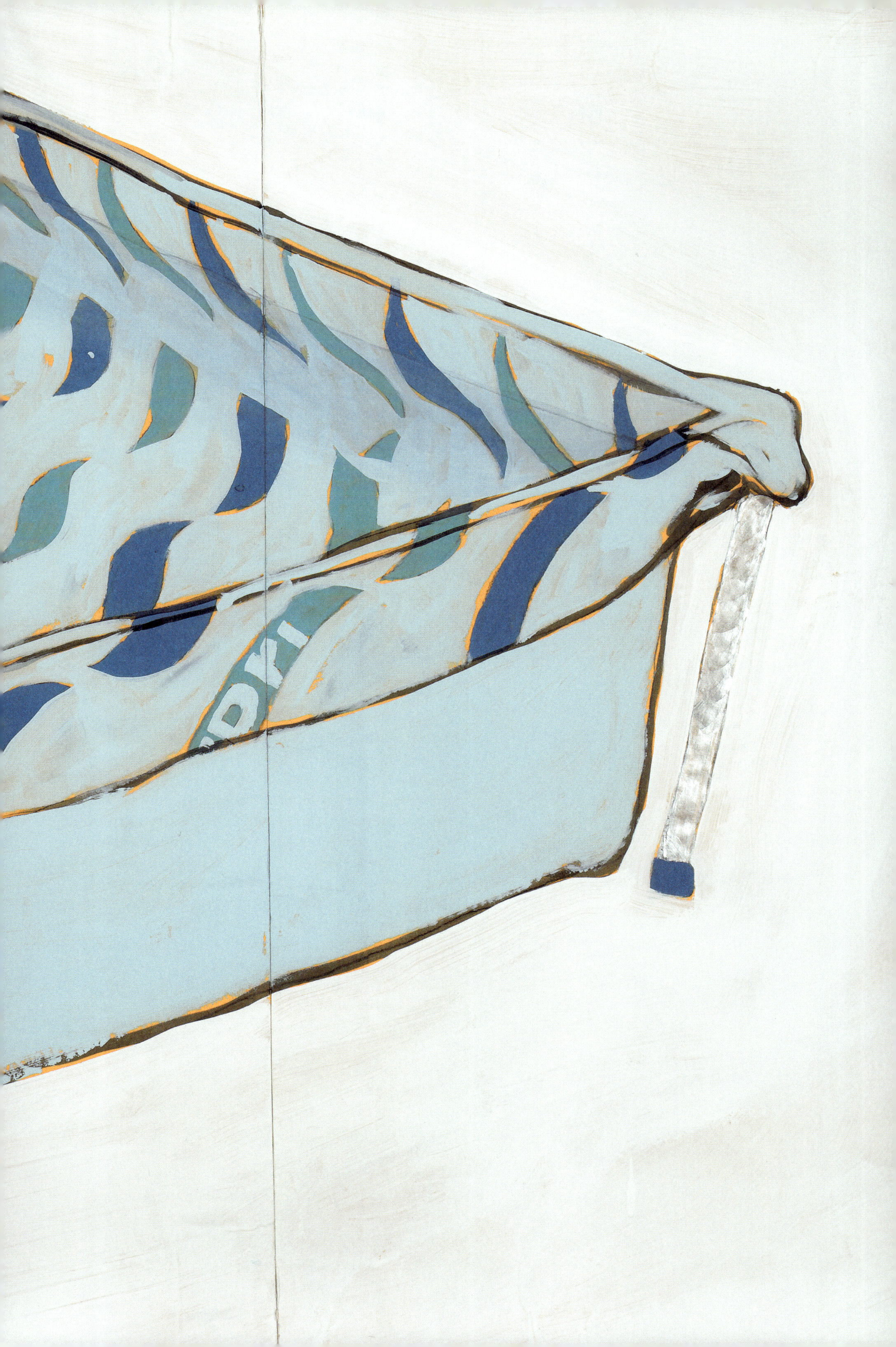

Maxwell Alexandre

Testemunho

Editado por
Daniel Frickmann,
Isadhora Müller,
Lucas Tolezano e
Raoni Azevedo

Traduzido por
John Norman e
Matthew Rinaldi

MUSEU DE ARTE DO RIO

Em maio de 2017, num desses dias de ateliê em que você vai sem saber muito o que fazer, eu pintei três autorretratos em folhas de papel pardo que estavam perdidas por ali. No dia seguinte, quando olhei as pinturas penduradas na parede, percebi que realmente havia uma sedução estética muito potente, mas somente quando fui fazer a quarta pintura me dei conta do ato político e conceitual que eu estava articulando ao pintar corpos negros sobre papel pardo, uma vez que a cor parda foi usada durante muito tempo para velar a negritude.

A designação "pardo" encontrada nas certidões de nascimento, em currículos e carteiras de identidade de negros do passado, foi necessária para o processo de redenção—em outras palavras, de clareamento—da nossa raça. Porém, nos dias de hoje, com o crescimento dos debates, a tomada de consciência e reivindicações das minorias, os negros passaram a projetar sua voz, a se entender e se orgulhar, assumindo seu nariz, seu cabelo e construindo sua autoestima por enaltecimento do que se é, de si mesmo. Esse fenômeno é tão forte e relevante que o termo "pardo" ganhou uma conotação pejorativa dentro dos coletivos negros. Dizer a um negro hoje que ele é moreno, ou pardo, pode ser um grande problema.

Maxwell Alexandre

Testimony[1]

Edited by
Daniel Frickmann,
Isadhora Müller,
Lucas Tolezano, and
Raoni Azevedo

Translated by
John Norman and
Matthew Rinaldi

MUSEU DE ARTE DO RIO

In May 2017, on one of those days in the studio when you go without really knowing what to do, I painted three self-portraits on sheets of kraft paper that were lying around. The next day, when I looked at the paintings hanging on the wall, I noticed that there really was a very powerful aesthetic appeal, but it was only when I went to do the fourth painting that it hit me that I was articulating a political and conceptual act by painting Black bodies on *papel pardo*, being that, for a long time, the color "pardo" was used to conceal Blackness.[2]

The designation "pardo" listed on the birth certificates, résumés, and ID cards of Black people in the past was necessary in the process of redeeming—in other words, whitening—our race. But, nowadays, with more debates, and the increased awareness and grievances on the part of minorities, Black people have begun to project their voices, to understand themselves and take pride, accepting their noses, their hair, and building their self-esteem through the validation of that which they are, of themselves. This phenomenon is so strong and relevant that the term pardo has taken on a pejorative connotation within Black collectives. Telling a Black person today that they're *moreno* or pardo can be a big problem.

1
This text by the artist recounts the history of the "Pardo é Papel" series as it has developed from exhibition to exhibition. Alexandre writes a new section for each subsequent iteration.

2
In Brazil, kraft paper is known as *papel pardo*, literally "brown paper." In Brazilian Portuguese, *pardo* is a term that refers to the tone between black and white, often used to categorize something as distinct from "a white norm," i.e., brown rice, brown paper, etc. For years, pardo was used as a racial designation to describe mixed-race Brazilians and was preferable to labeling someone as Black, an expression of the dominant Eurocentric point of view in Brazil, where the powers that be strove to whiten the population.

Tão saudável quanto um carinho foi a primeira pintura em grande formato que fiz, cobrindo toda a parede de meu ateliê com papel pardo. Fiz isso quatro vezes, e no final juntei tudo com fita crepe, formando uma folha única, de 320 × 480 cm.

Na ocasião estava preparando um trabalho para a exposição *Carpintaria para Todos*, na Carpintaria, braço da Galeria Fortes D'Aloia & Gabriel, no Rio de Janeiro. A exposição coletiva era aberta para qualquer artista, por ordem de chegada, até que se enchesse por completo o espaço expositivo. No comunicado online feito pela galeria, eram informadas as medidas dos portões, para evitar que artistas levassem obras que não pudessem adentrar o lugar.

A obra marcava o começo da série "Reprovados," que surgiu para tratar de questões mais ácidas da vivência preta, como o conflito da comunidade com a polícia, a dizimação e encarceramento da população negra, a falência do sistema público de educação.

Mesmo que esse tenha sido o primeiro momento em que minha obra entrava em contato com um grande público, o início de "Pardo é Papel" se deu pouco antes, quando eu estava pintando pequenos fragmentos de papel pardo que eu colecionava dos laboratórios de moda na época da faculdade. O material é muito usado pelos alunos no processo de criação de modelagem de roupas. Mas "Reprovados" é amargo, e por isso fui adiante com uma pintura dessa série para o contexto da Carpintaria. Eu não queria levar uma obra de "Pardo é Papel" que falasse de bonanças para uma galeria renomada de uma área abastada da zona sul. Eu precisava colocar um problema urgente ali, e por isso a primeira pintura em grande formato é de "Reprovados," mas utilizando o papel pardo como suporte, na estratégia de conseguir ocupar o maior espaço possível na mostra sem me preocupar com a possibilidade de o trabalho não passar pelos portões da galeria, uma vez que eu poderia entrar com ele dobrado, debaixo do braço.

Quando desdobrei a pintura dentro da galeria e viram o tamanho dela aberta, os organizadores a princípio quiseram vetar, pois consideraram a obra grande demais, e que ocuparia bastante espaço, deixando vários outros artistas que estavam na fila desde cedo sem a chance de participar também. Mas depois, olhando novamente, reconsideraram e optaram por tirar o texto curatorial da mostra para instalar meu trabalho. Essa pintura acabou sendo muito bem-sucedida, gerando uma comoção, e iniciando meu contato com o circuito e mercado de arte.

Embora existam distinções de abordagem entre as duas séries ("Reprovados" e "Pardo é Papel"), muitos símbolos tornaram-se comuns em ambas, estabelecendo um glossário com numerosas camadas e interpretações dentro do corpo de trabalho. Com isso as narrativas foram ganhando complexidade, e meu interesse em manipular símbolos e marcas de status e poder dentro da favela—como as famosas piscinas Capri, que marcaram minha infância, o logo da Prefeitura do Rio, a bandeira do estado do Rio de Janeiro, o brasão da Polícia Militar, Danone, Toddynho, entre outras—foi me permitindo criar uma mitologia própria a partir desses elementos emblemáticos na vivência do morro e da cidade como um todo.

A pintura é um lugar em que posso manipular essas marcas que são entidades e moldam as vidas das pessoas, ditam comportamentos, se impõem e invadem histórias e intimidades. Mas no campo fictício da arte, essas estão sujeitas ao artista, que tem o poder de gerar novos questionamentos simplesmente deslocando-as para o plano pictórico, atribuindo-lhe um novo tempo e espaço.

Junto disso, eu contava com um acervo pessoal de fotos de álbuns de família, imagens das redes sociais, de famosos e até publicitárias para construir um léxico que me permitisse elaborar cenários reais e especulativos.

Pós-Carpintaria, quando voltei ao estúdio para retomar a série "Pardo é Papel," achei pertinente assumir esse formato de pintura monumental, para intensificar o diálogo entre a quantidade de papel articulada e o número de corpos pretos em posições contemporâneas de poder. Eu queria densidade e contraste entre essas duas informações, corpo negro e papel pardo, por isso decidi seguir com pinturas de grande formato.

Eu queria que as pessoas sentissem a presença do papel. A própria maneira de instalar as obras ajuda nesse sentido. Queria que as fitas e os rasgos ficassem evidentes; a fragilidade das obras era importante para a poética do trabalho.

Mais adiante, terminei de entender que não se trata apenas de pintura, mas de ar, espaço, som... Não apresentar as obras em moldura ou qualquer estrutura rígida foi uma decisão tomada para enfatizar a precariedade dos materiais na construção do trabalho. A transparência do papel, a obra que se movimenta sutilmente no ambiente, as grandes folhas que cortam o espaço; todas essas características são importantes para a semântica de "Pardo é Papel."

Eu já tinha uma temática clara na minha cabeça, com uma estrutura conceitual e formal bastante definida. Ao mesmo tempo eu vinha acompanhando a cena de rap aqui no Brasil, que nos últimos quatro anos cresceu bastante, revelando vários novos talentos. Nessa onda, três rappers se destacaram e se tornaram uma referência muito forte na cena nacional: Baco Exu do Blues, da Bahia; Djonga, de Minas Gerais; e BK', meu conterrâneo, do Rio de Janeiro.

A música e a poesia dos manos do rap serviram para enriquecer e compor ainda mais meus trabalhos, tornando-se um eixo essencial para pensar as obras. Fiquei tão instigado com a qualidade das músicas que passei a ouvir os versos e enxergar

Tão saudável quanto um carinho [*As healthy as a caress*] was the first large-scale painting I ever made, covering the entire wall of my studio with kraft paper. I did this four times, and in the end I attached everything with masking tape, forming a single, approximately 126-by-189-inch sheet.

On the occasion, I was preparing a work for the exhibition *Carpintaria para Todos* [Carpentry for all] at Carpintaria, the Rio de Janeiro branch of the gallery Fortes D'Aloia & Gabriel. The group exhibition was open to all artists on a first-come, first-serve basis until the exhibition space was completely full. The gallery's online statement included the measurements of the gates to prevent artists from bringing works that wouldn't be able to fit inside.

The work marked the beginning of the series "Reprovados" ["Failed"], which addresses more toxic aspects of the Black experience, like the conflict between the community and police, the decimation and incarceration of the Black population, and the failure of the public education system.[3]

Though this was the first time my work came into contact with a large audience, the beginning of "Pardo é Papel" had happened right before that, when I was painting small scraps of kraft paper that I collected from fashion workshops when I was in college.[4] Students use that material a lot in the process of creating clothing models. But "Reprovados" is bitter, and that's why I went ahead with a painting from this series for the context at Carpintaria. I didn't want to take a work from "Pardo é Papel" that spoke of prosperity to a renowned gallery in an upscale neighborhood in the south zone. I needed to pose an urgent problem there, and that's why the first large-format painting is *Reprovados*, but using kraft paper as a support, as a strategy in order to be able to occupy as much space as possible in the show without having to worry about the work possibly not fitting through the gallery gates, since I could bring it inside rolled up under my arm.

When I unrolled the painting inside the gallery and the organizers saw the size of it all together, at first they wanted to veto it, because they thought the work was too big and would take up a lot of space, not leaving enough room for several other artists who'd been in line earlier. But later, after taking another look, they reconsidered and chose to remove the curatorial text from the exhibition in order to make space to install my work. This painting ended up being quite successful, causing a commotion and initiating my contact with the art circuit and the art market.

Though there are distinctions in approach between the two series ("Reprovados" and "Pardo é Papel"), both have various common symbols, establishing a glossary with a number of layers and interpretations within the body of work. As a result, the narratives started taking on more complexity, and my interest in manipulating symbols and brands of status and power inside the favela—like the famous Capri pools that marked my childhood, the City of Rio de Janeiro logo, the Rio de Janeiro state flag, the Military Police shield, Danone, Toddynho, among others—was allowing me to create my own mythology from these emblematic elements in the experience of the favela and the city as a whole.[5]

Painting is a place where I can manipulate these brands, which are entities that encroach on and shape people's lives, dictate behaviors, and invade stories and intimacies. But in the fictional field of art, they are subjected to the artist, who has the power to generate new questions simply by shifting them to the pictorial plane, assigning them a new time and space.

With this, I made use of a personal collection of photos from family albums, images from social networks, of celebrities, and even from advertising to build a lexicon that allowed me to develop real and speculative scenarios.

After the Carpintaria show, when I went back to the studio to resume the "Pardo é Papel" series, I found it pertinent to adapt this monumental painting format, to deepen the dialogue between the amount of paper used and the number of Black bodies in contemporary positions of power. I wanted density and contrast between these two pieces of information, Black bodies and brown paper, so I decided to move forward with large-format paintings.

I wanted people to feel the presence of the paper. The actual manner of installing the works helps in this regard. I wanted the tape and the rips to be evident: the fragility of the pieces was important for the poetics of the work.

Later on, I came to understand that it's not just about painting. It's about air, space, sound.... I made the decision not to present the works within a frame or any kind of rigid structure in order to emphasize the precariousness of the materials in the construction of the work. The transparency of the paper, the work that moves subtly in the environment, the large sheets that cut the space, all of these characteristics are important for the semantics of "Pardo é Papel."

3
Reprovados is a plural noun referring to students who have not passed an exam or whose failing marks prevent them from advancing to the next grade.

4
The title of the series makes use of a pun, as the Portuguese word *papel* has a double meaning and refers to "paper" or "role." As such, the title can be read as "Brown Is Paper," or "Brown Is a Role."

5
Capri is a brand of inflatable swimming pool, Danone is a popular yogurt snack, and Toddynho is a popular chocolate drink marketed to children.

imagens. Os caras estavam cantando coisas de que eu também estava tratando. Parti desse lugar comum e separei vários versos para traduzir em pinturas. Penso que o mais relevante disso tudo é poder afirmar que minha produção é pautada por poetas negros que têm vivências congruentes com a minha. Isso é forte, e uma quebra de paradigmas dentro da própria história da arte, quando sabemos que é comum que artistas, em sua maioria, buscam se alimentar de uma poesia branca e europeia para produzir.

Para além dessa afirmação, existe uma questão estratégica nessa decisão de pintar versos. O rap é conhecido por ser uma voz das periferias. Esse é o tipo de som que chega na favela e é assimilado, ao passo que a pintura ocupa um lugar muito exclusivo de circulação, dentro de um sistema codificado, elitista e privilegiado. Aqui onde eu moro, na favela da Rocinha, arte contemporânea não é um valor, a maioria das pessoas não se interessa ou nem sabe do que se trata. Então, pintar versos de rap é uma maneira de tentar diminuir esse abismo. É uma chance de aproximar o meu trabalho do interesse popular da comunidade.

A primeira vez que mostrei essas pinturas foi no Complexo Esportivo da Rocinha, onde tive meu primeiro ateliê. Eu tinha que deixar o espaço devido a problemas com a administração, então pedi 3 meses e uma data para mostrar minhas últimas peças criadas ali. Foi um período intenso, em que cumpri mais de 15 horas diárias de trabalho para produzir as 12 primeiras grandes obras da série "Pardo é Papel."

No dia 3 de março de 2018, ofereci as pinturas em meu 2° Dízimo, um ritual em que o artista simbolicamente apresenta 10% de sua produção no altar (espaço). O culto faz parte de um programa de uma Igreja que criei em comunhão com outros artistas: *A Noiva*, também conhecida como *Igreja do Reino da Arte*.

Sem equipe de montagem ou suporte institucional, eu e a Igreja começamos a suspender as grandes folhas de papel às 8 horas da manhã. Às 3 da tarde, horário previsto para o início do culto, estávamos longe de terminar a montagem. Nesse momento, uma questão importante da Igreja se validou: o processo de subida das obras sob a ideia de peregrinação ou sacrifício. Não só os membros da Igreja, mas todo o público que chegava, ia se inteirando em ajudar a instalar os trabalhos ou resolver qualquer outro tipo de problema.

Não era uma abertura de exposição ou vernissage para socializar e contemplar pinturas. Tratava-se de um ritual, no qual a montagem era parte divina da entrega também. Terminamos de subir tudo às 7 da noite. A única obra que não foi suspensa e ficou aberta no chão foi *Megazord só de Power Ranger preto*, que tinha altura maior que o pé-direito do lugar. Às 8 horas, o prédio fechava, então tivemos pouco tempo para ficar em comunhão, testemunhar as pinturas operando juntas no espaço, fazer a oração e desmontar tudo.

Ainda assim, a força das pinturas suspensas em exposição, flutuando no ambiente, ficou guardada em mim. Ali deu para ver que essa era uma exposição monumental, feita mesmo para grandes museus e espaços institucionais. Isso reforçou ainda mais minha ambição de ver essa série como uma exposição itinerante, viajando de cidade em cidade, de museu em museu.

O Dízimo no Complexo Esportivo foi marcante por ter sido a ocasião em que me aproximei e acabei fechando a parceria com a A Gentil Carioca, a galeria que vem me apoiando e representando desde então.

Somente um ano depois, em março de 2019, tive a chance de fazer pela primeira vez a exposição institucional de *Pardo é Papel*, no MAC Lyon (Museu de Arte Contemporânea de Lyon), na França. A oportunidade veio graças ao convite do curador francês Matthieu Lelièvre, que acreditou no trabalho quando viu uma pintura da série, *Um cigarro e a vida pela janela*, na SP-Arte, ocupando toda a parede externa do estande d'A Gentil Carioca. A pintura foi adquirida pela Pinacoteca de São Paulo naquele mesmo dia.

O show em Lyon iniciou a itinerância da mostra, que agora passou pelo MAR (Museu de Arte do Rio). Dessa vez, eu pude contar com uma grande parceira, a Frances Reynolds, uma colecionadora e mecenas que capitaneia o Instuto Inclusartiz, o grande responsável pela itinerância da mostra até então. Para o MAR a Inclusartiz trouxe como investidor da exposição a empresa, Grupo Petra Gold. Quando pintei essa primeira fase desta série, eu sonhava com essa dinâmica, por isso me anima ver que a exposição pode ganhar outros estados do Brasil e mundo afora.

Assim como havia acontecido em Lyon, tivemos alguns problemas no MAR com empréstimos de obras que foram vendidas para instituições. Foi frustrante saber que o conjunto de trabalhos que criei para serem exibidos juntos estaria desfalcado. Existe um sentimento confuso e comum aos artistas que veem suas criações ganharem o mundo sem poder controlar o destino, a exibição ou domicílio do trabalho. Eu precisava arrumar uma maneira de lidar com isso, então resolvi recriar três obras essenciais para o show que não havíamos conseguido resgatar.

Éramos as cinzas e agora somos o fogo, *Um cigarro e a vida pela janela* e *A lua quer ser preta, se pinta no eclipse* foram recriadas para a exposição no MAR com base nas obras originais. A ideia era que essas novas obras fossem exatamente fiéis às versões anteriores, mas durante o processo elas passaram por muitas atualizações, embora a mesma atmosfera tenha sido mantida.

Os mesmos títulos foram usados também, no entanto, com a adição da palavra *diss* no final, uma

I already had a clear theme in my head, with a well-defined conceptual and formal structure. At the same time, I had been following the rap scene here in Brazil, which has grown a lot in the last four years, revealing various new talents. In this wave, three rappers have stood out and become very strong references in Brazilian hip hop: Baco Exu do Blues, from Bahia; Djonga, from Minas Gerais; and BK', who, like me, is from Rio de Janeiro.

The music and poetry of these brothers in hip hop served to enrich and further structure my work, becoming an essential axis for thinking about the pieces. I was so inspired by the quality of the songs that I started to listen to the verses and see images. These guys were rapping about things that I was also addressing. I set out from this shared place and separated a number of verses to translate them into paintings. I think what is most relevant in all this is being able to affirm that my production is guided by Black poets whose experiences are congruent to my own. This is powerful, and it's a paradigm break within the history of art itself, knowing that it's common for artists, for the most part, to attempt to feed off of white European poetry to produce their work.

In addition to this affirmation, there is a strategic question in this decision to paint verses. Rap is known to be a voice of the outer-city neighborhoods. This is the kind of music that reaches the favelas and is assimilated, while painting occupies a very exclusive place of circulation within a codified, elitist, and privileged system. Here where I live, in the favela of Rocinha, contemporary art is not something of value. Most people aren't interested in it or they don't even know what it's about. So painting rap verses is a way to try to bridge that gap. It's a chance to bring my work closer to the popular interests of the community.

The first time I showed these paintings was at the Rocinha Sports Complex, where I had my first studio. I had to leave the space because of problems with the administration, so I asked for three months and scheduled a show with my latest pieces created there. It was an intense period in which I was putting in over 15 hours of work a day to produce the first 12 large pieces in the "Pardo é Papel" series.

On March 3, 2018, I offered the paintings for my tithe, a ritual in which artists symbolically present 10 percent of their production at the altar (space).[6] The ceremony is part of a program of a church that I created in communion with other artists: A Noiva [The Bride], also known as the Igreja do Reino da Arte [Church of the Kingdom of Art].

Without production staff or institutional support, the church members and I started hanging the large sheets of paper at 8 am. At 3 pm, the time scheduled for the ceremony to begin, we were still far from assembling everything. At that point, an important question of the church was validated: the process of putting up the works within the idea of a pilgrimage or sacrifice. The members of the church, as well as the entire public who arrived there, got involved in helping set up the works and solving all types of problems.

It wasn't an exhibition opening or vernissage for socializing and contemplating the paintings. It was a ritual in which the assembly was also part of the divine surrender. We finished putting everything up at 7 pm. The only work that didn't get hung and remained open on the floor was *Megazord só de Power Ranger preto* [Megazord only with Black Power Rangers], which was taller than the ceiling. The building closed at 8 pm so we had just a short time to be there in communion, to witness the paintings operating together in the space, to pray and take everything down.

But still, the power of the paintings hanging there on display, floating in the environment, has stayed with me. There, it was plain to see that this was a monumental exhibition made for large museums and institutional spaces. This further reinforced my ambition to see this series as a traveling exhibition going from city to city, from museum to museum.

The tithe at the Sports Complex was remarkable, because it was the occasion when I first made contact with and later formed a partnership with A Gentil Carioca, the gallery that has been supporting and representing me ever since.

Just one year later, in March of 2019, I had the honor of having the first institutional exhibition of *Pardo é Papel* mounted at MAC Lyon (Lyon Museum of Contemporary Art) in France. The opportunity came thanks to an invitation from French curator Matthieu Lelièvre, who believed in the work when he saw a painting from the series, *Um cigarro e a vida pela janela* [A cigarette and life through the window], occupying the entire outer wall of A Gentil Carioca's booth at SP-Arte [São Paulo's International Art Festival]. The painting was acquired by Pinacoteca de São Paulo that same day.

The show in Lyon was the beginning of the exhibition's touring, which then went to MAR (Museu de Arte do Rio). This time, I was able to count on a great partner, Frances Reynolds, a collector and patron who heads the Instituto Inclusartiz, largely responsible for the exhibition's itinerancy. For MAR, Inclusartiz brought in the company Grupo Petra Gold as an investor for the exhibition. When I painted this first phase of this series, I dreamed of this dynamic, which is why I am excited to see that the exhibition can reach other states in Brazil and around the world.

Just like in Lyon, we had some problems at MAR getting loans for works that were sold to institutions. It was frustrating to see that the set of

6
Tithing is a common practice in many of Brazil's Protestant churches in which church members hand over 10 percent of their salaries.

abreviação de *disrespect*, termo em inglês criado no cenário musical onde rappers produzem faixas para se atacarem ou discutirem entre si. Achei pertinente e honesto com meu sentimento de frustração fazer uma afirmação do poder de criação do artista em resposta às burocracias do jogo.

Além dessas três novas pinturas, criei também mais um trabalho da série "Novo Poder" para a passagem no MAR, que é um desdobramento de "Pardo é Papel." Nessa série, eu exploro a ideia da comunidade preta dentro dos templos consagrados para a contemplação de arte: galerias, fundações e museus.

A falta de interesse das periferias e favelas por arte contemporânea é um programa construído. Esse é um segmento de elite e também de distinção social mesmo entre os ricos. Para aqueles que têm iates, helicópteros, mansões e piscinas como bens corriqueiros, a arte torna-se uma referência para dizer quem é mais sofisticado. Nesse sentido, quem tem Picasso em casa e pode compreender Mark Rothko sai na frente.

Para além do capital financeiro, o campo da arte contemporânea é, sobretudo, detentor de um grande capital intelectual e simbólico. Tendo esse fator mapeado, eu entendi que a reivindicação desses lugares tem relação direta com uma posição de poder. Porque é nesses espaços que a história é legitimada, que narrativas e a construção de imagens são manipuladas.

Artistas, galeristas, críticos, curadores, historiadores, mecenas e colecionadores são agentes que detêm códigos desse campo específico, que constroem imagens, mundos, passados e futuros. A arte é um celeiro de cultura. Chamar a atenção da comunidade preta para esse campo é uma estratégia profética de ascensão e tomada de poder.

Inteirar-se dos códigos é uma maneira de começarmos a ocupar parte decisiva na construção da história. Hoje, eu ocupo uma posição de poder nesse jogo como um artista que pode criar mundos possíveis, que vão ser selados pelo sistema vigente. Mas sei que essa minha posição não é a regra, os agentes que atuam nessa estrutura são majoritariamente brancos.

Nos vernissages, os negros são encontrados em sua maioria servindo ou limpando, mesmo quando o assunto da exposição são eles próprios. Por isso é importante não só o artista negro ocupar seu local de representatividade num momento como este, mas também que a comunidade o ocupe fisicamente, porque a presença do corpo negro nesses espaços é política. Penso que a convivência real é a fronteira mais eficaz para desconfigurar estereótipos, caricaturas racistas, e por aí vai. Ter o negro apenas em pintura, bidimensional, ou em qualquer representação plástica não é suficiente.

No Museu de Arte do Rio, conforme fui preparando o espaço expositivo, visualizei essa pintura criando um corredor ao ser instalada em frente a uma parede branca, oportunidade perfeita para criar uma experiência de contemplação. No MAC Lyon eu já havia inserido três pinturas da série *Novo Poder*. Acredito que essa é uma maneira de ir anunciando esse assunto para a audiência, já que meu show em Paris, no Palais de Tokyo, programado para outubro, terá como foco exclusivo essa série.

A passagem da exposição pelo Rio de Janeiro foi a chance de apresentar pela primeira vez uma performance de "Pardo é Papel," com BK' e Baco Exu do Blues. Foi montado um palco nos pilotis do Museu para os poetas performarem seis faixas, com uma pintura ao fundo, de padrões de piscina Capri dourados, criada especialmente para a ocasião.

Como Baco falou em entrevista para o Museu de Arte do Rio, "foi uma noite importante de ocupação de um espaço de perspectiva branca, um encontro de arte preta, algo que vai ser histórico daqui a um tempo."[1] A performance aconteceu na inauguração da mostra e a divulgação causou alvoroço nas redes sociais, lotando o museu. A plenitude da série se deu ali, com toda a comunidade preta empoderada cantando "Minha vez de ganhar!," refrão da faixa "Vivos" de BK' com participação de Baco Exu do Blues.

A performance foi uma maneira também de desafiar as estruturas já estabelecidas da formatação de "Pardo é Papel." Apresentar a série em formato de show foi um dos caminhos que encontrei para colocar isso à prova. A articulação dessas crônicas não podia estar presa a um único suporte. Foi navegando por essa ideia que entendi que minha busca era pela valorização e reconhecimento do conteúdo da série: pretos empoderados, marrentos, ostentando, vencendo...

Eu já vinha interessado nessa questão quando resolvi migrar as narrativas de "Pardo é Papel" para a tela, a fim de excluir o papel. A pintura tinha que ser identificada como parte da série, mesmo se pintada em uma pedra. Para chegar a esse lugar, eu precisava tomar uma decisão radical: destruir a tradição da série, o papel, recorrendo, nesse primeiro momento, ao que há de mais tradicional na pintura, a tela.

A única tela da exposição no MAR é também um testemunho central dessa pesquisa; a obra sem título é um políptico da série "Golden Shower," um desdobramento de "Pardo é Papel" que tem como tema principal a urina.

O título da série vem da expressão usada para falar do ato de urinar no outro durante a relação

1 Essa afirmação pode ser encontrada na entrevista com Baco Exu do Blues, na abertura da exposição de Maxwell Alexandre, publicado no Youtube: https://youtu.be/oDg89gHA3Jc?t=184

works I created to be displayed together would be incomplete. There is a feeling of confusion common to artists who see their creations garner broad recognition, only to then lose control over their works' destination and how they are shown. I needed to figure out a way to deal with this, so I decided to re-create three of the pieces that we were unable to retrieve but that are essential to the show.

Éramos as cinzas e agora somos o fogo [We were the ashes and now we're the fire], *Um cigarro e a vida pela janela*, and *A lua quer ser preta, se pinta no eclipse* [The moon wants to be black, it paints itself in the eclipse] were re-created based on the original works for the exhibition at MAR. The idea was that these new works were entirely faithful to the previous versions, but during the process they were subjected to various updates while the same atmosphere was maintained.

The same titles were also used, but with the word *diss* tacked on at the end—"diss" being short for "disrespect" and used in the music scene to describe tracks produced by rappers to attack or argue with one another. I found it pertinent and honest with my feelings of frustration to make an assertion of the artist's creative power in response to the bureaucracies of the art game.

In addition to these three new paintings, I created another work in the series "New Power" that is an extension of "Pardo é Papel" for the exhibition at MAR. In this series, I explore the idea of the Black community inside the consecrated temples for the contemplation of art: galleries, foundations, and museums.

The favelas' and outlying urban neighborhoods' lack of interest in contemporary art is a construction of power systems. This interest is a marker of the elite and a marker of social distinction even among the rich. For those who have yachts, helicopters, mansions, and swimming pools as commonplace belongings, art becomes a reference, a way of understanding who is more sophisticated. In this sense, anyone who has a Picasso in their home and is able to understand Mark Rothko comes out on top.

In addition to financial capital, the field of contemporary art is, overall, the holder of great intellectual and symbolic capital. Having considered this factor, I understood that the reclaiming of these places is directly related to a position of power. Because it's in these spaces that history is legitimized, that narratives and the construction of images are manipulated.

Artists, gallery owners, critics, curators, historians, patrons, and collectors are the agents that control the codes in this specific field, that construct images, worlds, pasts, and futures. Art is a stockpile of culture. Drawing the Black community's attention to this field is a prophetic, uplifting strategy for taking power.

Familiarizing ourselves with the codes is a way for us to begin to occupy a crucial place in the construction of history. Today I occupy a position of power in this game as an artist who can create possible worlds that will be validated by the current system. But I know that my position is an exception to the rule. The agents who operate within this structure are almost always white.

At vernissages, Black people are mostly found serving or cleaning, even when they themselves are the subject of the exhibition. This is why it is important not only for Black artists to occupy their place of representation at a time like this but also for the community to occupy it physically, because the presence of the Black body in these spaces is political. I think that real coexistence is the most effective frontier for dismantling stereotypes, racist caricatures, and the like. Having Black people in two-dimensional paintings or any kind of visual representation is not enough.

As I was preparing the exhibition space at MAR, I visualized this painting as creating a corridor to be installed in front of a white wall, a perfect opportunity to create an experience of contemplation. At MAC Lyon, I had already included three paintings from the series "New Power." I believe this is a way to announce this subject to the audience, since my show scheduled for October at the Palais de Tokyo in Paris will focus exclusively on this series.

The exhibition's run in Rio de Janeiro was the chance to present a performance of "Pardo é Papel," with BK' and Baco Exu do Blues, for the first time. A stage was set up on the museum's pilotis for the poets to perform six tracks, with a golden Capri pool-pattern painting in the background created especially for the occasion.[7]

As Baco Exu do Blues said in an interview with MAR, "It was an important night for the occupation of a space of white perspective, a meeting of Black art, something that will be seen as historic further on in time."[8] The performance took place at the show's opening, and the publicity for it caused a commotion on social media, which brought crowds to the museum. It was there that the fulfillment of the series took place, with the whole Black community empowered, singing "Minha vez de ganhar!" (literally,

7
Pilotis are supports that lift a building above the ground or a body of water. They are similar to stilts, piers, columns, pillars, posts, and so on. It's one of the most used elements in Brazilian modern architecture. The MAR museum, even being a contemporary construction, follows a pattern of the 1940s and 1950s buildings. The word is frequently used to designate this architectural component.

8
Baco Exu do Blues, quoted in an interview on the occasion of Alexandre's exhibition opening, posted on YouTube: https://youtu.be/oDg89gHA3Jc?t=184.

sexual. A expressão ganhou as manchetes em 2019 quando Bolsonaro, atual presidente do Brasil, tuitou um vídeo no qual duas pessoas praticavam o ato na rua durante o carnaval e logo em seguida voltou ao Twitter perguntando: “o que é *golden shower*?” Foi uma polêmica total, o que me fez tratar desse assunto em uma pintura específica, que acabou desencadeando toda uma série.

As narrativas abordadas dão margem a interpretações escatológicas. Sabendo que o jugo sobre o corpo negro é pesado em qualquer situação, ainda mais quando se trata de uma prática que é tida como imunda e impura, “Golden Shower” se apresenta como um lugar de afirmação de liberdade de ser o que quiser, fazer o que quiser, independentemente dos estigmas atribuídos a corpos negros.

A tela de *Golden Shower* foi a única obra que conseguimos resgatar de uma coleção particular para esta mostra, embora eu tenha criado mais 12 pinturas com esse tema para uma instalação que fiz no estande d’A Gentil Carioca durante a Art Basel, na Suíça (2019). Envelopei todo o espaço com papel pardo e mostrei pinturas em telas, portas e papel em diálogo com obras de outros artistas representados pela galeria. O estande teve destaque naquele ano, aparecendo em algumas listas de avaliação como o número 1 da feira.

Tanto na forma quanto no conteúdo, o desenvolvimento da série e seus desdobramentos tratam intensamente de libertação/liberdade. Por isso quis levar trabalhos de “Golden Shower” para Basel, a maior feira de arte do mundo, um holofote relevante para esses embates e discussões.

Uma ativação que fiz para a exposição no MAR foi a *Descoloração Global*, ação na qual eu chamo cabeleireiros e compramos Blondor para a galera descolorir o cabelo. Na favela essa é sempre uma ocasião para se juntar, fazer uma bagunça. No meu estúdio mesmo, tem vários momentos em que a gente tá lá trabalhando com Blondor no cabelo. Oficialmente esse evento aconteceu outras duas vezes, uma em 2018 em meu *Batismo nas águas*—minha primeira exposição individual—, na encruzilhada da rua Gonçalves Ledo com a Luís de Camões, no centro do Rio, onde fica a galeria A Gentil Carioca, e outra em dezembro de 2019, na Rocinha, que foi um ritual para a virada do ano.

Eu pinto o cabelo de loiro desde 2013. Quando ainda era criança eu já queria descolorir, porque é uma cultura forte na favela, mas minha mãe nunca deixou, falava que era coisa de vagabundo. Muitos traficantes descolorem o cabelo, então essa estética ficou associada ao estilo de vida das facções. Nesse contexto, se você era negro e pintava o cabelo de loiro, acabava atraindo a atenção da polícia, de racistas e todo tipo de preconceito. Isso mudou bastante quando celebridades como o Chris Brown, Kanye West, Pharrell, Jaden Smith e, no Brasil, o Belo e até o Neymar adotaram esse estilo. Depois que eles assumiram essa estética também, a moda rapidamente a absorveu.

Pra mim, *Descoloração Global* é também um comentário de liberdade, de podermos ser o que quisermos ser. É uma afirmação de rebeldia e empoderamento diante de qualquer estrutura discreta e indiscreta de aprisionamento do corpo negro. Uma grande referência que tenho desde pequeno e me ajuda a ratificar essa estética é o famoso anime *Dragon Ball Z*, que marcou minha geração; seus personagens tinham cabelo preto mas ficavam loiros quando atingiam níveis superiores e viravam super saiyajins, aumentando seus superpoderes.

FUNDAÇÃO IBERÊ

A terceira parada da mostra *Pardo é Papel* foi na cidade de Porto Alegre. Emilio Kalil, diretor da Fundação Iberê, esteve na inauguração no MAR e ficou empolgado com a exposição. Por isso, Frances Reynolds e sua equipe do Instituto Inclusartiz, responsável pela itinerância da exposição, teve a generosa iniciativa de definir com Emilio que o show seguinte de *Pardo é Papel* seria na Fundação. O Inclusartiz mais uma vez contou com o apoio do Grupo Petra Gold para patrocinar essa empreitada, assim como foi no Museu de Arte do Rio. Estava tudo alinhado desde o início do ano para a exposição acontecer, mas fomos surpreendidos pela crise do Covid-19. A pandemia desestabilizou os planos de continuidade da itinerância da mostra.

Com a agenda congelada, e todos ansiosos sem saber o que aconteceria num breve futuro, resolvemos desmontar a exposição do MAR mais cedo. Foi uma pena para quem deixou a visita para os últimos dias, porém uma esperança com a concretização da passagem da exposição pelo Rio Grande do Sul, pois a desmontagem antecipada no Museu de Arte do Rio oferecia mais segurança para a próxima exposição. Digo isso pois existe um protocolo de preservação mínima das obras, que exige que elas fiquem guardadas durante um tempo considerável, antes de serem instaladas novamente, por conta da acidez e fragilidade do papel. Mesmo com essa margem de tempo para o repouso dos trabalhos, a pandemia dificultou um processo seguro de manutenção das pinturas mais antigas, de 2017 e 2018, que estavam realmente precisando de reparos. Esse grupo de obras teve que ficar de fora da nova exposição. De qualquer forma, não seria possível ter todos os trabalhos, considerando as propriedades físicas do novo espaço expositivo em relação aos outros por onde a mostra já havia passado. Esses fatores foram coautores da curadoria, que nos permitiu selecionar somente 11 pinturas. Mas uma novidade para a passagem de *Pardo é Papel* em Porto Alegre consistiu em uma obra em vídeo: o registro da performance de *Pardo é Papel* com BK’ e Baco Exu do Blues.

"My turn to win!"), the chorus of the track "Vivos" by BK' featuring Baco.

The performance was also a way to challenge the already established structures for the format of "Pardo é Papel." Presenting the series in a concert format was one of the ways I tested this. The articulation of these stories cannot be attached to one single medium. By navigating this idea, I understood that my aim was to encourage appreciation and recognition of the series' content: empowered Black people who are bold, showing off, winning.

I was interested in this issue before I decided to migrate the narratives of "Pardo é Papel" to the canvas, in order to move away from paper. Painting had to be identified as part of the series, even if it were painted on a stone. To come to this place, I needed to make a radical decision: to destroy what is traditional about this series—the paper—resorting instead to what is most traditional in painting—the canvas.

The only canvas in the exhibition at MAR is also a central testimony to this research; the untitled work is a polyptych of the "Golden Shower" series, an offshoot of "Pardo é Papel" with urine as its main subject.

The "Golden Shower" series title comes from the expression used to describe the act of urinating on one's partner during sexual intercourse. The expression made headlines in Brazil in 2019 when [Jair] Bolsonaro, the country's current president, tweeted a video of two people practicing the act on the street during Carnival, then went back to ask: "What's a golden shower?" It was a huge scandal, inspiring me to tackle the subject in a specific painting, which ended up inspiring an entire series.

The narratives addressed make room for eschatological interpretations. Knowing that the subject of the Black body is complex in any situation, especially when it comes to a practice considered unclean and impure, "Golden Shower" presents itself as a place of affirmation of the freedom to be what you want to be, to do what you want to do, regardless of the stigmas attributed to Black bodies.

The *Golden Shower* canvas was the only work we were able to retrieve from a private collection for this exhibition, though I created 12 more paintings with this theme for an installation I made for A Gentil Carioca's booth at Art Basel in Switzerland (2019). I wrapped the entire space with kraft paper and exhibited paintings on canvas, doors, and paper in dialogue with works by other artists represented by the gallery. The booth stood out that year and was ranked number one at the fair by some critics.

In both form and content, the development of the series and its extensions deal intensely with liberation/freedom. That's why I wanted to take the "Golden Shower" works to Art Basel, the biggest art fair in the world, a relevant spotlight for this kind of confrontation and discussion.

One action I did for the exhibition at MAR was *Descoloração Global* [Global bleaching], in which I hired hairdressers and bought Blondor for people to bleach their hair. In the favelas, this is always an occasion for people to get together, to make a mess. In my studio, there have been several occasions when we have worked there with Blondor, bleaching our hair. Officially, this event happened on two other occasions, once in 2018 for *Batismo nas águas* [Water baptism]—my first solo exhibition—at the intersection of Rua Gonçalves Ledo and Rua Luís de Camões in downtown Rio, where the A Gentil Carioca gallery is located, and another in December of 2019, in Rocinha, which was a New Year's Eve ritual.

I've been bleaching my hair blond since 2013. I used to want to bleach my hair when I was a kid, because this is a style in favela culture, but my mother never allowed me. She said it was something "good-for-nothings" do. Many drug dealers bleach their hair, so this aesthetic was associated with the gang lifestyle. In this context, if you're Black and you dye your hair blond, you end up attracting the attention of the police, racists, and all kinds of prejudice. This changed a lot when celebrities like Chris Brown, Kanye West, Pharrell, Jaden Smith, and, in Brazil, Belo and even Neymar adopted this style. After they assumed this aesthetic, the fashion world quickly absorbed it.

For me, *Descoloração Global* is also a commentary on freedom, of being able to be what we want to be. It's an affirmation of rebelliousness and empowerment in the face of any discreet or indiscreet structure for imprisonment of the Black body. One big reference that I've had ever since I was little and which helps me to legitimize this aesthetic is the famous anime *Dragon Ball Z*, which marked my generation. The characters had Black hair that would turn blond as they reached higher levels and became Super Saiyans, increasing their superpowers.

IBERÊ FOUNDATION

The third stop for the *Pardo é Papel* show was the city of Porto Alegre. Emilio Kalil, director of the Iberê Foundation, was at the inauguration at MAR and got excited about the exhibition. This is why Frances Reynolds and her team at Instituto Inclusartiz, responsible for the exhibition's travel schedule, took the generous initiative of working with Emilio to determine that the next *Pardo é Papel* show would be at the Foundation. Inclusartiz got support from the Petra Gold Group to sponsor this endeavor, just like at MAR. Since the beginning of the year, everything was aligned for the exhibition to take place, but we were surprised by the Covid-19 crisis. The pandemic destabilized the touring plans.

With the agenda on hold and everyone anxious, not knowing what would happen in the near future, we decided to take down the MAR show early. It was a disappointment for those who had intended to visit over those last few days, but a great prospect with the realization of the exhibition's run in Rio Grande do Sul, since taking down the show early

INSTITUTO TOMIE OHTAKE

A quarta parada de *Pardo é Papel* acontece no Instituto Tomie Ohtake, em São Paulo. A expectativa do público parece alta, muito por conta do sucesso das passagens anteriores e de todo o conteúdo gerado para promover o show, que continuará viajando e ganhando cada vez mais força. São Paulo tem um dos circuitos culturais mais aquecidos do país, e já estava aguardando a exposição chegar à cidade.

Alguns painéis da série já foram mostrados no estado, como as obras *Éramos as cinzas e agora somos o fogo*, na exposição *Histórias Afro-Atlânticas* no MASP em 2018, e *Um cigarro e a vida pela janela*, na SP-Arte, também em 2018. Inclusive esta mesma obra se encontra na atual exposição do acervo da Pinacoteca. Foram aparições isoladas. Mas desta vez a audiência vai ter a chance de ver os pares desses trabalhos juntos, reunidos pela primeira vez na cidade.

Para esta ocasião eu ampliei 4 vezes a obra sem título, com padrão de piscina Capri dourado, para circunscrever parte do espaço expositivo. Além disso, optei por não mostrar o vídeo da performance e reinserir uma das pinturas mais importantes de toda a série, a obra *Se eu fosse vocês olhava pra mim de novo*, que vou instalar isoladamente numa parte da sala. Neste capítulo, novamente, seguimos forte com o Instituto Inclusartiz e a Petra Gold realizando e financiando mais uma vez esta empreitada.

THE SHED

A passagem em Porto Alegre foi marcada pela reabertura da agenda cultural do país, devido ao hiato da primeira fase da pandemia. No entanto, *Pardo é Papel* no Instituto Tomie Ohtake, em São Paulo, nos mostrou a fragilidade das políticas de afrouxamento do isolamento social e medidas outras que tentavam normalizar a vida. Essa instabilidade ameaçou fechar a exposição no Instituto várias vezes. Eu havia me programado para realizar novamente a performance de "Pardo é Papel," desta vez com os três poetas; BK', Baco Exu do Blues e Djonga. A questão é que não poderíamos ter um grande público como foi no MAR. A alternativa seria a realização de uma live—algo que havia se tornado um fenômeno de comunicação explorado demasiadamente durante a quarentena. Realizaríamos a performance sem público, transmitindo ao vivo pelas redes sociais. Eu já tinha afinado tudo com os rappers para fazer essa ativação acontecer, mas a crise foi se acirrando. Inclusive, houve uma fatalidade no time do Instituto; um dos seguranças faleceu em decorrência de Covid-19. A situação sensibilizou a todos e a performance não aconteceu, porque mesmo sem o público, ainda teríamos que envolver muitas pessoas na logística e produção para que a ativação ocorresse.

Mesmo com o agravamento da crise, a mostra seguiu até o fim, com visitação normal, mas mantendo todos os protocolos de contenção do vírus. No último final de semana da mostra, eu reuni 8 pessoas, todas negras, de São Paulo, para fazer uma ativação que chamei de *Rolezinho*: inspirado em um movimento espontâneo de mesmo nome, que aconteceu por volta de 2013, onde jovens, a maioria de periferias, marcavam encontros (através das redes sociais) em lugares nobres da cidade, como praças, shoppings, etc.

O *Rolezinho* dentro de minha prática tem uma conotação similar a do original: ocupar, circular, permanecer em lugares onde certos grupos sociais não são bem-vindos pelas suas vestimentas, vocabulário, enfim, pelo seu ethos. A potência desta ativação se dá em juntar o máximo de pessoas possível, uma vez que a ação é sobre gerar estranhamento e desconforto. No entanto, num contexto de pandemia, eu precisava reunir o mínimo de pessoas—seguindo as normas de segurança estabelecidas—mas que ainda gerasse um impacto da presença de um grupo de pessoas negras, circulando e se afirmando na fachada de uma instituição de arte, assim como nos corredores, banheiros, bibliotecas e galerias daquele espaço. A escolha para os integrantes da ativação se deu a partir de fotos que encontrei no instagram, registros feitos dentro da minha exposição. O *Rolezinho* que aconteceu no dia 26 de Junho de 2021 foi uma ativação até então inédita no curso da itinerância de *Pardo é Papel*.

Em 18 de dezembro de 2021, inaugurou a segunda Bienal da Tailândia, da qual fui convidado a participar através da curadora-chefe do evento, Yuko Hasegawa que, por intermédio de Frances Reynolds, foi ver *Pardo é Papel* em sua primeira parada, ainda em Lyon, no ano de 2019. Minha primeira presença significativa no circuito asiático é fruto dessa história: a passagem de *Pardo é Papel*, ainda que de forma reduzida, com menos trabalhos, pela Tailândia. Essa foi a quinta parada da série em sua itinerância.

O convite para mostrar no The Shed veio por indicação do curador e crítico Hans Ulrich Obrist, que demonstrou vontade de trabalhar comigo desde nosso primeiro encontro em Basel, durante a feira de arte, em junho de 2019. Frances Reynolds foi quem, mais uma vez, mediou o encontro. De lá pra cá, eu e Hans colaboramos em alguns projetos menores até que a carta oficial do The Shed chegou, em fevereiro de 2020. Desde então eu e minha equipe passamos a conversar mais especificamente com a curadora responsável pela exposição, Alessandra Gómez.

Enquanto a itinerância acontecia, eu fiz mais dois lançamentos significativos para a série. O primeiro foi em Londres na galeria David Zwirner em 2020, onde mostrei 9 obras inéditas de "Pardo é Papel." Embora não tivesse uma conexão precisa com a exposição itinerante, esse lançamento foi decisivo para eu repensar, classificar e renomear a exibição que viajava. A produção de "Pardo é Papel" para a David Zwirner teve uma densidade e

offered more security for the next exhibition. I say this because there is a protocol for minimally preserving the works, which requires that they be stored for a considerable time before being installed again, due to the acidity and fragility of the paper. Even with this margin of time for the work to settle, the pandemic hindered a safe process of maintenance on the oldest paintings, from 2017 and 2018, which were really in need of repairs. This group of works had to be left out of the new exhibition. In any case, it would not have been possible to include all the works, considering the physical properties of the new exhibition space in relation to the others where the show had been held previously. These factors were co-authors of the curatorship, which allowed us to select just 11 paintings. But one novelty of the *Pardo é Papel* run in Porto Alegre consisted in a video work: a recording of the *Pardo é Papel* performance with BK' and Baco Exu do Blues.

TOMIE OHTAKE INSTITUTE

Pardo é Papel's fourth stop was at the Tomie Ohtake Institute in São Paulo. The public's expectations seemed high due to the success of the show's previous runs and all the content generated to promote it, which would continue to travel and gain more and more strength. São Paulo has one of the hottest cultural circuits in the country, and I had been eagerly waiting for the exhibition to arrive in the city.

Some panels in the series had already been shown in São Paulo: *Éramos as cinzas e agora somos o fogo* was part of the exhibition *Afro-Atlantic Stories* at MASP [Museu de Arte de São Paulo] in 2018, and *Um cigarro e a vida pela janela* was displayed at SP-Arte, also in 2018. The latter work was also found in the current exhibition of the Pinacoteca de São Paulo's collection. They were isolated appearances. But this time, the audience would have a chance to see the counterparts of these works together, gathered for the first time in the city.

For this occasion, I quadrupled the size of the untitled work, with the gold Capri pool pattern, to circumscribe part of the exhibition space. In addition, I chose not to show the video of the performance and to reinsert one of the most important paintings in the whole series, the piece *Se eu fosse vocês olhava pra mim de novo* [If I were you I'd look at me again], which I installed on its own in one part of the room. For this chapter, we were still going strong, with Instituto Inclusartiz and Petra Gold once again financing and executing this undertaking.

THE SHED

The show's run in Porto Alegre was marked by the reopening of the country's cultural scene following the hiatus brought on by the first phase of the pandemic. When it traveled to Tomie Ohtake Institute in São Paulo, however, *Pardo é Papel* showed us the fragility of the policies for relaxing the social isolation rules and other measures in an attempt to return to normal life. That instability threatened to shut down the exhibition at Tomie Ohtake Institute multiple times. I had been planning another staging of the *Pardo é Papel* performance, this time with the three poets BK', Baco Exu do Blues, and Djonga. We would have liked to have done it with a large crowd as we had in Rio de Janeiro at MAR. Instead, the alternative would be to hold a livestream, which had become somewhat of a communication fad during the quarantine. We held the performance without a physical audience, broadcasting it live through social networks. I had already fine-tuned everything with the rappers for this activation to take place, but the crisis was worsening. Someone had even died on the Ohtake Institute's team: one of the security guards had passed away from Covid-19. That situation was felt by everyone, and so the performance did not take place, because even without a physical audience we would still need to involve many people in the activation's logistics and production.

Despite the worsening of the crisis, the show continued to the end, with normal visitation while maintaining all protocols for controlling the virus. In the last week of the show, I gathered eight people, all of them Black from São Paulo, to carry out an activation that I called *Rolezinho*, inspired by a grassroots movement of the same name, which arose in around 2013, where young people, mostly from the city's outskirts, used social networks to organize gatherings at upscale places in the city, such as prominent public squares and shopping malls.

Within my practice, *Rolezinho* has a similar connotation: to occupy, circulate, and hang out in places where certain social groups are not welcome due to the way they dress, the way they talk; in short, due to their ethos. The potential of this activation lies in gathering the largest number of people possible, since the action is about generating strangeness and uneasiness. In the context of the pandemic, however, I needed to gather a minimal number of people—in accordance with established safety protocols—that would still generate the impact arising from a group of Black people, circulating and affirming their presence along the façade of an art institution and in the hallways, bathrooms, libraries, and galleries of that space. I chose the members of the activation group based on images I found on Instagram, photos taken at my exhibition. The *Rolezinho* that took place on June 26, 2021, was an utterly new sort of activation in the course of the *Pardo é Papel* traveling exhibitions.

On December 18, 2021, the second Thailand Biennale was held, in which I was invited to participate by the event's chief curator, Yuko Hasegawa, who, through the intermediation of Frances Reynolds, had seen *Pardo é Papel* at its first stop in Lyon in 2019. That led to my first significant presence on the

relevância de criação muito parecida com a das obras que criei em 2017 e 2018, e que agora viajam de instituição a instituição. Os contextos e condições eram, porém, absolutamente distintos. Como então distinguir esses dois períodos, sem que houvesse uma confusão quanto ao que pertencia à exposição itinerante e o que estava sendo mostrado em Londres?

Para compreender esta questão, trago parte do testemunho que escrevi na ocasião:

> [...] A interseção entre artes plásticas e música em minha prática me fez naturalmente estabelecer relações entre os dois campos para além de apenas pintar versos. Eu comecei a me interessar, por exemplo, em como os músicos organizam suas obras a partir de um sistema composto por álbuns, mixtapes, EPs e singles. Normalmente álbuns são construídos dentro de um período limitado de tempo, englobando um momento da pesquisa de um músico, e frequentemente construídos com um conceito ou tema específicos. Enquanto isso mixtapes são junções mais aleatórias de um conteúdo, e EPs apresentam trabalhos interligados porém concisos, com menos faixas. Já o single é uma música lançada isoladamente dessas divisões e, por mais que ela entre em uma dessas categorias, é comum seu uso como forma de promover o artista, chamar atenção para um outro projeto maior, sendo mais estratégico no sentido de apresentar uma potência que está por vir e angariar público. Enquanto isso, na pintura, a organização mais tradicional se dá a partir de séries, que dividem a produção do artista mais por motivos/temas que por períodos.
>
> Essa reflexão me aparece exatamente neste momento onde começo a preparar *Pardo é Papel: Close a door to open a window*, minha próxima exposição individual para a galeria David Zwirner em Londres. A mostra foi desenhada para ocupar os dois andares da galeria com 9 pinturas em grande formato, sendo três delas dois dípticos e um tríptico. A densidade de trabalho e assuntos articulados nesse show me levou a querer de alguma maneira separar essas obras em uma coletânea delineada, e foi nesse momento que o conceito de álbum surgiu como uma forma de organização de minhas pinturas.
>
> Olhando retroativamente, precisei renomear o primeiro período de "Pardo é Papel," que acontece em 2017-2018, onde crio as 12 primeiras pinturas da série e mostro no Complexo Esportivo da Rocinha, ainda no contexto religioso da Igreja do Reino da Arte, em forma de Dízimo, culto. Incluo ainda como parte deste mesmo período, obras que realizei em 2019 quando essa mesma mostra passou a ser institucionalizada e viajar, começando este processo no MAC-Lyon, na França. A obra que mais sintetiza este período é *A vitória gloriosa*. Seria esta obra, portanto, a capa de meu primeiro álbum.
>
> Construindo agora este segundo álbum que será lançado no estrangeiro, eu resolvi inserir versos de mais 3 artistas internacionais dos quais eu sou muito fã e que já vinham inspirando esteticamente "Pardo é Papel." São eles: Frank Ocean, Solange e Tyler, the Creator. O título da exposição, *Close a door to open a window*, é a pintura deste verso que selecionei da faixa "Magic Wand" de *Igor*, disco de Tyler. Essa é a capa deste meu novo momento com "Pardo é Papel" [...]

O segundo lançamento significativo foi o de "Novo Poder," que contou com 3 aberturas simultâneas: um show principal no Palais de Tokyo, e dois pela A Gentil Carioca, em suas galerias do Rio de Janeiro e São Paulo. Ainda que a série só viesse a ser lançada definitivamente em 2021, eu já vinha incluindo pelo menos uma uma obra de "Novo Poder" em paradas anteriores de "Pardo é Papel," uma espécie de introdução para o público. No trecho estão questões e pensamentos ao redor desse lançamento:

> [...] Pouco mais de um ano desenvolvendo pesquisa, conceito e sketches para fazer esse projeto, no dia 5 de abril começamos as primeiras execuções das pinturas no estúdio novo. Como a série "Novo Poder" é monotemática (figuras pretas dentro de espaços expositivos, como museus, galerias e fundações, se relacionando com arte contemporânea, principalmente contemplando pintura), eu a encaro quase como a prática de pintura de natureza morta: articular objetos numa mesa para pintar suas variações a fim de entender sutilezas de tais objetos de estudo. Em "Novo Poder" eu escolhi trabalhar exatamente desta maneira, de tal forma que a investigação ficou tão prolífera que eu não me preocupei em montar uma expografia a priori. A idéia era trabalhar com densidade e levar o assunto à exaustão até que eu pudesse olhar para o todo mais tarde, e só então começar a curar cuidadosamente o que entraria na exposição, de modo que o lançamento e apresentação desta série pudesse acontecer de forma básica, em sua gênese, mas que ao mesmo tempo fosse o mais integral possível. Eu criei mais de 100 novos trabalhos, sem contar com os esboços inacabados. Eram tantas obras realizadas que eu tinha o suficiente em mãos para fazer pelo menos mais dois shows nos próximos anos.

Asian circuit: the exhibition of *Pardo é Papel*—albeit in a reduced form, with fewer works—traveled to Thailand. This was the fifth stop on the tour.

The invitation to show at The Shed arose through the recommendation of curator and critic Hans Ulrich Obrist, who had demonstrated a desire to work with me since the first time we met at Art Basel in June 2019. Frances Reynolds helped to set up the meeting. Since then, Hans and I had collaborated on some smaller projects until the official letter from The Shed arrived in February 2020. From then on, my team and I have spoken more specifically with the curator responsible for the exhibition, Alessandra Gómez.

While the show was traveling, I made two more significant releases in the series. The first was in London, at David Zwirner Gallery in 2020–21, where I showed nine brand-new "Pardo é Papel" works. Although it did not have a precise connection with the traveling show, that release was decisive for me to rethink, classify, and rename the exhibition that was traveling. The production of "Pardo é Papel" works for David Zwirner had a density and impact very similar to that of the works I created in 2017 and 2018, which are now traveling from institution to institution. The context and conditions were therefore completely different. How, then, can these two periods be distinguished without confusing what belongs to the traveling exhibition and what was shown in London?

To understand this question, I refer to part of the testimony I wrote on that occasion:

> [...] The intersection between visual arts and music in my practice naturally makes me establish relationships between the two fields beyond just painting song lyrics. I began to be interested, for example, in how the musicians organize their works based on a system composed of albums, mixtapes, EPs, and singles. Normally albums are constructed within a limited period of time, covering a moment of research by a musician and often built around a specific theme or concept. While mixtapes are more random combinations of contents, EPs present works that are interlinked yet concise, with fewer tracks. The single is a song that is released separately from these divisions. Even though the single might otherwise fit into one of these categories, it is released on its own as a way of promoting the artist, calling attention to another, larger project, more strategic in the sense of presenting a potential that is about to arrive, to engage the public. Meanwhile, in painting, the more traditional organization takes place based on series, which divides the artist's production more by motifs/themes than by periods.
>
> This reflection appeared to me precisely at the moment when I was beginning to prepare *Pardo é Papel: Close a door to open a window*, my next solo show for the David Zwirner Gallery in London. The show was designed to occupy the gallery's two floors with nine large-format paintings, including three diptychs and one triptych. Due to the density of the work and subjects articulated in the show, I sought a way to separate these paintings into a delineated collection, and it was at this moment that the concept of the album arose as a way of organizing them.
>
> This need that I felt to create a separation by periods led me to look back on my production and to retroactively classify it. The first moment of the "Pardo é Papel" series took place in late 2017 and early 2018, in connection with a symbolic ritual of A Igreja do Reino da Arte—A Noiva (The Church of the Kingdom of Art—The Bride), where I presented the first 12 large sheets of paper shown previously at the Rocinha Sports Complex, where I had my first studio. One year later, this vision was already a reality, and the show *Pardo é Papel* was opened in March 2019 at MAC Lyon in France. This context is summarized in the painting *A vitória gloriosa* [The glorious victory], which became a sort of emblematic banner and the cover of the first album.
>
> Now, constructing this second album to be released abroad, I decided to insert lyrics from another three international artists of whom I am a great fan and who had already been inspiring "Pardo é Papel" aesthetically—namely, Frank Ocean, Solange, and Tyler, the Creator. The exhibition's title, *Close a door to open a window*, is after the painting I made as a translation of this line from the lyrics of the track "New Magic Wand" from *Igor*, Tyler's most recent album. This is the cover of this new moment with "Pardo é Papel." [...]

The second significant release was that of the subseries "New Power," which had three simultaneous openings: a main show at the Palais de Tokyo and two at A Gentil Carioca in its galleries in Rio de Janeiro and São Paulo. Even though the series was only definitively launched in 2021, I had already included at least one work from "New Power" at previous stops of *Pardo é Papel*, a sort of introduction to the public. The following passage presents questions and thoughts regarding that launch:

> [...] After a little more than one year developing the research, concept, and sketches for this project, on April 5 we began the first

Foi pensando nisso, junto da abertura de um novo espaço d'A Gentil Carioca em São Paulo, que tive a ideia de ocupar o novo ambiente, e também o antigo e tradicional espaço no Rio de Janeiro, com as obras que não entraram no show principal em Paris, no Palais de Tokyo. Encontrei neste *insight*, também, uma maneira conceitual de falar precisamente desse período de pandemia global que estamos vivendo, uma vez que se reunir ou viajar torna-se uma realidade a ser ponderada. Abrir a mesma exposição em 3 diferentes lugares do mundo, poeticamente dá conta dessas ponderações, já que eu consigo dividir minha audiência entre os 3 shows. Sem contar na ideia de trazer um pedaço de Paris, centro do mundo, onde acontecerá o show principal, para o centro do Rio de Janeiro, onde o acesso e a possibilidade de contato entre a periferia, o público principal a quem o trabalho se refere, se potencializam. Este último ponto é muito especial para mim.

Além das 3 exposições produzidas, eu ainda planejei algumas inserções de "Novo Poder" em feiras de arte como parte deste grande lançamento da série. Comecei com 3 painéis que foram exibidos no estande d'A Gentil Carioca no retorno da maior feira do circuito, Art Basel, na Suíça, no mês de outubro. Em novembro foi a vez de retornar também com a maior feira de arte da América Latina, a SP-Arte, em São Paulo, onde a galeria instalou 4 painéis inéditos de "Novo Poder" distribuídos em todos os dias da feira. A continuação dessas inserções que deram apoio ao lançamento da exposição em Paris, Rio e São Paulo, aconteceu em dezembro na Art Basel Miami com mais 4 novos painéis: sendo 3 instalados no estande da galeria durante os dias de feira, e 1 painel principal que estará disponível no Meridians, uma seção especial de projetos de arte em larga escala inspirado na seção Unlimited de Art Basel Suíça, que inaugura nesta edição da feira, nos Estados Unidos. [. . .]

A confirmação da exposição no The Shed me pareceu uma boa oportunidade para juntar esse primeiro momento de "A Vitória Gloriosa," e o mais recente desenvolvimento da série, "Novo Poder." Essa aproximação revela a evolução desse corpo de obra nos últimos cinco anos, criando paralelos e tensões entre os dois momentos. Como parte de *Pardo é Papel*, tanto "A Vitória Gloriosa" quanto "Novo Poder" elaboram aspectos diferentes dos temas centrais da série que os envolve: retratos e profecias de um futuro de benção, glória e bonança para a comunidade preta.

"A Vitória Gloriosa" inicia essa intenção pintando as formas mais materiais e terrenas de poder e acesso: roupas, joias, carros, jatos, comida, festas... Além de enaltecer amigos, personalidades famosas, e carreiras que marcaram a subida de pessoas pretas no Brasil, como a música e o futebol. A ostentação nas periferias é um símbolo de poder que incita recorrentemente a imaginação, e é uma maneira direta de mostrar que é possível conquistar, de que dinheiro e pele preta também combinam, como diz Baco Exú do Blues. A ostentação é também uma das fortes características do funk e do rap. É cultural.

Nesse primeiro momento, ao fazer referência a essas linguagens, já surgia uma preocupação que veio a se tornar central em minha prática: criar trabalhos, séries e narrativas que levem o público preto para os museus e espaços da arte contemporânea.

A concretização dessa intenção é a gênese de "Novo Poder" que, embora só viesse a ser lançada oficialmente anos depois, já existia ali, nas primeiras exposições de "Pardo é Papel," pela presença massiva de pessoas pretas em um espaço que não foi desenhado para recebê-las. Muitos dos visitantes de minhas exposições estavam pela primeira vez num ambiente de arte contemporânea, contemplando as obras daquelas que agora faziam parte, quer dizer, retratados em pinturas, sentiam-se orgulhosos e valorizados.

Desse modo, ambas as séries simultaneamente contém, e estão contidas, uma na outra. "A Vitória Gloriosa," ao falar das muitas formas de empoderamento e orgulho preto, atrai essas pessoas para o universo da arte, enquanto "Novo Poder" espelha e reflete sobre esse movimento. Sendo assim, ao mesmo tempo, é feito um recorte estreito, focado em uma das muitas carreiras de ascensão contidas em "A Vitória Gloriosa," e um olhar expandido, meta, se afastando e ampliando a perspectiva sobre o sistema em que suas obras estão contidas.

Por outro lado, como em todo meu corpo de trabalho, "Novo Poder" tem o aspecto de autorretrato, onde eu me debruço sobre o universo particular que me permitiu chegar aqui. Não por acaso a cor parda, traduzida como os objetos de arte, frequentemente remete, pelos grandes formatos retangulares, às próprias obras de "Pardo é Papel." Sob um olhar biográfico, a série fala sobre como, ao chegar numa posição de sucesso—, olhei em volta e me vi envolvido em um mundo dominado quase exclusivamente por brancos. A série é um estudo e mapeamento das contradições, armadilhas e oportunidades desse campo para que mais pessoas pretas possam se infiltrar, não só como espectadores ou objetos das obras, mas enquanto agentes em posições de poder: curadores, artistas, colecionadores, diretores, financiadores, galeristas, etc.

execution of paintings in the new studio. As the series is monothematic (figures of Black people in exhibition spaces, such as museums, galleries, and foundations, in relation to contemporary art, mainly the contemplation of painting), I look at these works as being akin to the practice of still-life painting, where objects are articulated on a table to paint their variations, with the aim of understanding the subtleties of those objects of study. In "New Power" I chose precisely to work in this way, and the investigation became so prolific that I did not concern myself with conceiving an a priori exhibition design. The idea was to work with density and to push the subject matter to exhaustion, for me to later look at the work as a whole, and only then begin to carefully curate what would enter the exhibition. Thus, the release and presentation of this series could take place in a basic way, at its genesis, while also being as integral as possible. I created more than 100 new works, not counting the unfinished sketches. So many works were made that there were enough to hold at least two more shows in the years to come.

It was while thinking about this, together with the opening of a new space of A Gentil Carioca gallery in São Paulo, that I had the idea of occupying not only that new setting, but also the old traditional space in Rio de Janeiro, with the works that did not enter the main show in Paris at the Palais de Tokyo. This same insight also led me to a conceptual approach suited precisely to this period of global pandemic we are all experiencing, since getting together for a meeting or traveling is something that must be carefully planned and considered. The simultaneous opening of the same exhibition in three different places around the world is a poetic solution for these concerns, since with this format the audience is divided in the three locations for the three shows. Coupled with this, there is the further possibility of bringing a piece from Paris—the center of the world, where the main show is to take place—to downtown Rio de Janeiro, where the access to and the possibility of contact with the periphery, the main public to which my work refers, are leveraged. This last point is very special for me.

Besides the three exhibitions produced, I also planned some insertions of "New Power" in art fairs as a part of this large release of the series. I began with three panels that were shown at A Gentil Carioca's stall for the return of the largest art fair in the circuit, Art Basel in Switzerland, in October. November also saw the return of the largest art fair in Latin America, SP Arte, in São Paulo, where A Gentil Carioca installed four never-before-shown panels displayed each day of the fair. The continuation of these installations that lend support to the launching of the exhibition in Paris, Rio, and São Paulo, will take place in December at Art Basel Miami Beach with four more new panels: three installed at the gallery's stall during the days of the fair and one main panel that will be available at the Meridians, a special section of large-scale art projects inspired by the Unlimited section of Art Basel Switzerland, which is being opened at this edition of the fair in the United States. [...]

When the exhibition at The Shed was confirmed, I considered this a good opportunity to combine two periods of the "Pardo é Papel" series: the initial phase, "The Glorious Victory," and the more recent development, "New Power." This combination reveals the evolution of this body of work over the last five years, creating parallels and tensions between the two. As part of "Pardo é Papel," both "The Glorious Victory" and "New Power" elaborate different aspects of the central themes of the series: portraits and prophecies of a future of blessings, glory, and abundance for the Black community.

"The Glorious Victory" attempts this by painting the more material and earthly forms of power and access: clothes, jewelry, cars, jets, food, parties. It also exalts friends, famous personalities, and the careers often associated with the rise of Black people in Brazil, such as music and soccer. Ostentation in the urban outskirts is a symbol of power that recurrently incites the imagination; it is a direct way of showing that it is possible to achieve, that money and Black skin can go well together, as stated by Baco Exu do Blues. Ostentation is also a strong characteristic of Brazilian funk and rap. It is cultural.

During that first phase, while making reference to those languages, a concern arose that became central in my practice: to create works and narratives that bring the Black public to the museums and spaces of contemporary art.

The concretization of this aim was the genesis of "New Power," which, although it was only officially released years later, already existed back then, in the first exhibitions of "Pardo é Papel," as indicated by the massive presence of Black people in a space that was not designed to host them. Many of the visitors to my exhibitions were in an environment of contemporary art for the first time. Contemplating the works of those who were enjoying a new sort of inclusion—that is, portrayed in paintings—they felt proud and validated.

Thus, each of the series contains—and is simultaneously contained in—the other. By talking

Mas ainda assim é preciso ir além, e "Novo Poder" então aprofunda e imagina o futuro desse plano do qual "A Vitória Gloriosa" deu os primeiros passos, ultrapassando as formas mais materiais e terrenas de acesso—roupas, poses, joias, carros, jatos, comida, festas—e concebendo o acesso a valores mais imateriais e etéreos—contemplação, vadiagem, irreverência, intelectualidade, filosofia, tempo livre, ambiguidade, incerteza, inutilidades.

A profecia está mais adiante na análise e proposição do que seria não só a ocupação física, mas também metafórica dos espaços de arte e os privilégios que eles contém. A arte é um lugar de disputar narrativas, que são produzidas e legitimadas. Imagens que moldam o imaginário coletivo, guardando o passado e profetizando o futuro. Apontando o que tem valor ou não, o que e como vai ser mostrado.

No futuro de "Novo Poder" a comunidade preta está a par dos códigos da arte contemporânea, capaz de se relacionar sem ressalva com os objetos, performances, instalações, pinturas e tudo mais. Onde essa audiência não sente mais repulsa no espaço branco, que sempre lhe foi hostil. Onde a relação com a abstração e a não-finalidade não são mais uma culpa, pois o peso político e social de um negro vencer e ser funcional foi diluído. Esse é um aspecto na arte que me interessa particularmente enquanto reivindicação de poder e liberdade para um povo: objetos de arte como alimento do espírito. O gozo estético é um privilégio. E a arte oferece esse lugar na máxima potência, ao se visitar uma exposição de arte contemporânea, principalmente de pinturas abstratas; um privilégio e uma necessidade que não sabíamos que podíamos ter. Não fomos educados para isso, esse lugar nos foi roubado: o das experiências que transcendem a finalidade prática das coisas, dos objetos e até mesmo dos comportamentos e afazeres.

A contemplação e o fazer artístico, a rotina, os ateliês, foram inicialmente idealizados e romantizados por e para os brancos. Viver a arte como um lugar religioso, de alimento da alma, do encontro com o sublime. Aos artistas são autorizadas a excentricidade, a exceção, a inutilidade. O privilégio de não precisar se apressar, ou dar certo, de funcionar, mas de ser vadio e intelectual. O luxo imaterial máximo; do tempo livre, do descanso, da ingenuidade, da loucura. O direito à displicência e à irreverência, com o dinheiro, com os bens, a autoridade, com o próprio foco, e o próprio tempo. Quem pode estudar, entender, dar sentido, criar e fetichizar objetos com valor prático tão reduzido? Essa tensão é importante porque ela fala muito especificamente de questões de classe e culturais. Vindo de um lugar onde tudo é permitido. Fruto de um berço farto onde tudo se pode, onde se é acostumado com o poder e o luxo, com não se preocupar com a aparência das coisas, inclusive a própria.

"Novo Poder" é portanto também a ocupação desses ideais romantizados e utópicos da arte. Não à toa, por vezes, os espaços brancos, que envolvem obras e personagens, beiram a abstração sem definição espacial clara, completamente higienizados, herméticos, como lojas de joias caras, ou marcas de grife, assépticos. São espaços liminares, entre o que foi e o que vai ser, transitórios entre a partida e a chegada. E a profecia é a ocupação dessa aura, desse subconsciente, da tranquilidade branca, com pessoas pretas calmamente circulando em meio ao branco, à branquitude, absorvendo seus códigos, seus símbolos.

Por fim, assim retratada em "A Vitória Gloriosa," uma pintura é um objeto único, tradicional, certamente também com seu valor de ostentação, uma posse, um bem de consumo. É uma ostentação mais sutil—imagina chegar na casa de alguém e se deparar com um dos trípticos de Francis Bacon bem na sala? No entanto, em "Novo Poder" esses objetos passam a ser considerados por seu valor intelectual, filosófico e religioso. São *tokens*, de alto valor especulativo e simbólico. E talvez a transformação mais interessante seja que deixem de ser o objeto final do desejo, e se tornem um meio para a ascensão que eu vejo para as pessoas pretas, que ao criar, contemplar, vender, colecionar, curar e dominá-los, possam desfrutar a sutileza, sublimação e gozo antes reservados aos brancos.

about the many forms of Black empowerment and pride, "The Glorious Victory" attracts these people to the universe of art, while "New Power" mirrors and reflects on this movement. Consequently, while "New Power" is a narrow cross section focused on one of the many careers of upward mobility contained in "The Glorious Victory," it is also a broadened viewpoint, a meta-approach, gaining a more distanced view and enlarging the perspective on the system into which its works are inserted.

On the other hand, as in my entire body of work, "New Power" involves an aspect of self-portraiture, where I deal with the particular universe that allowed me to get to this point. In these works, the color *pardo* [a term for "brown," used in Brazilian society to gloss over negritude] often appears in large rectangular formats, in a sort of self-reference to the works of "Pardo é Papel." From a biographical perspective, the series talks about how I, upon arriving at a position of success, looked around and found myself in a world dominated almost exclusively by white people. The series is a study and mapping of the contradictions, pitfalls, and opportunities in this field so that more Black people can infiltrate it, not only as spectators or subjects in the works but also as agents in positions of power: curators, artists, collectors, directors, funders, gallerists, and so on.

But it is moreover necessary to go beyond this, and so "New Power" deepens and imagines the future of this plan in which "The Glorious Victory" took the first steps, surpassing the more material and worldly forms of access—clothes, possessions, jewelry, cars, jets, food, parties—to consider access to more immaterial and ethereal values: contemplation, idleness, irreverence, intellectuality, philosophy, free time, ambiguity, uncertainty, futility.

This prophesizes the analysis and proposal of what would be not only the physical but also the metaphorical occupation of the spaces of art and the privileges they contain. Art is a place for disputing narratives, which are produced and legitimized. Images that mold the collective imaginary, conserving the past and prophesizing the future. Pointing out what has value or what does not have value, what will be shown, and how it will be presented.

In the future of "New Power," the Black community is informed about the codes of contemporary art and is able to relate fully, without restrictions, to the objects, performances, installations, paintings, and so forth. It is a place where these audiences will no longer feel repulsed in the white space, which was always hostile to them. A place where the relationship with aimlessness and abstraction is no longer a cause for guilt, since the political and social onus on a Black person to achieve and be functional has been diluted. This is an aspect in art that interests me particularly as a demand of a people for power and freedom: art objects as food for the spirit. Aesthetic enjoyment is a privilege. And art offers this place of maximum power, as when one visits an exhibition of contemporary art, especially of abstract painting, which is both a privilege and a need that we never knew we could have. We were not educated for this. This place, the place of experiences that transcend the practical purpose of things, of objects, and even of behaviors and practices, was stolen from us.

The idealization and romanticization of the making and contemplation of art were initially generated by and for white people to experience art as a religious place, a place of food for the soul, for an encounter with the sublime. In this ideal, the artists have a special license for eccentricity, exception, and uselessness. The privilege of not needing to hurry, to be successful or functional, and the right to be idle and intellectual. The maximum immaterial luxury—of free time, of rest, of ingenuity, of craziness and carelessness. The right to indifference and irreverence in regard to money, assets, authority, one's focus, one's appearance, one's time. Who can study, understand, give meaning to, create, and fetishize objects of such limited practical value? This tension is important because it has much to say specifically about questions concerning class and culture.

"New Power" is therefore also the occupation of these romanticized and utopian ideals of art. Not by chance, sometimes the white spaces, which involve works and subjects, border on abstraction without a clear spatial definition, being completely sanitary, hermetic, and aseptic—like stores selling expensive jewelry or designer goods. They are borderline, transitory spaces between what was and what will be, spaces of transition between the starting point and the finish line. And the prophecy is the occupation of this aura, of this subconscious, of white tranquility, with Black people calmly circulating among the white, among the whiteness, absorbing its codes, its symbols.

As portrayed in "The Glorious Victory," a painting is a unique, traditional object, and certainly with its ostentatious value, a possession, a consumer good. It is a more subtle ostentation—imagine arriving at someone's house and finding one of Francis Bacon's triptychs right there in the living room. In "New Power," however, these objects are seen in another light: they are considered for their intellectual, philosophical, and religious value. They are tokens with a high speculative and symbolic value. Perhaps the most interesting transformation is that they are no longer the final object of desire. Rather, they become a means for the ascension I see for Black people, who, by creating, contemplating, selling, collecting, curating, and mastering them, can appreciate the subtlety, sublimation, and enjoyment that were previously reserved only for white people.

Contributor Biographies

MAXWELL ALEXANDRE was born in 1990 in Rio de Janeiro. Raised in an evangelical home, the artist served in the army and was a professional street in-line skater for 12 years. He graduated in design from PUC-RJ (Pontifícia Universidade Católica of Rio de Janeiro) in 2016. In 2018, he received an award from the Arquidiocese of Rio de Janeiro and the São Sebastião Culture Prize. Alexandre was elected artist of the year by Deutsche Bank and is one of the 35 artists worldwide included on Artsy's Vanguard list. His work figures in the collections of various prestigious institutions, including the Pinacoteca do Estado de São Paulo, the Museu de Arte de São Paulo, the Museu de Arte Moderna do Rio de Janeiro, the Museu de Arte do Rio, the Musée d'Art Contemporain de Lyon, Perez Art Museum Miami, and Guggenheim Abu Dhabi. Alexandre considers his works prayers and his studio a temple.

TINA M. CAMPT is Owen F. Walker Professor of Humanities and Modern Culture and Media at Brown University. She is a Black feminist theorist of visual culture and contemporary art. She is the author of five books, including *A Black Gaze* (MIT Press, 2021), *Listening to Images* (Duke University Press, 2017), *Image Matters: Archive, Photography, and the African Diaspora in Europe* (Duke University Press, 2012), and *Other Germans: Black Germans and the Politics of Race, Gender and Memory in the Third Reich* (University of Michigan Press, 2004). Her co-edited collection, *Imagining Everyday Life: Engagements with Vernacular Photography* (Steidl, 2020), received the 2020 Photography Catalogue of the Year award from Paris Photo and Aperture Foundation.

ALESSANDRA GÓMEZ is the curator of *Pardo é Papel: The Glorious Victory and New Power* and associate curator at The Shed. She graduated from Columbia University's Modern and Contemporary Art: Critical and Curatorial Studies master's program and was a curatorial fellow at the university's Wallach Art Gallery. She conceived and organized the gallery's first performance program, *Into Darkness* (2019), which featured commissions by artists Trajal Harrell, Dean Moss, and Eiko Otake & DonChristian Jones. At The Shed, she organized *HEADLESS: The Demonstration* (2022) by Anonymous Club, the creative studio led by Shayne Oliver. She was an assistant curator on *Tomás Saraceno: Particular Matter(s)* (2022), *Ian Cheng: Life After BOB* (2021), and *Open Call* (2021), and a curatorial assistant on *Manual Override* (2019) and *Open Call* (2019). Her independent curatorial projects include *As If You Me* (2017) and *Ember Ground* (2018) at the Center for Performance Research, *Material Witness Witness Material* (2018) at Knockdown Center, and *Public Setting* (2017) as part of the Queens Museum partnership with Bulova Center. She was previously part of the editorial collective for *Women & Performance: a journal of feminist theory*.

HANS ULRICH OBRIST is artistic director of the Serpentine Galleries in London, senior advisor at LUMA Arles, and senior program advisor at The Shed. Prior to this, he was curator of the Musée d'Art Moderne de la Ville de Paris. Since his first show, *World Soup (The Kitchen Show)*, in 1991, he has curated more than 350 exhibitions, including most recently *IT'S URGENT* at LUMA Arles (2019–21) and *Enzo Mari* at Triennale Milano (2020). In 2011, Obrist received the CCS Bard Award for Curatorial Excellence, and in 2015 he was awarded the International Folkwang Prize. He was honored by the Appraisers Association of America with the 2018 Award for Excellence in the Arts. Obrist's publications include *Ways of Curating* (2015), *The Age of Earthquakes* (2015), *Lives of the Artists, Lives of Architects* (2015), *Mondialité* (2017), *Somewhere Totally Else* (2018), *The Athens Dialogues* (2018), *Maria Lassnig: Letters* (2020), *Entrevistas Brasileiras: Volume 2* (2020), *An Exhibition Always Hides Another Exhibition* (2019), *The Extreme Self: Age of You* (2021), and *140 Ideas for Planet Earth* (2021).

Acknowledgments

FROM ALESSANDRA GÓMEZ: Organizing an exhibition affords the privilege of working with visionary and gifted artists such as Maxwell Alexandre. This exhibition and this publication have been made possible through the careful, intelligent, and generous work of many colleagues and supporters. It has truly been a tremendous honor and privilege to work with Maxwell over these past few years and witness the exponential growth of his artistic practice. Thank you, Maxwell, for your trust in working together, and to your studio; your gallery, A Gentil Carioca; and Frances Reynolds, who have all been wonderful partners. I would also like to express my most sincere gratitude and admiration to scholar Tina M. Campt, who wrote a beautiful, compelling essay on Maxwell's work for this publication. I am also grateful to Hans Ulrich Obrist for his insightful interview with Maxwell, which offers deeper context for his life and artistic practice. Thank you to Alex Poots, Emma Enderby, and Andria Hickey for their support and enthusiasm for this project. I've also been lucky to have incredible mentors, one of whom is Christina Yang. I am grateful for her advice and persistent encouragement of my work as a scholar and interdisciplinary curator over the years. Thank you to my wonderful colleagues, especially Phillip Griffith for his editorial guidance; Keri Bronk for her design input; our publication designers Renata Graw and Lucas Reif of Normal studio, who designed this extraordinary book; this book's proofreader, Dianne Woo, for her scrupulous attention; and Matthew Rinaldi for his translations from Portuguese to English. Thank you to my exhibitions colleagues, Yayoi Sakurai, Amanda Singer, and Elizabeth Berridge, for facilitating the production and installation of this exhibition. Finally, thank you to my friends and family, and especially to my parents for their endless support and for instilling in me an appreciation for the arts.

FROM MAXWELL ALEXANDRE: I express my special thanks to A Gentil Carioca gallery and all its team; to Alessandra Gómez, who made the show happen with care and patience; to Álvaro Piquet, who is always by my side; to the rappers Baco Exu do Blues, BK', and Djonga, who inspired me in so many ways; to some of the important mentors I had during college: Cadu Felix, Eduardo Berliner, Fernando Cocchiaralle, Roberta Portas, and Ligia Saramago; to the David Zwirner Gallery and team; to Eduardo Braule-Wanderley; to Edu de Barros; to Fortes D'Aloia & Gabriel; to Frances Reynolds, who, in addition to always being by my side, made the *Pardo é Papel* tour possible; to Fundação Iberê; to Hugo Vitrani, who through his efforts made my last show at the Palais de Tokyo happen; to A Igreja do Reino da Arte—A Noiva; to Instituto Tomie Ohtake; to Isabelle Berlotti and the MAC Lyon team; to Museu de Arte do Rio; to Emma Lavigne; to James Green; to Maria Klabin; to Marisa da Silva, my mom; to Mari Stockler, who has believed in my professional paths since the beginning; to Matthieu Lelièvre, who is always sensitive to my work; to the Palais de Tokyo and team; to Paulo Herkenhoff; to Primo da Cruz, my cousin; to my beloved Raissa Caroline; to the movement Roda Cultural da Rocinha; to Rosa Melo; to Samuel Alexandre, my brother; to Tina Campt; to Vanessa Carlos; and to the Megazord Studio team, who made this exhibition happen: Daniel Frickmann, Douglas Bastos, Isadhora Müller, Ingrid Kita, Lucas Tolezano, Mari Santos, Michel Moreira, Raoni Azevedo, Carlos Renato, and Vall Lloveras.

FROM ALEX POOTS, HANS ULRICH OBRIST, AND ANDRIA HICKEY: We would like to jointly thank the many people who have been essential in realizing this exhibition and publication. We would also like to thank the wider Shed team, listed at the back of this publication, all of whom have played an important role in *Pardo é Papel: The Glorious Victory and New Power*. We thank The Shed's Board of Directors, notably Chair Jonathan M. Tisch, as well as Debbie August, Heather Baker, Peter A. Boyce II, Neeraj Chandra, Misty Copeland, Roberta Denning, Founding Chair Daniel L. Doctoroff, Lew Frankfort, Dexter G. Goei, Robert Goldstein, Glenda G. Grace, Gary Hoberman, Todd Kahn, Monish Kumar, Kate D. Levin, Christina Weiss Lurie, Frank H. McCourt Jr., Marigay McKee, Darla Moore, Colby Mugrabi, Dasha Zhukova Niarchos, Claudia Rankine, Maria Catalina Saieh Guzman, Andres Santo Domingo, Ann Sarnoff, Dean Shapiro, Harvey J. Spevak, Jed Walentas, Fred Wilson, Deborah Winshel, and Kenneth P. Wong, and our ex officio members, Hons. Adrienne E. Adams, Laurie Cumbo, Mark Levine, and Maria Torres-Springer. The creation of new work at The Shed has been generously supported by the Lizzie and Jonathan Tisch Commissioning Fund. Special thanks to the following Shed Commissioners, a group of visionary philanthropists providing essential early support for our mission to produce and welcome innovative art and ideas, across all forms of creativity: Bruce A. Beal Jr., Jeff and Lisa Blau, Sherry Brous and Doug Oliver, Lisa and Dick Cashin, R. Martin Chavez, David C. Drummond, Eva and Glenn Dubin, Larry and Lori Fink, Julis Romo Rabinowitz Family, Kirsh Foundation, Adam and Margaret Korn, Judy and Leonard Lauder, Leni and Peter May, Greg and Alexandra Mondre, Eric and Wendy Schmidt, Robert K. Steel Family Foundation, Laurie M. Tisch Illumination Fund, Steve Tisch, and two anonymous Commissioners. Thank you, Maxwell, for partnering with us on both this exhibition and this publication, along with the teams at your studio and gallery, A Gentil Carioca.

Captions

Page 2
O mundo é nosso [The world is ours] (detail), 2018, from "Pardo é Papel: The Glorious Victory," 2017–. Shoe polish on brown kraft paper. Courtesy the artist, Fortes D'Aloia & Gabriel, and A Gentil Carioca.

Page 3
Maxwell Alexandre in his studio in Gávea, Rio de Janeiro, 2021.

Page 4
Maxwell Alexandre's studio in Gávea, Rio de Janeiro, 2021.

Page 5
Meus manos, minhas minas, meus irmãos, minhas irmãs e meus cães [My homies, my homegirls, my brothers, my sisters, my dogs] (detail), 2017–18, from "Pardo é Papel: The Glorious Victory," 2017–. Latex, grease, henna, bitumen, dye, acrylic, graphite, charcoal on brown kraft paper. Courtesy Fortes D'Aloia & Gabriel.

Page 6
Gazing ball 2, 2021, from "Pardo é Papel: New Power," 2019–. Charcoal and latex on brown kraft paper. 94 ½ × 47 ¼ inches. Courtesy the artist and A Gentil Carioca.

Page 7
Olhar embriagado no espelho [Drunk look in the mirror] (detail), 2018, from "Pardo é Papel: The Glorious Victory," 2017–. Latex, grease, henna, bitumen, acrylic, graphite, and charcoal on brown kraft paper. Courtesy Fortes D'Aloia & Gabriel and A Gentil Carioca.

Pages 8–9
Pintei o Éden de preto [I painted Eden black] (detail), 2020, from "Pardo é Papel: Close a door to open a window," 2020–. Latex, shoe polish, bitumen, colored pencil, and acrylic on brown kraft paper. Courtesy the artist and David Zwirner Gallery.

Page 10
Novo Poder [New Power] (detail), 2019, from "Pardo é Papel: New Power," 2019–. Latex, shoe polish, hair relaxer, bitumen, dye, ballpoint pen, graphite, vinyl, acrylic, charcoal, and oil stick on brown kraft paper. Courtesy the artist and A Gentil Carioca.

Page 11
Maxwell Alexandre in his studio in Gávea, Rio de Janeiro, 2021.

Page 12
Maxwell Alexandre's studio in Gávea, Rio de Janeiro, 2021.

Page 13
sem título [untitled] (detail), 2021, from "Pardo é Papel: New Power," 2019–. Latex, acrylic, shoe polish, bitumen, charcoal, dye, and graphite on brown kraft paper. Courtesy the artist and A Gentil Carioca.

Page 14
Dois quadros SAMO na parede [Two SAMO paintings on the wall] (detail), 2020, from "Pardo é Papel: New Power," 2019–. Latex, bitumen and acrylic on brown kraft paper. Courtesy the artist and David Zwirner Gallery.

Page 33
sem título [untitled] (detail), 2021, from "Pardo é Papel: New Power," 2019–. Shoe polish, graphite, latex, acrylic, and photocopy transfer on brown kraft paper. Courtesy the artist and A Gentil Carioca.

Pages 34–5
sem título [untitled], 2021, from "Pardo é Papel: New Power," 2019–. Shoe polish, graphite, latex, acrylic, and photocopy transfer on brown kraft paper. 126 × 189 inches. Courtesy artist and A Gentil Carioca.

Pages 36–7
Concetto spaziale (detail), 2021, from "Pardo é Papel: New Power," 2019–. Shoe polish, bitumen, charcoal, graphite, latex, and acrylic on brown kraft paper. Courtesy the artist and A Gentil Carioca.

Pages 38–9
Concetto spaziale, 2021, from "Pardo é Papel: New Power," 2019–. Shoe polish, bitumen, charcoal, graphite, latex, and acrylic on brown kraft paper. Diptych: 63 × 94 ½ and 63 × 47 ¼ inches. Courtesy the artist and A Gentil Carioca.

Pages 40–1
sem título [untitled] (detail), 2021, from "Pardo é Papel: New Power," 2019–. Shoe polish, bitumen, charcoal, graphite, latex, and acrylic on brown kraft paper. Courtesy the artist and A Gentil Carioca.

Pages 42–3
sem título [untitled], 2021, from "Pardo é Papel: New Power," 2019–. Shoe polish, bitumen, charcoal, graphite, latex, and acrylic on brown kraft paper. 126 × 189 inches. Courtesy the artist and A Gentil Carioca.

Page 44
sem título [untitled] (detail), 2021, from "Pardo é Papel: New Power," 2019–. Shoe polish, bitumen, charcoal, graphite, latex, and acrylic on brown kraft paper. Courtesy the artist and A Gentil Carioca.

Page 45
sem título [untitled], 2021, from "Pardo é Papel: New Power," 2019–. Shoe polish, bitumen, charcoal, graphite, latex, and acrylic on brown kraft paper. 27 × 32 11⁄16 inches. Courtesy the artist and A Gentil Carioca.

Pages 46–7
sem título [untitled], 2021, from "Pardo é Papel: New Power," 2019–. Shoe polish, bitumen, charcoal, graphite, dye, latex, oil stick, and acrylic on brown kraft paper. Diptych: 126 × 189 inches each. Courtesy the artist and A Gentil Carioca.

Pages 48–9
sem título [untitled] (detail), 2021, from "Pardo é Papel: New Power," 2019–. Shoe polish, bitumen, charcoal, graphite, dye, latex, oil stick, and acrylic on brown kraft paper. Courtesy the artist and A Gentil Carioca.

Page 50
sem título [untitled], 2021, from "Pardo é Papel: New Power," 2019–. Shoe polish, graphite, latex, and acrylic on brown kraft paper. 126 × 189 inches. Courtesy of the artist and A Gentil Carioca.

Page 53
sem título [untitled] (detail), 2021, from "Pardo é Papel: New Power," 2019–. Shoe polish, graphite, latex, and acrylic on brown kraft paper. Courtesy the artist and A Gentil Carioca.

Pages 54–5
sem título [untitled] (detail), 2021, from "Pardo é Papel: New Power," 2019–. Latex, shoe polish, bitumen, graphite, charcoal, and acrylic on brown kraft paper. Courtesy the artist and A Gentil Carioca.

Pages 56–7
sem título [untitled] (detail), 2021, from "Pardo é Papel: New Power," 2019–. Latex, shoe polish, bitumen, graphite, charcoal, and acrylic on brown kraft paper. Courtesy the artist and A Gentil Carioca.

Pages 58–9
sem título [untitled] (detail), 2021, from "Pardo é Papel: New Power," 2019–. Latex, shoe polish, bitumen, dye, graphite, charcoal, and acrylic on brown kraft paper. Courtesy the artist and A Gentil Carioca.

Pages 60–1
sem título [untitled], 2021, from "Pardo é Papel: New Power," 2019–. Latex, shoe polish, bitumen, dye, graphite, charcoal, and acrylic on brown kraft paper. 94 ½ × 566 15⁄16 inches. Courtesy the artist and A Gentil Carioca.

Page 62
sem título [untitled] (detail), 2021, from "Pardo é Papel: New Power," 2019–. Shoe polish, graphite, latex, and acrylic on brown kraft paper. Courtesy the artist and A Gentil Carioca.

Page 63
sem título [untitled], 2021, from "Pardo é Papel: New Power," 2019–. Shoe polish, graphite, latex, and acrylic on brown kraft paper. 63 × 63 ¾ inches. Courtesy the artist and A Gentil Carioca.

Pages 64–5
sem título [untitled], 2021, from "Pardo é Papel: New Power," 2019–. bitumen, charcoal, latex, and acrylic on brown kraft paper. 126 × 189 inches. Courtesy the artist and A Gentil Carioca.

Page 85
Crianças atrás de telas [Kids behind canvases], 2018, from "Pardo é Papel: The Glorious Victory," 2017–. Latex, shoe polish, hair relaxer, bitumen, dye, acrylic, graphite, charcoal, and oil stick on brown kraft paper. 141 ¾ × 141 ¾ inches. Courtesy the artist and A Gentil Carioca.

Page 86
Bilionário escuro [Dark Billionaire], 2018, from "Pardo é Papel: The Glorious Victory," 2017–. Latex, grease, henna, bitumen, dye, acrylic, vinyl, graphite, ballpoint pen, charcoal, oil stick, and powdered chocolate wrapping paper on brown kraft paper. 126 × 189 inches. Courtesy Fortes D'Aloia & Gabriel and A Gentil Carioca.

Page 87
A lua quer ser preta, se pinta no eclipse [The moon wants to be black, it paints itself in the eclipse] (detail), 2017–18, from "Pardo é Papel: The Glorious Victory," 2017–. Latex, grease, henna, bitumen, dye, acrylic, graphite, vinyl, ballpoint pen charcoal, and oil stick on brown kraft paper. Courtesy the artist and A Gentil Carioca.

Page 88
A lua quer ser preta, se pinta no eclipse (diss) [The moon wants to be black, it paints itself in the eclipse (diss)], (detail) 2019, from "Pardo é Papel: The Glorious Victory," 2017–. Latex, grease, henna, bitumen, dye, acrylic, graphite, vinyl, charcoal and oil stick on brown kraft paper. Courtesy the artist and A Gentil Carioca.

Page 89
Meus manos, minhas minas, meus irmãos, minhas irmãs e meus cães [My homies, my homegirls, my brothers, my sisters, my dogs] (detail), 2017–18, from "Pardo é Papel: The Glorious Victory," 2017–. Latex, grease, henna, bitumen, dye, acrylic, graphite, and charcoal on brown kraft paper. Courtesy Fortes D'Aloia & Gabriel.

Page 90
Olhar embriagado no espelho [Drunk look in the mirror] (detail), 2018, from "Pardo é Papel: The Glorious Victory," 2017–. Latex, grease, henna, bitumen, acrylic, graphite, and charcoal on brown kraft paper. Courtesy Fortes D'Aloia & Gabriel and A Gentil Carioca.

Page 91
Olhar embriagado no espelho [Drunk look in the mirror], 2018, from "Pardo é Papel: The Glorious Victory," 2017–. Latex, grease, henna, bitumen, acrylic, graphite, and charcoal on brown kraft paper. 126 × 189 inches. Courtesy Fortes D'Aloia & Gabriel and A Gentil Carioca.

Page 92
Só quando tu tá com as folhas geral gosta de salada [Only when you're with leaves do people like salad], 2018, from "Pardo é Papel: The Glorious Victory," 2017–. Latex, shoe polish, hair relaxer, bitumen, dye, acrylic, graphite, charcoal, and oil stick on brown kraft paper. 126 × 189 inches. Courtesy private collection.

Page 93
Um cigarro e a vida pela janela (diss) [A cigarette and life through the window (diss)], 2019, from "Pardo é Papel: The Glorious Victory," 2017–. Latex, grease, henna, bitumen, dye, acrylic, graphite, ballpoint pen, charcoal, and oil stick on brown kraft paper. 126 × 189 inches. Courtesy the artist and A Gentil Carioca.

Page 94
Não foi pedindo licença que chegamos até aqui [We didn't get here by apologizing], 2018, from "Pardo é Papel: The Glorious Victory," 2017–. Latex, grease, henna, bitumen, dye, acrylic, vinyl paint, graphite, ballpoint pen, charcoal, oil stick, and chocolate drink package on brown kraft paper. 126 × 189 inches. Courtesy Fortes D'Aloia & Gabriel.

Page 95
Não foi pedindo licença que chegamos até aqui [We didn't get here by apologizing] (detail), 2018, from "Pardo é Papel: The Glorious Victory," 2017–. Latex, grease, henna, bitumen, dye, acrylic, vinyl paint, graphite, ballpoint pen, charcoal, oil stick, and chocolate drink package on brown kraft paper. Courtesy Fortes D'Aloia & Gabriel.

Pages 96–7
Contos de esquinas [Street corner songs], 2019, from "Pardo é Papel: The Glorious Victory," 2017–. Latex, grease, henna, bitumen, dye, acrylic, graphite, charcoal, and oil stick on brown kraft paper. Diptych: 126 × 364 3⁄16 inches. Courtesy the artist and A Gentil Carioca.

Pages 98–9
Contos de esquinas [Street corner Songs] (detail), 2019, from "Pardo é Papel: The Glorious Victory," 2017–. Latex, grease, henna, bitumen, dye, acrylic, graphite, charcoal, and oil stick on brown kraft paper. Courtesy the artist and A Gentil Carioca.

Page 100
A vitória gloriosa [The glorious victory], 2018, from "Pardo é Papel: The Glorious Victory," 2017–. Latex, shoe polish, hair relaxer, bitumen, acrylic, graphite, charcoal, and oil stick on brown kraft paper. 126 × 189 inches. Courtesy Fortes D'Aloia & Gabriel and A Gentil Carioca.

Page 101
Insatisfeito com o tamanho do mundo [Displeased with the size of the world], 2018, from "Pardo é Papel: The Glorious Victory," 2017–. Latex, shoe polish, hair relaxer, bitumen, dye, acrylic, graphite, and charcoal on brown kraft paper. 126 × 563 inches. Courtesy Fortes D'Aloia & Gabriel and A Gentil Carioca.

Page 102
Insatisfeito com o tamanho do mundo [Displeased with the size of the world] (detail), 2018, from "Pardo é Papel: The Glorious Victory," 2017–. Latex, shoe polish, hair relaxer, bitumen, dye, acrylic, graphite, and charcoal on brown kraft paper. Courtesy Fortes D'Aloia & Gabriel and A Gentil Carioca.

Pages 103
Até Deus inveja o homem preto [Even God envies the Black man], 2018, from "Pardo é Papel: The Glorious Victory," 2017–. Latex, acrylic and oil stick on brown kraft paper. 169 5⁄16 × 200 13⁄16 inches. Courtesy Fortes D'Aloia & Gabriel and A Gentil Carioca.

Pages 104–5
Se eu fosse vocês olhava pra mim de novo [If I were you I'd look at me again], 2018, from "Pardo é Papel: The Glorious Victory," 2017–. Latex, hair relaxer, bitumen, acrylic, and charcoal on brown kraft paper. 126 × 189 inches. Courtesy Fortes D'Aloia & Gabriel and A Gentil Carioca.

Pages 106–7
sem título [untitled], 2021, from "Pardo é Papel: New Power," 2019–. Bitumen, latex, graphite, and acrylic on brown kraft paper. 31 ½ × 94 ½ inches. Courtesy the artist and A Gentil Carioca.

Pages 108–9
sem titulo [untitled] (detail), 2021, from "Pardo é Papel: New Power," 2019–. Bitumen, latex, graphite, and acrylic on brown kraft paper. Courtesy the artist and A Gentil Carioca.

Page 137
sem titulo [untitled] (detail), 2021, from "Pardo é Papel: New Power," 2019–. Latex, bitumen, and acrylic on brown kraft paper. Courtesy the artist and A Gentil Carioca.

Pages 138–9
sem titulo [untitled] (detail), 2021, from "Pardo é Papel: New Power," 2019–. Latex, shoe polish, charcoal, graphite, and acrylic on brown kraft paper. Courtesy the artist and A Gentil Carioca.

Page 140
Maxwell Alexandre's studio in Gávea, Rio de Janeiro, 2021.

Page 141
Gazing ball 2 (detail), 2021, from "Pardo é Papel: New Power," 2019–. Charcoal and latex on brown kraft paper. Courtesy the artist and A Gentil Carioca.

Page 142
I saw things I imagined (detail), 2020, from "Pardo é Papel: Close a door to open a window," 2020–. Shoe polish on brown kraft paper. Courtesy the artist and David Zwirner.

Page 143
Olhar embriagado no espelho [Drunk look in the mirror] (detail), 2018, from "Pardo é Papel: The Glorious Victory," 2017–. Latex, grease, henna, bitumen, acrylic, graphite, and charcoal on brown kraft paper. Courtesy Fortes D'Aloia & Gabriel and A Gentil Carioca.

Page 144
Maxwell Alexandre's studio in Gávea, Rio de Janeiro, 2021.

Page 145
sem titulo [untitled] (detail), 2021, from "Pardo é Papel: New Power," 2019–. Shoe polish, graphite, latex and acrylic on brown kraft paper. Courtesy the artist and A Gentil Carioca.

Page 146
sem titulo [untitled] (detail), 2021, from "Pardo é Papel: New Power," 2019–. Latex and shoe polish on brown kraft paper. Courtesy the artist and A Gentil Carioca.

Page 147
Maxwell Alexandre in his studio in Gávea, Rio de Janeiro, 2021.

Page 148
Maxwell Alexandre's studio in Gávea, Rio de Janeiro, 2021.

Page 149
sem titulo [untitled] (detail), 2021, from "Pardo é Papel: New Power," 2019–. Latex on brown kraft paper. Courtesy the artist and A Gentil Carioca.

Reproduction Credits

Page 2
© Maxwell Alexandre. Photo: Gabi Carrera. Courtesy Instituto Inclusartiz and Museu de Arte do Rio – MAR.

Page 3, 4
© Maxwell Alexandre. Photo: Megazord Studio. Courtesy the artist.

Page 5
© Maxwell Alexandre. Photo: Gabi Carrera. Courtesy Instituto Inclusartiz and Museu de Arte do Rio – MAR.

Page 6
© Maxwell Alexandre. Courtesy the artist and A Gentil Carioca;

Page 7
© Maxwell Alexandre. Photo: Gabi Carrera. Courtesy Instituto Inclusartiz and Museu de Arte do Rio – MAR.

Pages 8–9
© Maxwell Alexandre. Photo: Gabi Carrera. Courtesy David Zwirner Gallery.

Page 10
© Maxwell Alexandre. Courtesy the artist and A Gentil Carioca.

Page 11
© Maxwell Alexandre. Photo: Megazord Studio. Courtesy the artist.

Page 12
© Maxwell Alexandre. Photo: Megazord Studio. Courtesy the artist.

Page 13
© Maxwell Alexandre. Courtesy the artist and A Gentil Carioca.

Page 14
© Maxwell Alexandre. Photo: Gabi Carrera. Courtesy David Zwirner Gallery.

Page 20
Figs 1, 2: Courtesy Fortes D'Aloia & Gabriel. © macLYON. © Photo: Blaise Adilon.

Page 21
Fig. 3: © Maxwell Alexandre. Photo: Megazord Studio. Courtesy the artist.

Page 22
Fig. 4: Courtesy Fortes D'Aloia & Gabriel and A Gentil Carioca. © Maxwell Alexandre. Photo: Gabi Carrera. Courtesy Instituto Inclusartiz and Museu de Arte do Rio – MAR.

Page 23
Fig. 5: Courtesy Fortes D'Aloia & Gabriel and A Gentil Carioca. © Maxwell Alexandre. Photo: Gabi Carrera. Courtesy Instituto Inclusartiz and Museu de Arte do Rio – MAR; Fig. 6: Courtesy the artist and A Gentil Carioca. © Maxwell Alexandre. Photo: Gabi Carrera. Courtesy Instituto Inclusartiz and Museu de Arte do Rio – MAR.

Page 24
Fig. 7: Courtesy Fortes D'Aloia & Gabriel and A Gentil Carioca. © Maxwell Alexandre. Photo: Gabi Carrera. Courtesy Instituto Inclusartiz and Museu de Arte do Rio – MAR.

Page 25
Fig. 8: Courtesy the artist and David Zwirner. © Maxwell Alexandre. Photo: Gabi Carerra. Courtesy David Zwirner Gallery.

Page 26
Figs. 9, 10: © Maxwell Alexandre. Photo: Wagner Kox. Courtesy Instituto Inclusartiz and Museu de Arte do Rio – MAR.

Page 27
Fig. 11, 12: © macLYON collection. © Blaise Adilon.

Page 28
Fig. 13: Courtesy the artist, Fortes D'Aloia & Gabriel and A Gentil Carioca. © Maxwell Alexandre. Photo: Gabi Carrera. Courtesy Instituto Inclusartiz and Museu de Arte do Rio – MAR.

Page 29
Fig. 14: Courtesy the artist, Fortes D'Aloia & Gabriel and A Gentil Carioca. © Maxwell Alexandre. Photo: Gabi Carrera. Courtesy Instituto Inclusartiz and Museu de Arte do Rio – MAR; Fig. 15: © Maxwell Alexandre. Photo: Megazord Studio. Courtesy the artist.

Page 30
Fig. 16: Photo: Aurélien Mole. Courtesy the artist and Palais de Tokyo, Paris; Fig. 17: Courtesy the artist and A Gentil Carioca. © Maxwell Alexandre. Photo: Aurélien Mole. Courtesy the artist and Palais de Tokyo, Paris.

Page 31
Fig. 18: Courtesy the artist and A Gentil Carioca. © Maxwell Alexandre. Photo: Aurélien Mole. Courtesy the artist and Palais de Tokyo, Paris.

Pages 33–65
© Maxwell Alexandre. Courtesy the artist and A Gentil Carioca.

Page 67
Fig. 1: © Maxwell Alexandre. Photo: Aurélien Mole. Courtesy the artist and Palais de Tokyo, Paris.

Page 68
Figs. 2, 3: © Maxwell Alexandre. Courtesy the artist and A Gentil Carioca.

Pages 69–70
Figs. 4, 5: © Maxwell Alexandre. Photo: Aurélien Mole. Courtesy Palais de Tokyo, Paris.

Page 71
Fig. 6: Courtesy the artist and A Gentil Carioca. © Maxwell Alexandre.

Pages 72–4
Figs. 7–9: © Maxwell Alexandre. Photo: Aurélien Mole. Courtesy Palais de Tokyo, Paris.

Page 76
Figs. 10, 11: © Maxwell Alexandre. Courtesy the artist and A Gentil Carioca.

Page 77
Fig. 12: © Maxwell Alexandre. Photo: Aurélien Mole. Courtesy the artist and Palais de Tokyo, Paris.

Pages 82–3
Figs. 1–4: © Maxwell Alexandre. Photo: Megazord Studio. Courtesy the artist.

Page 85–105
Courtesy the artist and A Gentil Carioca. © Maxwell Alexandre. Photo: Gabi Carrera. Courtesy Instituto Inclusartiz and Museu de Arte do Rio – MAR.

Pages 106–9
© Maxwell Alexandre. Courtesy the artist and A Gentil Carioca.

Page 137
© Maxwell Alexandre. Courtesy the artist and A Gentil Carioca.

Pages 138–9
© Maxwell Alexandre. Courtesy the artist and A Gentil Carioca.

Page 140
© Maxwell Alexandre. Photo: Megazord Studio. Courtesy the artist.

Page 141
© Maxwell Alexandre. Courtesy the artist and A Gentil Carioca.

Page 142
© Maxwell Alexandre. Photo: Gabi Carrera. Courtesy David Zwirner Gallery.

Page 143
© Maxwell Alexandre. Photo: Gabi Carrera. Courtesy Instituto Inclusartiz and Museu de Arte do Rio – MAR.

Page 144
© Maxwell Alexandre. Photo: Megazord Studio. Courtesy the artist.

Page 145
© Maxwell Alexandre. Courtesy the artist and A Gentil Carioca.

Page 146
© Maxwell Alexandre. Courtesy the artist and A Gentil Carioca.

Page 147
© Maxwell Alexandre. Photo: Megazord Studio. Courtesy the artist.

Page 148
© Maxwell Alexandre. Photo: Megazord Studio. Courtesy the artist.

Page 149
© Maxwell Alexandre. Courtesy the artist and A Gentil Carioca.

Board of Directors

Jonathan M. Tisch,
Chair

Daniel L. Doctoroff,
Founding Chair

Alex Poots,
Artistic Director and CEO

Debbie August
Heather Baker
Peter A. Boyce II
Neeraj Chandra
Misty Copeland
Roberta Denning
Lew Frankfort
Dexter G. Goei
Robert Goldstein
Glenda G. Grace
Gary Hoberman
Todd Kahn
Monish Kumar
Kate D. Levin
Christina Weiss Lurie
Frank H. McCourt Jr.
Marigay McKee
Darla Moore
Colby Mugrabi
Dasha Zhukova Niarchos
Claudia Rankine
Maria Catalina Saieh Guzman
Andres Santo Domingo
Ann Sarnoff
Dean Shapiro
Harvey J. Spevak
Jed Walentas
Fred Wilson
Deborah Winshel
Kenneth P. Wong

Ex Officio
Hon. Adrienne E. Adams
Hon. Laurie Cumbo
Hon. Mark Levine
Hon. Maria Torres-Springer

As of April 28, 2022

Staff

Alex Poots,
Artistic Director and CEO

Maryann Jordan,
President and
Chief Operating Officer

Bader AlAwadhi
Miranda Alicea
Lance Anderson
Laura Aswad
Ryan Bailey
Kleigh Balugo
Matthew Barrows
Elizabeth Bell
Miles Bentley
Elizabeth Berridge
Nkosi Boulware
Keri Bronk
Stuart Burgess
Abra Burkett
Christina Burnette
Frank Butler
Robert Carotenuto
Stefan Carrillo
Julio Catano
Emily Cazares
Solana Chehtman
Vilma Clausen
DaeQuan Alexander Collier
Chaya Coppersmith
Amber Rosio Cruz
Augustin Cruz
Catherine Daniel
Wayne Dean
LaWanda Dezil
Sarah Khalid Dhobhany
Mike Diaz
Carlos Diaz
Kyle Dubin
Gina Dyches
Olivia Ellis
Dani Farula
Desiree Fernandez
Kevin Figueroa
Ivy Mace Firtell
Jade Fortune
Kishawn Francis
Josh Galitzer
Brian Gee
Peter Gee
Christopher Genovese
Alessandra Gómez
Jason Granado
Phillip Griffith
Jaydah Grullon
Marlen Gumny
Andrew Hannaoui
Andria Hickey
Shakira Hill
Destiny Howlett
Seth Huling
Geovanni Hyman
Maria Inkateshta
Onyekachi Iwu
Kiana Jackson
Pope Jackson
Bridgeanand James
Tracie Jaramillo
Kierrah Jeffrey
Joanny Jimenez
Erickson Joachim
Terrelle Jones
Bobby Kean
Julien Khurey
Jean Kwartler
Jennifer Lam
Marcos Lamberty
Michael Lanier
Steffi Lee
Beckett Levine
Jeff Levine
Dorothy Lin
Alexander Lopez
Andrea Lopez
Julio Lugo
Vanessa Luna
Maggie MacTiernan
Angel Martinez
Gabriela Martinez
Maytté Martinez
Sarah Mathison
Tamara McCaw
Emma McIntosh
Edwin Medina
Aleksandar Milicevic
Angela Moncayo
NaQuay Morales
Marisol Moreno
Kamar Devin Adriane Morris
Hans Ulrich Obrist
Nick Panopoulos
Teddy Panopoulos
Daisy Peele
Gil Perez
Matthew Pezzolo
Josh Phagoo
Sarah Pier
Peter Pimentel
Henry Pinckney
Steven Quinones
Sadaf Qurashi
Cassandra Ramos
Emilio Philippe Ramos
Sara Ramsawak
Lauren Ranson
Christina Riley
Jose Rivera
Chris Roberts
Emmanuel Rosario
Keith Sainten
Yayoi Sakurai
Kim Sanchez
Ines Santos
Erica Sattin
Whitney Alexis Scott
Ariel Seaman
Amanda Singer
Milange Solano
Kristy Solomon
Mary Steffens
Sarah-Elisabeth Stein
Kin Tam
Mariam Tarin
Jessie Thiele
Annabel Thompson
Kaylon Thompson
Britney Tusa
Kewanna Upshur
Jim Van Bergen
Miguel Angel Vasquez
Vladimir Vince
Isabelle Vincent
Kodie-Ann Walcott
Jeter Jahari West
Ezra Wiesner
Ryan Witte
Jai Woods
Tiffanie Yakum
Madani Younis
Deborah Zebeda
Jennifer Zuniga

As of June 11, 2022

This catalogue was published on the occasion of the exhibition *Pardo é Papel: The Glorious Victory and New Power* at The Shed, October 26, 2022–January 8, 2023, organized by Alessandra Gómez, Associate Curator; exhibition management by Elizabeth Berridge, Assistant Exhibitions Producer. Special thanks to Amanda Singer, former Senior Exhibitions Producer.

This publication has been generously supported by Elaine Goldman and John Benis.

The creation of new work at The Shed has been generously supported by the Lizzie and Jonathan Tisch Commissioning Fund.

Special thanks to the following Shed Commissioners, a group of visionary philanthropists providing early support for our mission to produce and welcome innovative art and ideas, across all forms of creativity: Bruce A. Beal Jr., Jeff and Lisa Blau, Sherry Brous and Doug Oliver, Lisa and Dick Cashin, R. Martin Chavez, David C. Drummond, Eva and Glenn Dubin, Larry and Lori Fink, Julis Romo Rabinowitz Family, Kirsh Foundation, Adam and Margaret Korn, Judy and Leonard Lauder, Leni and Peter May, Greg and Alexandra Mondre, Eric and Wendy Schmidt, Robert K. Steel Family Foundation, Laurie M. Tisch Illumination Fund, and Steve Tisch.

Editor: Alessandra Gómez
Project Editor: Phillip Griffith
Design: Renata Graw and
Lucas Reif at the Normal studio
Proofreader: Dianne Woo
Translation (Portuguese to English):
Matthew Rinaldi and John Norman

Produced by the Curatorial, Design, and Editorial Departments, The Shed:
Andria Hickey, Chief Curator
Alessandra Gómez, Associate Curator
Keri Bronk, Design Director
Dorothy Lin, Graphic Designer
Phillip Griffith, Editorial Director

First published by
Verlag der Buchhandlung Walther
und Franz König
Ehrenstraße 4, D-50672 Köln

Bibliographic information published by the Deutsche Nationalbibliothek. The Deutsche Nationalbibliothek lists this publication in the Deutsche Nationalbibliografie; detailed bibliographic data are available on the Internet at http://dnb.d-nb.de.

Printed by die Keure in Belgium

Distribution

Europe
Buchhandlung Walther König
Ehrenstraße 4
D-50672 Köln
Tel: +49 (0) 221 / 20 59 6 53
verlag@buchhandlung-walther-koenig.de

UK & Ireland
Cornerhouse Publications Ltd, HOME
2 Tony Wilson Place
UK—Manchester M15 4FN
Tel: +44 (0) 161 212 3466
publications@cornerhouse.org

Outside Europe
D.A.P. / Distributed Art Publishers, Inc.
75 Broad Street, Suite 630
USA—New York, NY 10004
Tel: +1 (0) 212 627 1999
orders@dapinc.com

ISBN 978-3-7533-0309-3

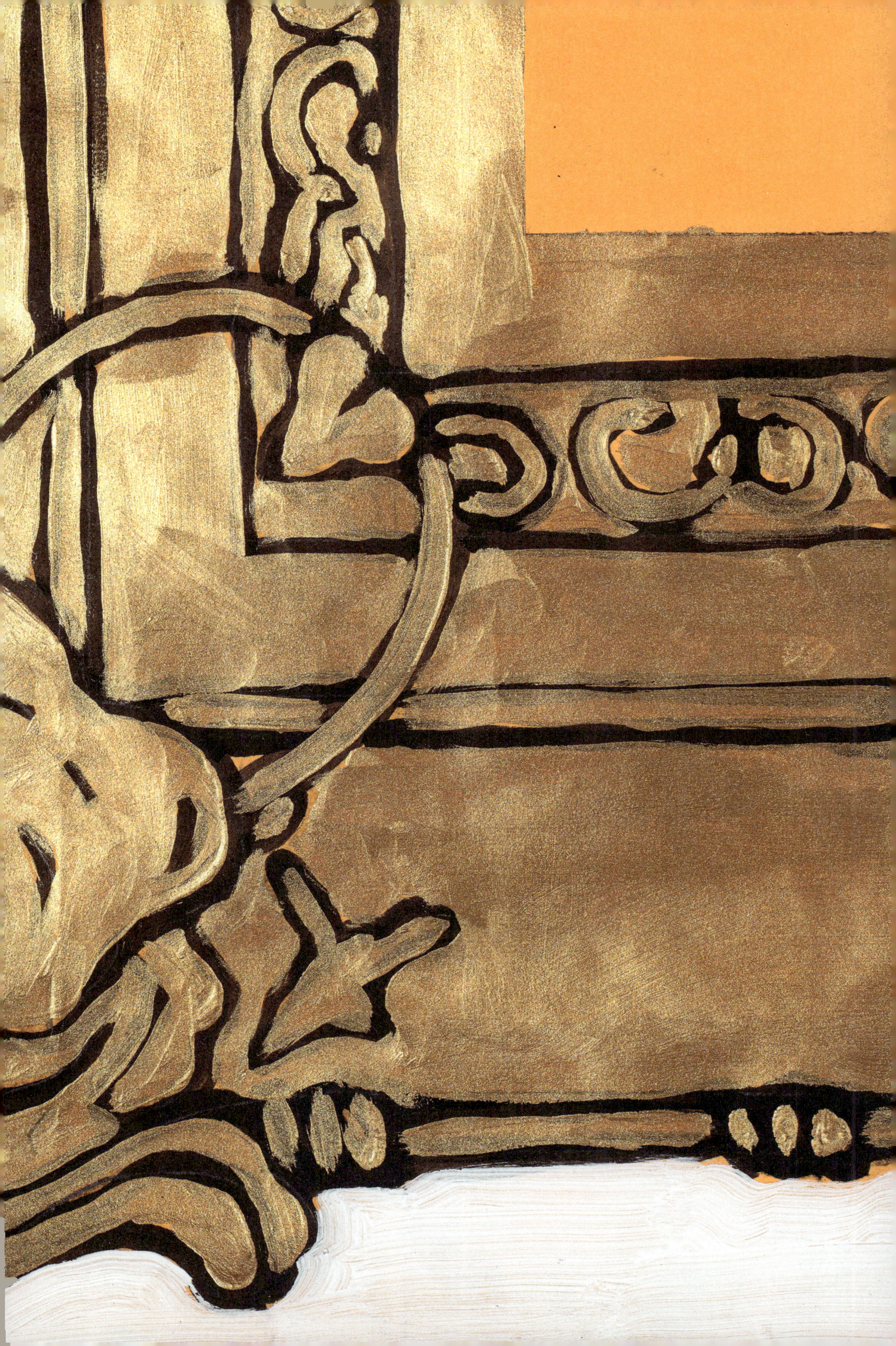

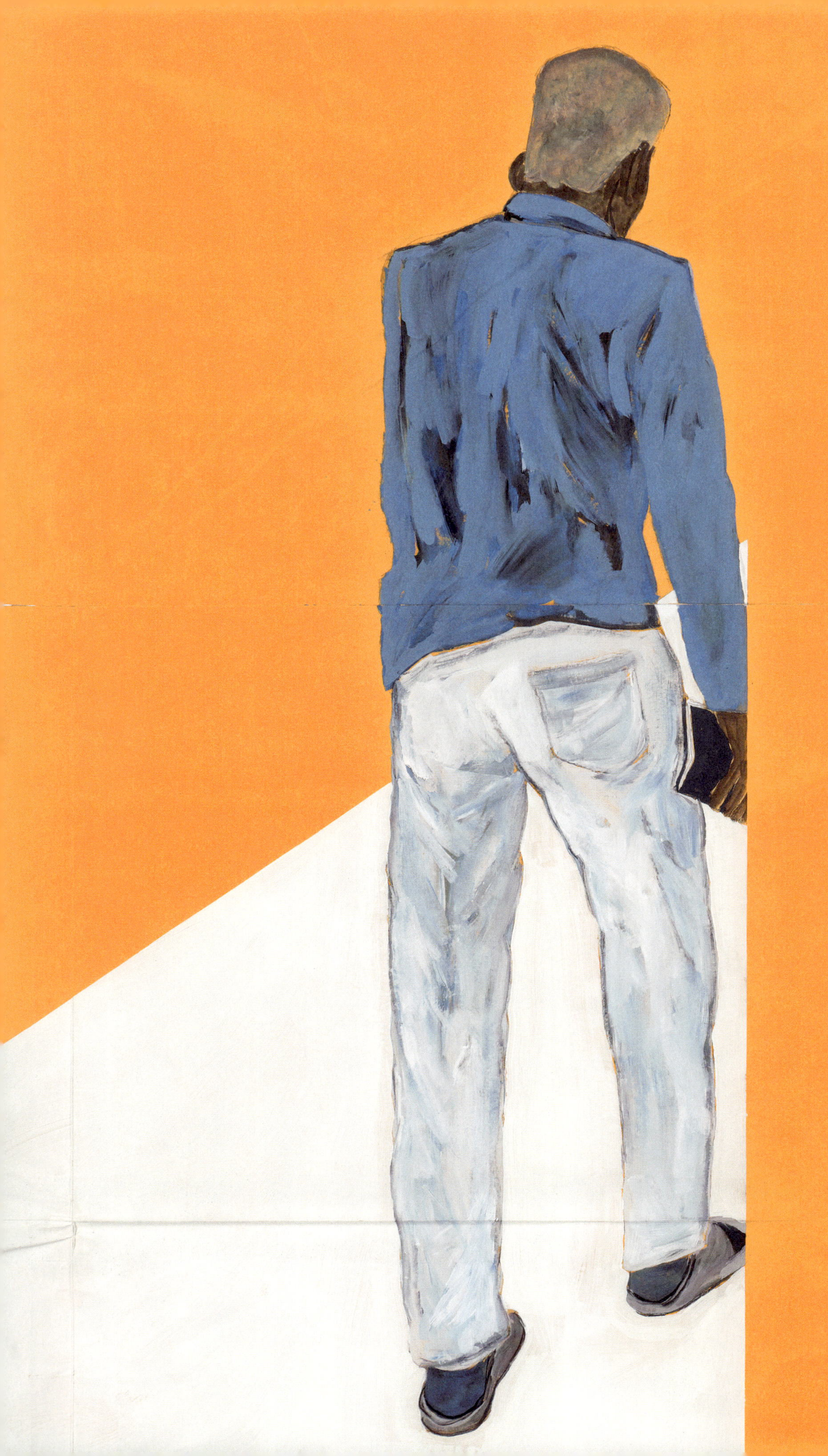

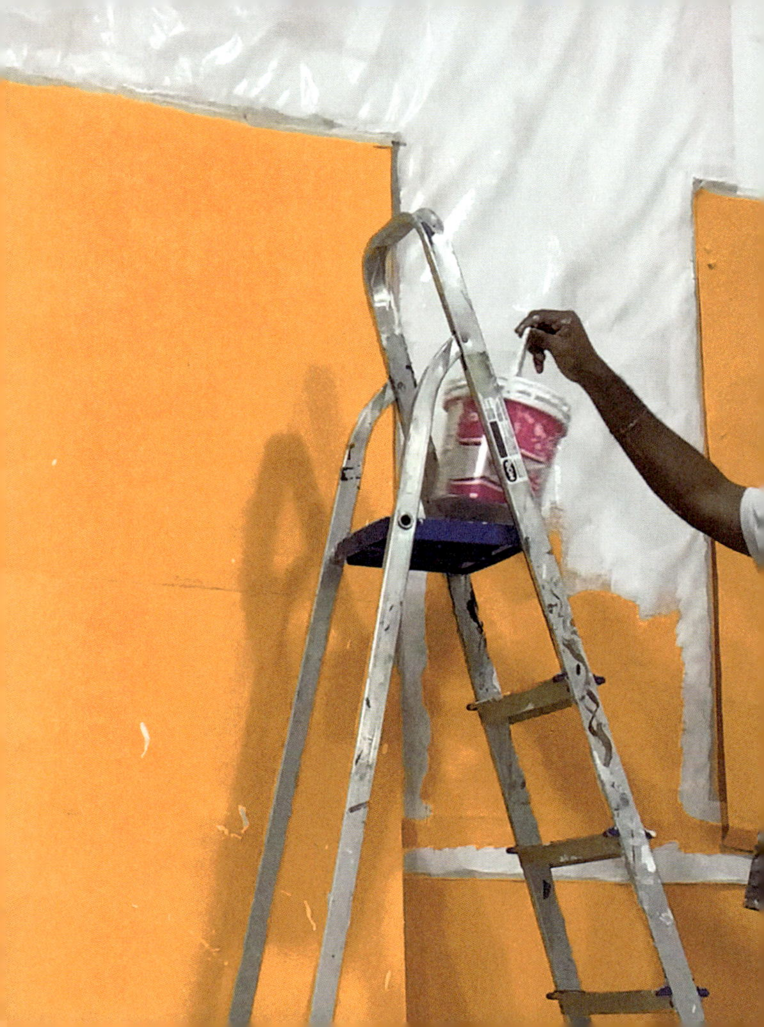

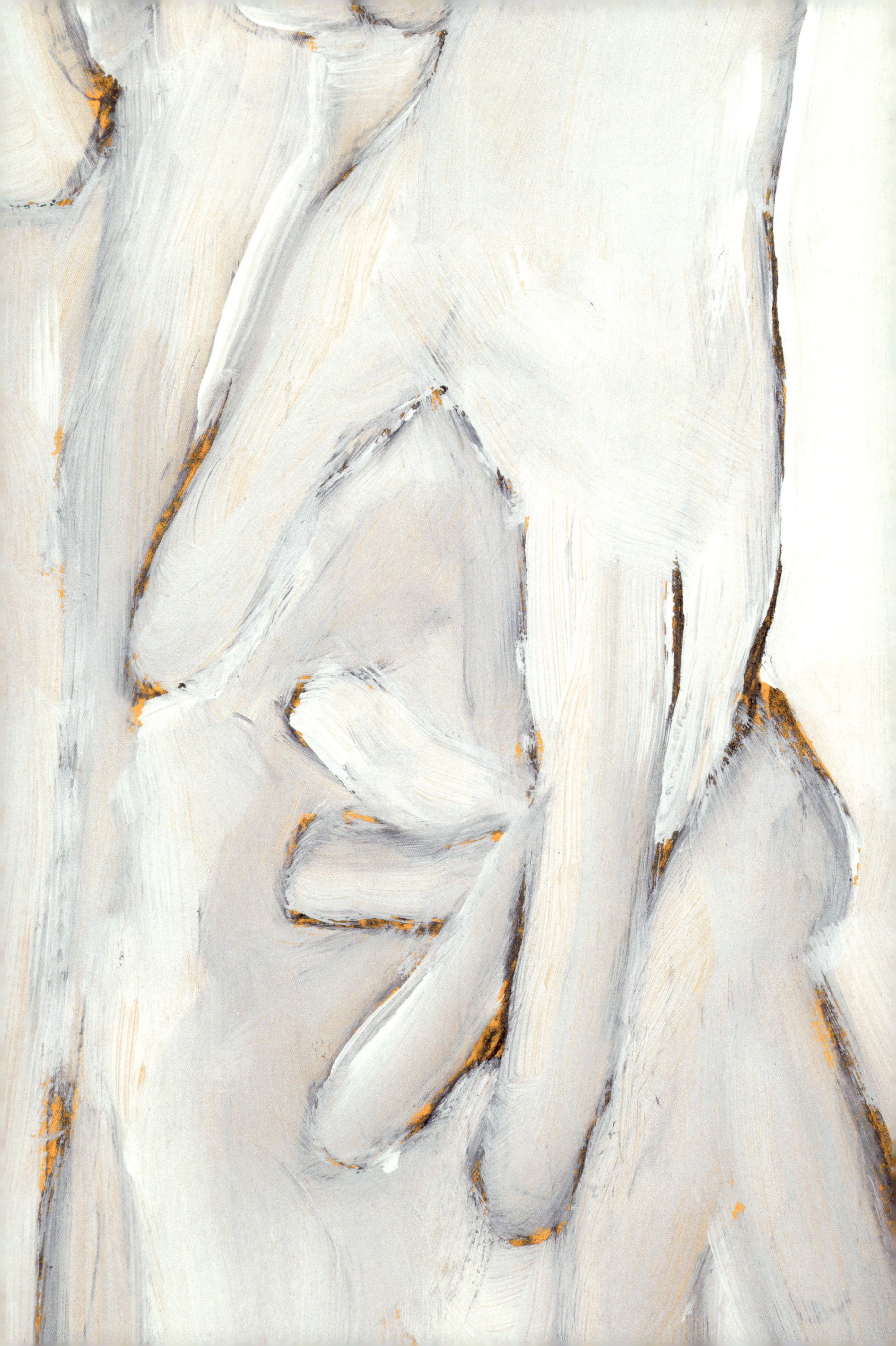

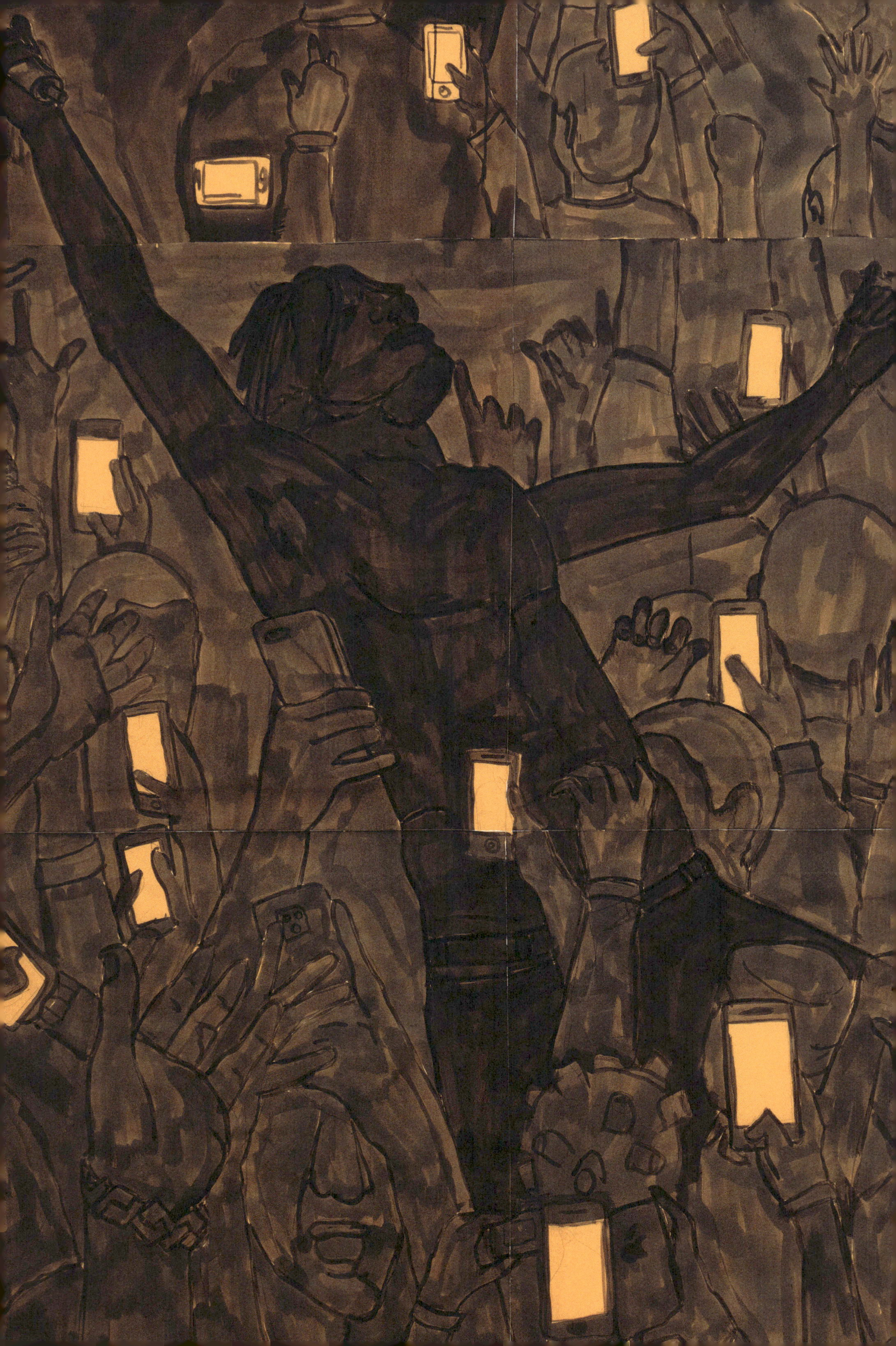

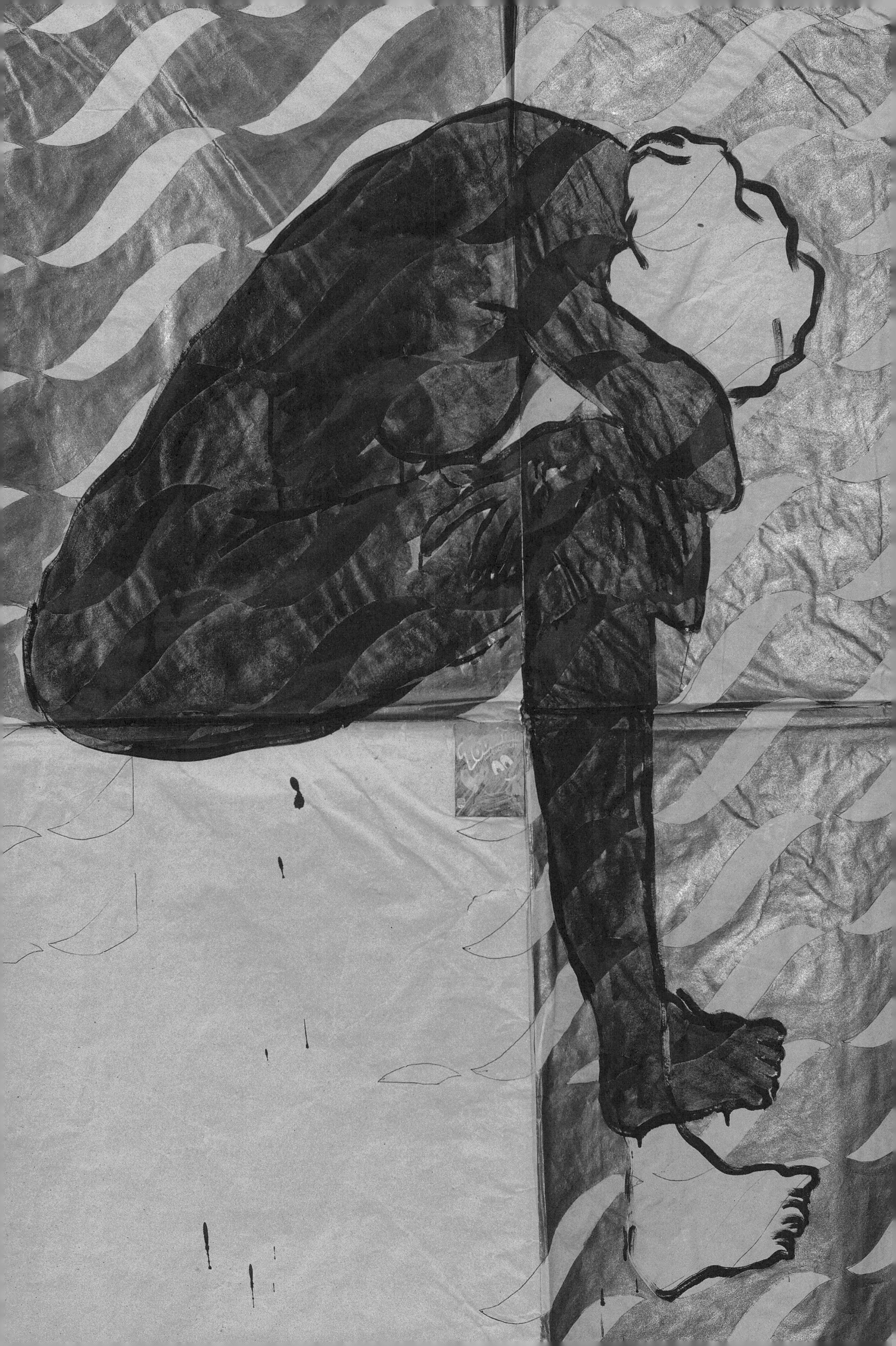

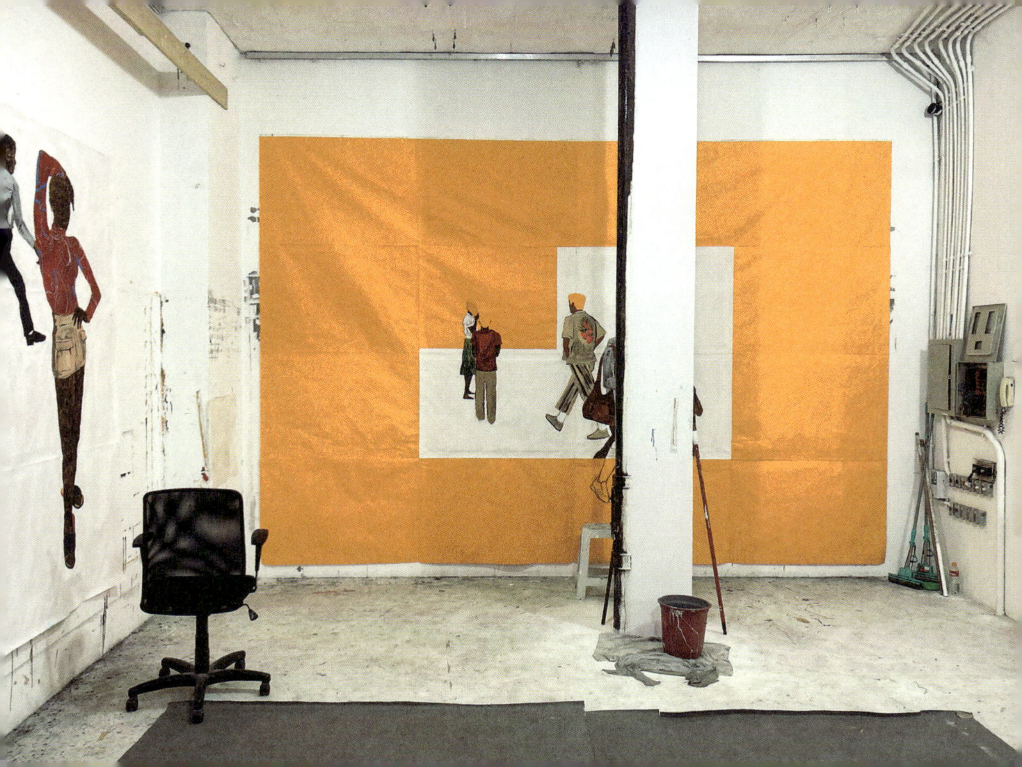

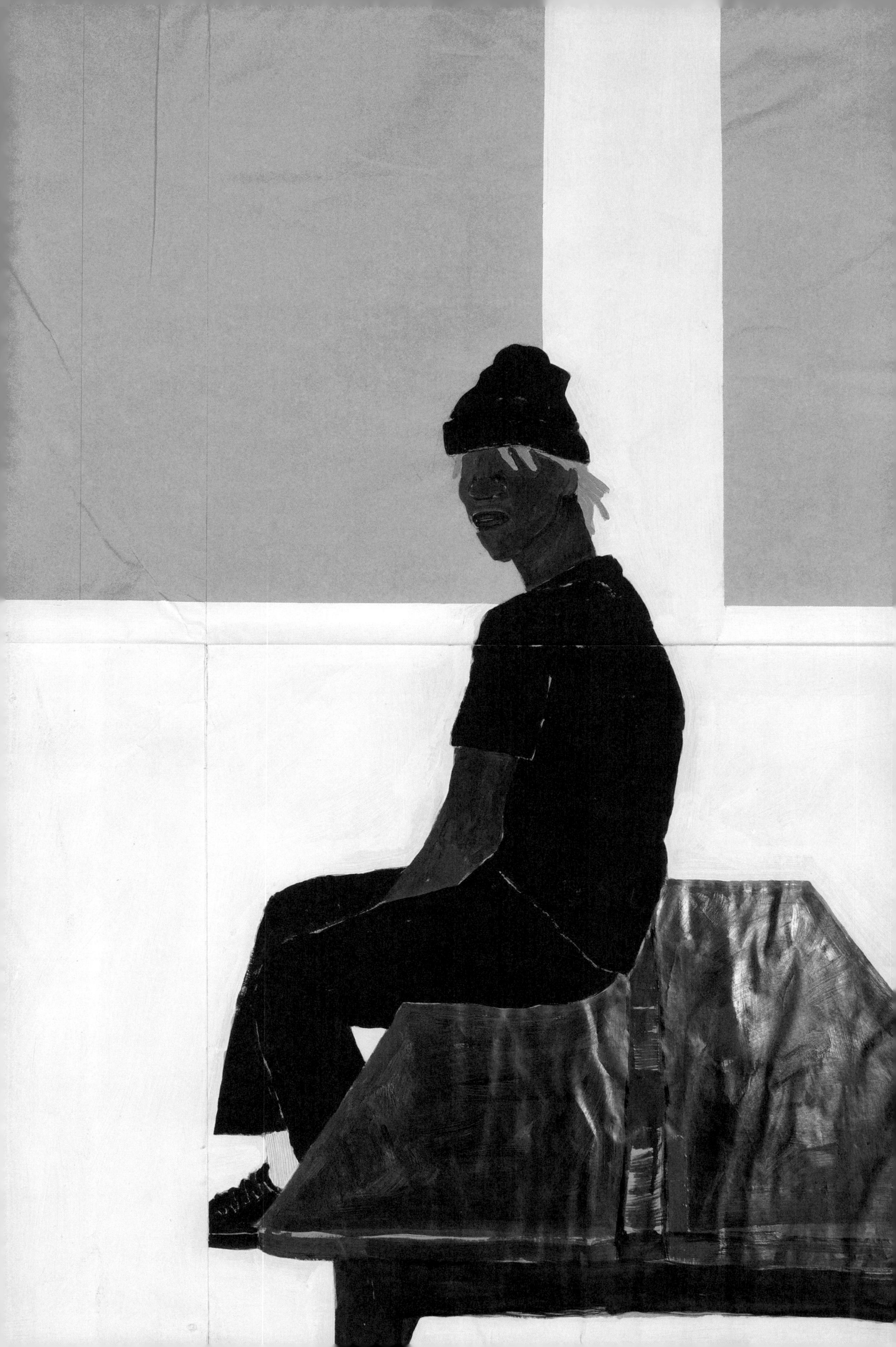

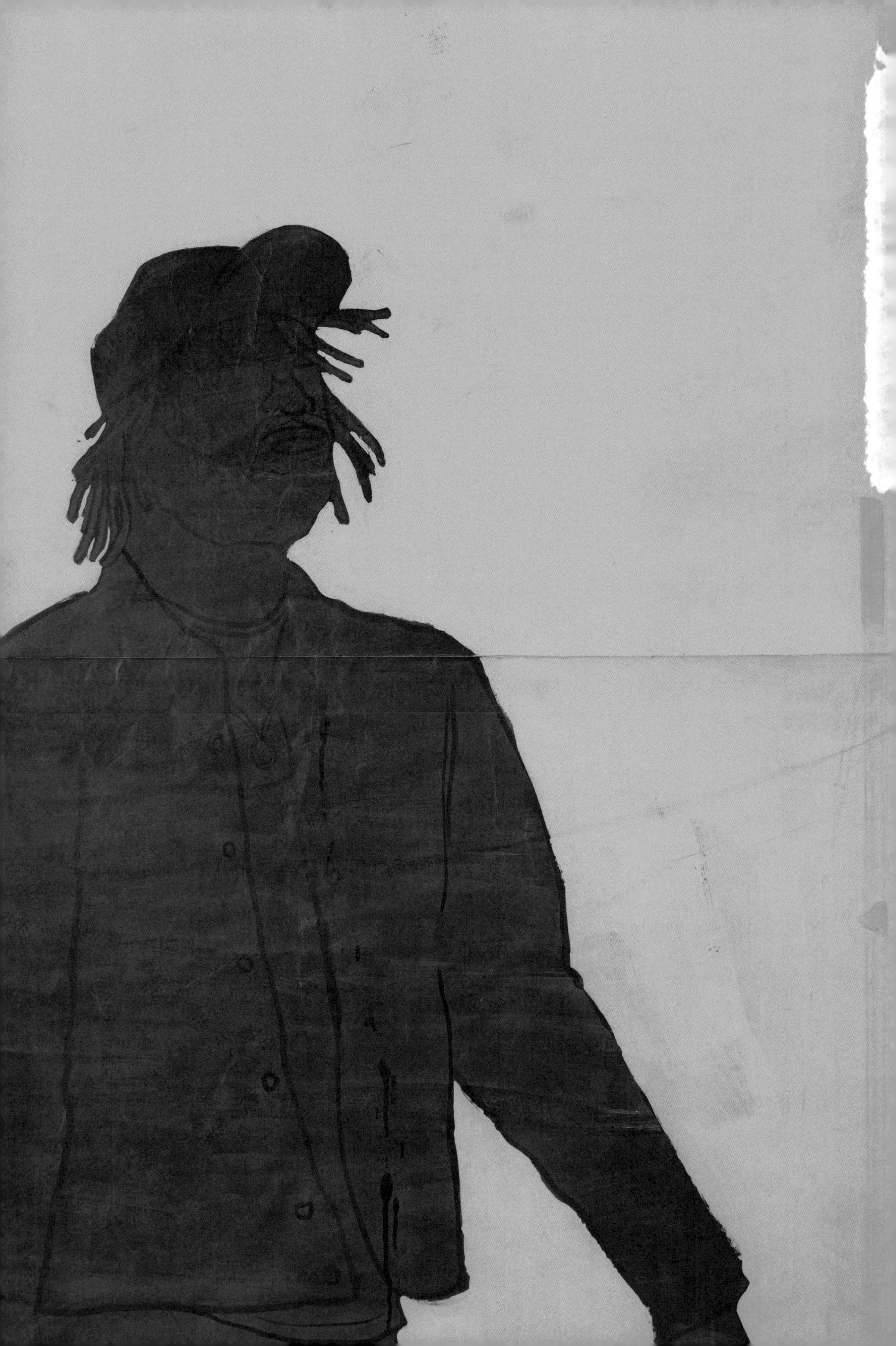

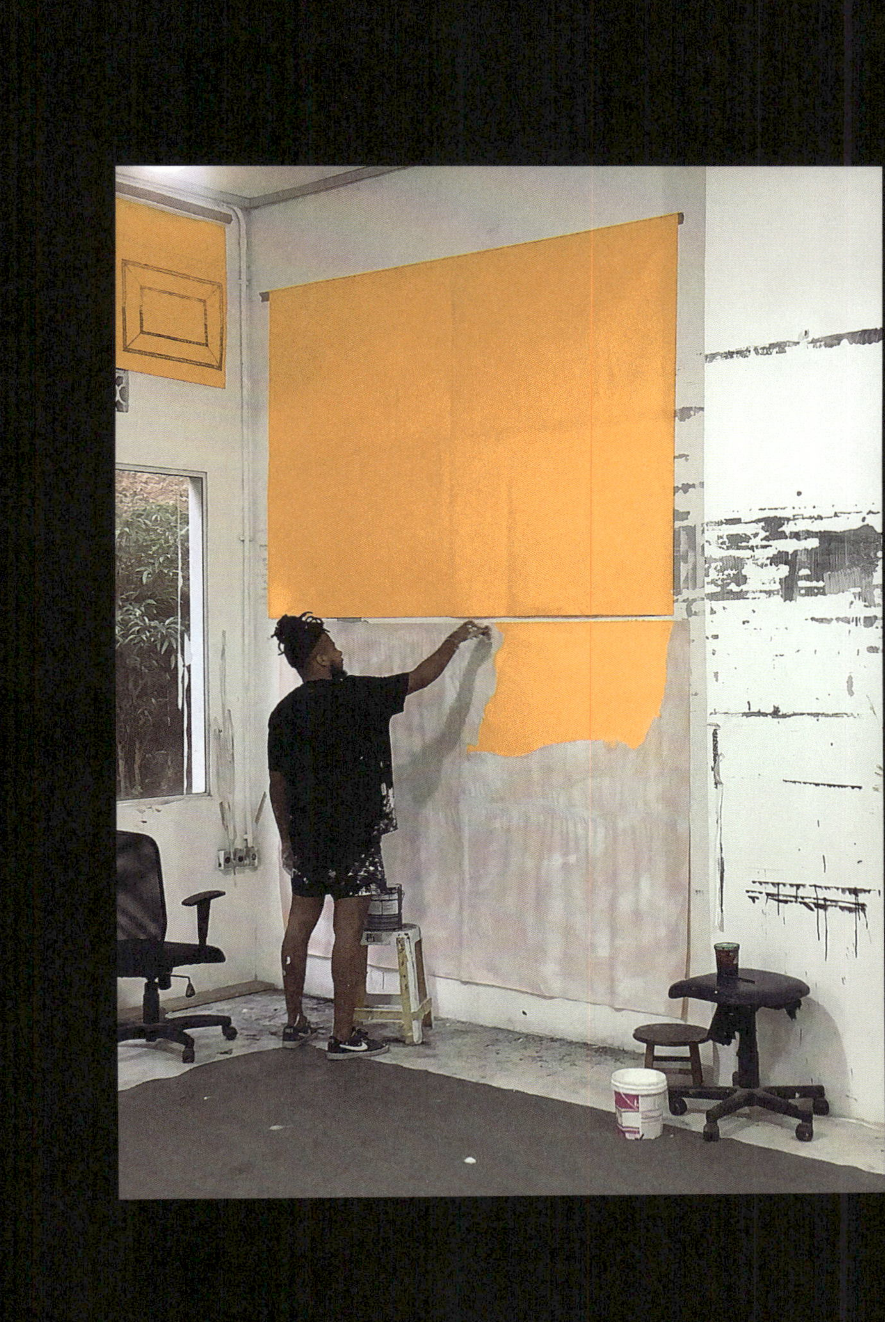

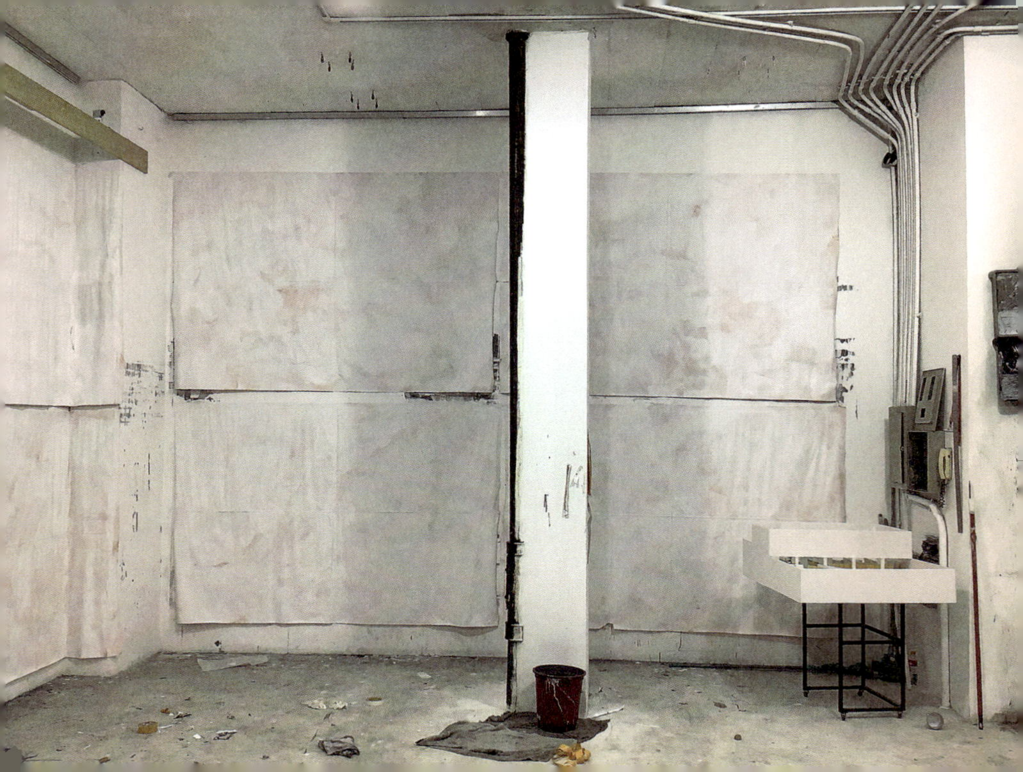